'Race', ethnicity and education

KEY ISSUES IN EDUCATION

The politics of reorganizing schools
Stuart Ranson

Parental choice in education
Daphne Johnson

Forthcoming in this series

Women in primary teaching:
career contexts and strategies
Julia Evetts

ALSO FROM UNWIN HYMAN

Action research in classrooms and schools
edited by David Hustler, A. Cassidy and E. C. Cuff

The behaviourist in the classroom
edited by Kevin Wheldall

Equality and freedom in education:
a comparative study
edited by Brian Holmes

Understanding educational aims
Colin Wringe

The curriculum
Brian Holmes and Martin McLean

Examinations
John C. Mathews

KEY ISSUES IN EDUCATION

Series editor:
Dr Robert Burgess, *University of Warwick*

'Race', ethnicity and education

Teaching and learning in multi-ethnic schools

David Gillborn

University of Sheffield

London
UNWIN HYMAN
Boston   Sydney   Wellington

Published by the Academic Division of
Unwin Hyman Ltd
15/17 Broadwick Street, London W1V 1FP, UK

Unwin Hyman Inc.,
955 Massachusetts Avenue, Cambridge, Mass. 02139, USA

Allen & Unwin (Australia) Ltd,
8 Napier Street, North Sydney, NSW 2060, Australia

Allen & Unwin (New Zealand) Ltd in association with the
Port Nicholson Press Ltd,
Compusales Building, 75 Ghuznee Street, Wellington 1, New Zealand

First published in 1990

British Library Cataloguing in Publication Data
Gillborn, David
'Race', ethnicity and education:teaching and learning in
multi-ethnic schools. – (Key issues in education)
1. Great Britain. Education. Racial discrimination
I. Title
370.193420941

ISBN 0–04–445398–1

Library of Congress Cataloging in Publication Data
Gillborn, David.
'Race', ethnicity, and education:teaching and learning in multi-
ethnic schools/David Gillborn.
p. cm. — (Key issues in education)
Includes bibliographical references and index.
ISBN 0–04–445397–3. — ISBN 0–04–445398–1 (pbk.)
1. Children of minorities—Education—Great Britain—Case studies.
2. Intercultural education—Great Britain—Case studies. 3. Urban
schools—Great Britain—Case studies. 4. Educational equalization—
Great Britain—Case studies. I. Title. II. Series.
LC3736.G6G53 1990
370.19'341—dc20   90–39837
                                                        CIP

Typeset in 10/12 Garamond and printed in Great Britain by
Billing and Sons, Ltd., London and Worcester

Contents

List of tables and figures

Key to transcripts   xi

Series editor's preface   xiii

Preface   xv

1   'Race', ethnicity and education   1

PART ONE: *City Road – Teaching and learning in a multi-ethnic comprehensive*   17

2   Discipline and control   19

3   Resistance and accommodation   45

4   South Asian pupils   72

PART TWO: *Beyond City Road – Issues for education in a multi-ethnic society*   103

5   Achievement and opportunity   105

6   'Race', ethnicity and the curriculum   142

7   Language issues   173

8   'Race' matters   198

Notes   210

Guide to further reading   217

References   219

Index   236

List of tables

2.1 The frequency of detentions per pupil detained during the third, fourth and fifth years in City Road Comprehensive (by gender and ethnic origin) *page* 36

2.2 'Reason for detention' given during the third, fourth and fifth years in City Road Comprehensive (by gender and ethnic origin) *page* 41

5.1 Sixteen-plus examination results by ethnic origin: six surveys compared (percentages) *pages* 108–9

5.2 Sixteen-year-olds' examination achievements in ILEA (1985) by ethnic origin *page* 111

5.3 Fifth-form examination performance by ethnic origin and social class in an Outer London borough (percentages) *page* 125

5.4 The fifth-year examination results of YCS respondents by ethnic origin *page* 127

5.5 Average exam score broken down by ethnic origin, gender and socioeconomic group *page* 130

5.6 Percentage of children obtaining an 'O' level (or equivalent) pass grade in each subject group by ethnic origin in eighteen urban comprehensive schools (percentages) *page* 134

7.1 Proportions of bilingual pupils in five LEAs *page* 186

7.2 Main languages reported in five LEAs *page* 187

List of figures

5.1 Distribution of exam scores by ethnic group *page* 128

To Joyce and Jim
for all their love and support

Key to transcripts

Fieldwork data from the City Road study are presented according to the following conventions:

italicized text	Denotes emphasized speech or raised voice.
[square brackets]	Background information or where speech has been paraphrased for sake of clarity.
...	Pause.
(...)	Material has been edited out.
(field notes)	Denotes that data are taken from my field notes (written shortly after the interview/observation) rather than an audiotape transcript.

Series Editor's Preface

Each volume in the *Key Issues in Education* series is designed to provide a precise, authoritative guide to a topic of current concern to teachers, researchers and educational policy-makers. The books in the series comprise an introduction to some of the key debates in the contemporary practice of education. In particular, each author demonstrates how the social sciences can help us to analyse, explain and understand educational issues. The books in the series review key debates, and the authors complement this material by making detailed reference to their own research, which helps to illustrate the way research evidence in the social sciences and education can contribute to our understanding of educational policy and practice.

All the contributors to this series have extensive experience of their chosen field and have worked with teachers and other educational personnel. The volumes have been written to appeal to students who are intending to become teachers, working teachers who seek to familiarize themselves with new research and research evidence, as well as social scientists who are engaged in the study of education. Each author seeks to make educational research and debate accessible to those engaged in the practice of education. At the end of each volume there is a short guide to further reading for those who wish to pursue the topic in greater depth. The series provides a comprehensive guide to contemporary issues in education and demonstrates the importance of social science research for understanding educational practice.

Much has been written on race, ethnicity and education but relatively little material has been based on first hand observational studies. In this respect, David Gillborn's volume breaks new ground by using ethnographic data from his study of City Road Comprehensive School. In the first part of the book he uses the data to explore teacher–pupil interactions in multi-ethnic settings, while Part Two uses data to consider key educational issues such as the development of educational opportunity, achievement, curriculum and assessment in a multi-ethnic society. The evidence that David Gillborn makes available extends our understanding of race, ethnicity and education and raises issues for policy-makers and practitioners, as well as students and their teachers.

Robert Burgess
University of Warwick

Preface

This book is about 'race' in schools. It is about the day-to-day interaction, conflict and negotiation between teachers and pupils of different ethnic backgrounds. It is about education in an unequal society where many white people believe that the best way to handle ethnic diversity is to ignore it.

The book blends an up-to-date review of major research findings with an analysis of life in 'City Road Comprehensive' — my name for a multi-ethnic inner-city school which I studied intensively over a two-year period.

The text was written with a diverse audience in mind. Primarily I am addressing intending and practising teachers, educational researchers and those studying the fields of 'race' and/or education in further and higher education. I hope, however, that the relevance of the material will be evident to anyone with an interest in education in the 1990s.

The first chapter acts as a general introduction. It provides a discussion of key concepts in the field of 'race', ethnicity and education, plus a description of City Road and the methods I used to study the school. The rest of the book is divided into two parts. The first focuses on the experiences of Afro-Caribbean and Asian pupils in schools dominated by the perspectives of white teachers. In particular, I examine teachers' expectations (concerning discipline, ability and 'attitude') and the way that, as a result, Afro-Caribbean and Asian pupils experienced school very differently. The pupils' experiences and responses are discussed using a variety of data, including material from in-depth interviews and classroom observations.

The second part of the book addresses particular areas of current controversy and debate. Recent research findings are discussed in relation to the issues of equality of opportunity, academic achievement, language use and changes in curriculum content and classroom practice. This part of the book includes a discussion of the clashes between multicultural and anti-racist approaches, and critically considers the possible consequences of the national curriculum.

Throughout the book I draw upon the views and experiences of teachers and pupils. My first debt of gratitude must, therefore, be to the staff and students of City Road Comprehensive who allowed me into their lives for two years. My research in City Road was made possible by a postgraduate studentship from Nottingham University, where the staff of the Sociology Department gave so generously of their time, patience and support. In particular I want to thank Julia Evetts, Mike King, Danny Lawrence and Ken Levine who kept me critical, whilst Suzy Harris — a fellow postgraduate — kept me sane.

Various people gave their time to read and comment upon the chapters in draft form; their views were invaluable and the book has been much improved as a result. My thanks to Ranjit Kaur Arora, Claudette Clarke, David Drew, Julia Evetts, John Gray, Danny Lawrence, Máirtín Mac an Ghaill, Jon Nixon, Jean Rudduck and Sally Tomlinson. Any remaining errors or omissions are entirely my own responsibility. Bob Burgess made detailed comments on the entire draft; his encouragement and support have been very important to me.

I was also allowed to see several academic papers before their publication. My thanks to the authors: David Drew, Harvey Goldstein, John Gray, Desmond Nuttall, Robert Prosser and Jon Rasbash.

Finally, and most of all, I want to thank my family and friends for believing in me, especially my mother and father, and wife Dorn. Without their love and understanding the book could not have been written.

David Gillborn
Sheffield, February 1990

KEY ISSUES IN EDUCATION

'Race', ethnicity and education

Chapter 1

'Race', ethnicity and education

Key concepts and ideas

Want it again, Paki?

You stupid white Bastard.

These are reportedly the words of two Manchester school-boys, one with a bloody knife, the other about to die from his wound. Half a year later, the mother of the Pakistani boy killed in a school playground is quoted as saying: 'It might take 100 years to change the world. *But the schools can change now...*' (Cohn, 1987, p. 8; emphasis added)

Questions of 'racial' equality, discrimination and harassment have become a familiar part of late twentieth century life. The ethnic diversity of society has consequences for every area of social policy, not least education. The 'race issue' cannot be adequately met by actions in any single area. Alone, the education system cannot provide all the answers, yet it does have the opportunity, and obligation, to make a significant contribution towards the creation of a more just society.

schools cannot 'solve' the problem of racism in our society. But they should surely not contribute to it, to the extent that they do. There is no simple or doctrinaire solution to the problem but the teaching profession can make a much larger contribution than they do at present. (Lacey, 1988, p. vii)

1

Race as an issue in contemporary education

'Race' issues frequently grab the headlines. When a Local Education Authority (LEA) designed a 'Development Programme for Race Equality', which included school-based evaluation and in-service training, national newspapers responded with banner headlines proclaiming a 'Race Spies Shock', involving the use of 'race commissars' in the classroom. When a Bradford headteacher published articles which offended many parents (both white and ethnic minority), the ensuing legal battle dominated media interest in education and led to a man whom many felt was 'racist' being hailed as a hero in the tabloid press.[1] 'Race' is, therefore, a highly political matter; it is also a key educational issue. 'Race' is perhaps one of *the* most controversial areas of contemporary educational debate.

The area of 'race' and education is characterized by a lack of coherence and seemingly endless change and controversy. There are many different theories of race relations but very little agreement (cf. Rex and Mason, 1986). Scholars have argued over the relative importance of economic, gender and ethnic factors; the origins and mechanisms of group difference; even the validity of the very term 'race'. In fact, terminology is one of the most frequently changing and disputed aspects of the whole field. Before going any further, therefore, it may be useful to outline briefly something of the main concepts which are used at present.

Defining and studying 'race'

Key words and phrases have changed to reflect the variety of political and educational perspectives which have evolved over the last few decades. Consequently, words which were once quite proper are now scorned as insulting, and vice versa. In their struggle for political recognition and social equality, several groups have glorified previously derogatory terms – as has been the case with the Black Power and Chicano movements in the USA (Cashmore, 1988). During the early 1960s, the words 'negro' and 'coloured' were used by Civil Rights leaders such as Martin Luther King, yet by the end of the decade the same words were viewed as insulting (Demaine, 1989, p. 198). Similarly, social science researchers in the field of 'race' and ethnic relations have used a succession of words and phrases to describe different groups (cf. Bulmer, 1986).

Changes in the acceptability of different terms have important consequences for teachers. In Britain many teachers still refer to 'coloured' people without realizing the messages which they may be transmitting to pupils and parents. At the very least, such a phrase reveals a lack of sensitivity and understanding which cannot help communities' confidence in their children's schooling.

The following descriptions are, therefore, offered as a brief guide to some of the most frequently used concepts. The words reappear throughout this book – where other writers have used a term differently I will note this in the text.

Race

BIOLOGICAL RACE: During the nineteenth century, biologists used the term 'race' to place human beings in apparently distinct groups (types) thought to share a common biological ancestry. These races were primarily defined in terms of physical differences (known as phenotypes), such as skin colour. Consequently, geographical factors also became bound up in the competing racial categorizations proposed by different physical anthropologists. Assumptions about physical and mental differences were conflated so that supposed scientific 'fact' was used as 'an explanation of and justification for the exploitation and subordination of blacks by whites' (Mason, 1986, pp. 5–6) – what is sometimes known as 'scientific racism' (cf. Banton, 1988a).

Although such a view of 'race' still survives among some political and lay groups, in biological terms the notion of separate human races is now discredited. Quite apart from the fact that physical anthropologists could not agree 'as to where the genetic boundaries between human groups were to be drawn, or even on how many such groups there were' (van den Berghe, 1988, p. 238), advances in the biological sciences have established that all human beings are members of a single species, *Homo sapiens*, which has no meaningful sub-species.

[The human species] shares a largely common genetic structure in which minute variation controls differences in individual phenotypes (apparent characteristics). For

3

example, skin colour in humans is thought to be controlled by just four out of about a hundred thousand genes. (Demaine, 1989, p. 199).

SOCIAL RACE: Although the idea of biologically distinct human races is now discredited, the term is still very widely used to refer to groups of people who are socially defined as sharing common characteristics. Again, physical characteristics play a major part in this. Such groupings are, therefore, socially constructed; they are not a biological fact, but are defined into existence.

In this sense, 'race' is no longer supposed to be a permanent, fixed genetic feature but is recognized as a variable, contested and changing social category. This is a crucial point, and can be illustrated with reference to the different conceptions of 'race' which have been constructed in different societies. In the United States, for example, any physical indication of even partial African ancestry might define someone as 'black', whereas the same person could well be be viewed as 'white' in Brazil (cf. Banton, 1983; van den Berghe, 1988).

The notion of 'social race' underlies almost all current use of the word 'race' in social science literature and research. Consequently, unless otherwise stated, this understanding is assumed wherever the term 'race' appears in the rest of this book.

Ethnic Group

Members of ethnic groups see themselves as culturally distinct from other groupings in a society, and are seen by those others to be so. Many different characteristics may serve to distinguish ethnic groups from one another, but the most usual are language, history or ancestry (real or imagined), religion, and styles of dress or adornment. Ethnic differences are *wholly learned* (Giddens, 1989, pp. 243–4; original emphasis)

There are several important points about this definition. Ethnic groups exist within larger cultural systems and are distinguished by their cultural distinctiveness (for example, language or history). Ethnic groups may, or may not, also be visibly distinct (for instance, through dress customs or physical characteristics). Where ethnic groups are visibly distinct this may reinforce the group's separation from the wider society.

The notion of ethnic group is often confused with that of 'ethnic minority'. It should be noted, however, that the latter is usually taken as implying minority status not only in numerical terms, but also in power terms. Consequently, although white South Africans account for a very small proportion of that state's total population they are not an ethnic minority in the usual sense of the term: as a group, white South Africans have systematically exploited black Africans to a degree which is unprecedented elsewhere in the modern world.

In the UK the largest (and longest established) ethnic minority group is of Irish decent (Dickinson, 1982). Italians, Jews, Ukranians, and travellers are also important ethnic groups in Britain (cf. Jeffcoate, 1984; Swann, 1985). However, in political and everyday language, the terms ethnic group and ethnic minority are frequently equated with groups who are physically distinct from the 'white' (European) majority – an example of racist stereotyping.

The identification and naming of ethnic groups is a complex and political issue, as witnessed by the continuing controversies over an 'ethnic question' for the UK census (cf. Bulmer, 1986; Cross, 1989). In 1984 the Commission for Racial Equality (CRE) adopted the practice of distinguishing between 'black' and 'white' groups, with 'further sub-divisions' in terms of regional origins (for example, 'Afro-Caribbean', 'Asian', 'European', etc.). This classification was based on the belief that 'discrimination on the basis of *colour* was the prime enemy to overcome' (Cross, 1989; original emphasis). Similarly, many people use the term 'black' to refer to people of different national, ethnic and religious backgrounds who are believed to share a 'common experience of white racism' (Mukherjee, 1984, p. 8; Mac an Ghaill, 1988, p. 156). This use of the term is currently very popular; its strength lies in highlighting the shared experiences of different ethnic groups. However, such an interpretation is not without its problems; many people of South Asian descent, for example, do not describe themselves as 'black'. Furthermore, by combining different ethnic groups together under crude general headings we may lose sight of important differences in opportunity and experience (Banton, 1977).

5

In this book I draw on the work of many different authors and, consequently, have to reproduce the changing use of a wide variety of terms. Wherever I quote from another study I will indicate which interpretations were used in the original. My own data were collected during a two-year study of life in an inner-city school which I call 'City Road Comprehensive'.[2] I have classified the City Road data according to the following distinctions:

AFRO-CARIBBEAN: This term is used where both parents were of black African or Caribbean origin. Within City Road and the surrounding community these pupils were known as, and referred to themselves as, 'West Indian' and/or 'black'. I decided against adopting the term 'black' because (a) it is not used consistently in the literature, and (b) within the school the term was also used by, and about, some (but not all) pupils of mixed race (see below). Almost all the 'West Indian' pupils in City Road had parents who were born in the West Indies (usually Jamaica) and so I repeated the term when I first wrote about the school (Gillborn, 1987, 1988). As I have already noted, terminology changes rapidly and this label is now used much less frequently. Consequently, I have chosen to adopt the more common (and in some cases, more accurate) term, 'Afro-Caribbean' which 'Somehow implies roots without denying Britishness' (Gaine, 1984, p. 6).

SOUTH ASIAN: This phrase (often shortened to 'Asian' for the sake of convenience) is commonly used to denote pupils whose parents emigrated to this country from the Indian subcontinent. The term can obscure important historical, religious, linguistic, political and national differences; between people of Indian, Pakistani and Bangladeshi ethnic origin, for example. Within City Road, however, the term has some merit, since the majority of South Asian males shared the same religion and were linked by a common friendship network. Where differences of religion and experience were apparent these are identified in the text.

MIXED RACE: Within City Road pupils with one parent of Afro-Caribbean origin were usually referred to by teachers as 'half-castes' — now widely viewed by the black community as a derogatory term. Within academic studies such pupils have sometimes been referred to as 'mixed race' (cf. Wilson, 1981,

6

1987). As I have noted, there is only one human race; the phrase mixed race is, therefore, potentially misleading. Unfortunately, no better term has yet been suggested and for the sake of continuity I have decided to follow Wilson's example.

WHITE: Any pupils not included in the previous categories are understood to fall within this general grouping, which might more accurately be termed 'white European' (in City Road this group included pupils of UK, Irish, Scandinavian and Italian parentage).

These classifications are far from perfect and each group is heterogeneous, reflecting the sheer complexity of the field (and the basic problem of defining ethnic groups). As Malcolm Cross has observed, 'The fact is that no one classification is likely to please all observers because the data are intended to reflect social constructions which are not held totally in common' (Cross, 1989).

The situation is further complicated by the fact that, depending upon the circumstances, the same person might describe themselves as 'black' in one context (say on a census form) and as Jamaican or African in another (such as in a conversation relating to their sense of nationality or cultural heritage). Hence it cannot be assumed that one label is appropriate in all cases, even for the same person; the complexity of the situation reflects the dynamic and political nature of the issues at stake.

Ethnicity

Closely related to the concept of ethnic group, 'ethnicity' emphasizes the *'sense* of difference which can occur where members of a particular [ethnic] group interact with non-members. *Real* differences between groups of people are no more (and no less) than *potential* identity markers for the members of those groups' (Wallman, 1979, p. x; original emphasis). Ethnicity concerns the sense and expression of ethnic difference. To acknowledge and glorify one's ethnicity does not necessarily involve passing judgement on other ethnic groups. It is where such judgements are made that we begin to move into the realms of 'racism'.

Racism

An increasingly widespread understanding of racism combines individual and group *prejudice* with a structural position whereby the individual or group has the *power* to influence others' experiences and life-chances (cf. AMMA, 1987). Consequently,

PREJUDICE + POWER = RACISM

In its emphasis on power, this view deliberately recognizes the importance of wider social structures. Consequently, although an individual of Afro-Caribbean ethnic origin might, for example, hold stereotyped and negative images of white culture, s/he is unlikely to be in a position to put those views into effect because people of Afro-Caribbean ethnic origin are a relatively powerless minority in the UK. Hence racism becomes synonymous with 'white racism'.

The simplicity and force of this definition make it particularly attractive to many practitioners. However, the term prejudice might be understood to imply fixed, easily recognized and hostile beliefs about members of another ethnic group, but such a view would be too limiting (cf. Wellman, 1977). Minorities often suffer through actions which have discriminatory effects despite their benign or even liberal intent. In order to deal with this complexity it is necessary to distinguish between crude 'popular' racism and the less obvious (but equally damaging) institutional racism and ethnocentrism.

'Popular' racism:

> Societies that recognize social races are invariably *racist* societies, in the sense that people, especially members of the dominant racial group, believe that physical phenotype is linked with intellectual, moral and behavioural characteristics. Race and racism thus go hand in hand. (van den Berghe, 1988, p. 239; original emphasis)

This quotation describes many elements of a classical nineteenth century racism, including (a) a belief in the existence of discrete human races, and (b) a belief that the races are not equal – the user's own race being supposed innately superior. As I have noted, 'scientific racism' based on such a doctrine has

8

now been demolished by advances in biological science. Elements of this view remain, however, and are often put into practice in the 'demeaning and prejudiced attitudes or discriminatory and antagonistic behaviour that members of one racial group direct against those of another' (Jeffcoate, 1984, p. 23). These kind of crude beliefs and actions have sometimes been termed, 'folk' or 'popular' racism.

Popular racism is, therefore, racism in its crudest form, yet individuals and groups who would denounce popular racism might themselves act in ways which disadvantage one or more ethnic minority groups. In order to analyse such instances, two further concepts are useful: 'institutional racism' and 'ethno-centrism'.

INSTITUTIONAL RACISM: In the USA this term was used by the Black Power campaigners Stokely Carmichael and Charles Hamilton (1967) to highlight the 'active and pervasive operation of anti-black attitudes and practices', not only at an individual, but also at an institutional (corporate and state) level (Banton, 1988b). Although the term is still used in this way by some writers (cf. Brandt, 1986; Solomos, 1988), the dominant understanding in the UK is related but somewhat more specialized. The CRE, for example, has stated that:

> For too long racism has been thought of in individual psychological terms reducible to the actions of prejudiced individuals. The concept of institutional racism draws attention to the structural workings of institutions which exclude black people regardless of individuals' attitudes. (CRE, 1985, pp. 2–3)

Hence institutional racism can operate 'through the normal workings of the system' where rules, regulations, formal procedures and informal practices have the effect of discriminating against members of an ethnic group (CRE, 1985, p. 2). The Swann report, for example, condemned separate provision (in language centres) for pupils for whom English was a second language. These centres draw their pupils primarily from South Asian communities and, by therefore excluding them from the mainstream of education, deny 'an individual child access to the full range of educational opportunities' (Swann, 1985, p. 389). The CRE has noted the similarity between institutional racism and the legal definition of 'indirect discrimination',

9

which makes it unlawful to apply conditions which 'disproportionately affect particular racial groups' (CRE, 1985, p. 3). For
instance, a private school's rule requiring pupils to wear a
uniform (and not a turban) has been judged to be discriminatory against Sikhs (Malone, 1983, pp. 6–7).

The concept of institutional racism is of great importance: it
establishes the simple but crucial fact that *a rule which is
applied to everyone is not automatically fair or just*. This
principle is particularly useful when examining the workings of
multi-ethnic schools where teachers who would strongly reject
crude popular racism may act in ways which are (in their
effects) discriminatory. Such actions may be examples of
institutional racism. However, because of the different uses of
that term it is useful to adopt instead the notion of
'ethnocentrism', a related concept which allows us to explore
more fully the complexity of life in multi-ethnic schools.

ETHNOCENTRISM: I wish to use this term in its most basic form,
meaning the tendency to evaluate other ethnic groups from the
standpoint of one's own ethnic group and experience. Ethnocentric judgements of others' behaviour, culture and experience
may lead to misunderstandings and even to conflict and
control. In some circumstances ethnocentrism on the part of
power-holders will lead to consequences which are 'racist'
in as much as they act against the interests of other ethnic
groups.

On many occasions, therefore, it is not possible to distinguish
between ethnocentrism and institutional racism. At this point,
however, it is useful to retain the concept of ethnocentrism
since it may help to illuminate important aspects of teacher–
pupil interactions which could otherwise be obscured by the
blanket term 'racism'. For example, several writers have
commented upon the stereotypes which teachers hold of South
Asian pupils as being more positive than those they hold of
Afro-Caribbeans (cf. Tomlinson, 1981; Mac an Ghaill, 1988).
Although the stereotypes differ, teachers' assumptions about
Asian and Afro-Caribbean pupils are both likely to operate in
racist ways. The concept of ethnocentrism acts as a useful
analytical tool which allows us to examine some of the more
complex ways in which apparently well-meaning, even liberal
teachers may act in racist ways.

Interaction and education

Focusing on the school

Throughout this book, my main concern is with life in multi-ethnic schools. I focus on the school-based practices, experiences and perspectives of those who are involved on a day-to-day basis: teachers and pupils. This does not mean, however, that I ignore wider structural forces; the complex nature of human society is such that the structures of economic and political power interrelate with individual human actions. We cannot understand life in multi-ethnic comprehensives without reference to the economic, gender and 'racial' inequalities at work in society as a whole. These inequalities are brought into the school and modified, re-created or reinforced through its workings (cf. Giddens, 1984).

By taking the school as the main level for analysis I wish to avoid the dehumanizing nature of some previous approaches. If we are to understand the workings of the educational system we have to consider the problems and solutions which are experienced and created 'at the chalk-face'. Both academics and ethnic minority communities have criticized research projects, government inquiries and local initiatives which have failed to address problems at the school level (cf. Troyna, 1986; *Issues in Race and Education*, 1987).

Large-scale surveys have charted the influences which individual schools can have upon the academic achievement of their pupils (Rutter, *et al.* 1979; Gray, McPherson and Raffe, 1983; Smith and Tomlinson, 1989; Nuttall, *et al.* 1989); unfortunately, because of their distance from the day-to-day pressures and realities of the classroom, such quantitative approaches have not been completely successful in discovering the reasons for success or failure, and exploring the complexities of life in school. Small-scale, detailed qualitative research can be more useful here; it gains in insight what it loses in sample size. In writing this book I have tried to draw on the strengths of both approaches.

Before considering the organization of the book in more detail, it may be useful to say a few words about the style of qualitative research which informed my study of City Road Comprehensive.

11

Qualitative research and ethnographic methods

In the past, qualitative research has sometimes been dismissed as dealing in 'soft' and 'unscientific' data (cf. Burgess, 1985; Gherardi and Turner, 1987). Such views reveal ignorance of a now well-established and vital part of social science methodology. Although the general term 'qualitative research' may be used in relation to a wide variety of different methods, there is no intrinsic reason why such work should be any less scientific than experimental or survey approaches — indeed, a growing literature has established the rigorous and systematic nature of good qualitative research (cf. Becker, 1970, especially part 1; Hammersley and Atkinson, 1983; Burgess, 1984).

There are many different styles of qualitative research, but they tend to share certain fundamental concerns and characteristics which may be summarized as follows (after Burgess, 1985):

(i) The researcher works in a natural setting: Qualitative work takes us 'where the action is'. Rather than theorizing about schools from a distance, the researcher actually enters the institution: s/he might observe life in classrooms and staffrooms, and/or talk to those involved on a day-to-day basis (ranging from the headteacher to the school's cleaning staff).

(ii) Studies may be designed and redesigned: Flexibility is the key to successful qualitative work, in terms both of the methods used and the issues which are addressed. Because qualitative work is intimately tied to the day-to-day life of institutions and individuals, the researcher must be ready to adapt to changes in the field which cannot be predicted in advance.

(iii) The research is concerned with social processes and with meaning: A great deal of qualitative sociological research is conducted from an 'interactionist' viewpoint (Woods, 1980a, 1983) which stresses the need to understand how participants perceive their role and experiences. Different social actors see the same situation in different ways; the interaction between them may have consequences of which neither is fully aware. In some respects the situation is analogous to the narrator's role in dramatic monologues, 'They don't quite know what they are saying and are telling a story to the meaning of which they are not entirely privy' (Bennett, 1988, p. 7). The qualitative

researcher must understand the actors' perspectives, but will also try to highlight something of the wider processes (that is, the full story).

(iv) Data collection and data analysis occur simultaneously: There are no rigid distinctions between the phases of data collection and analysis. Throughout the life of a project, researchers constantly shift and reappraise their understanding of the data. This process feeds back into the generation of new data (asking new questions, watching different groups in action). In this way qualitative theories are 'grounded' in the life of institutions and actors (cf. Glaser and Strauss, 1967; Strauss, 1987).[3]

The term 'ethnography' originally referred to detailed studies written by social anthropologists who spent years living in other cultures in order to understand something of their way of life. Some sociologists have used the same term in relation to detailed studies of life in more familiar settings, such as schools, hospitals, prisons and factories (cf. Hammersley and Atkinson, 1983). Ethnographies are characterized by a concern to chart the realities of day-to-day institutional life (usually over a period of months or even years) and by the great variety of data which are used. During my study of City Road Comprehensive, for example, I taped interviews with pupils and teachers; observed lessons, assemblies, formal and informal conversations; designed and administered questionnaires, and made use of existing documentary evidence within the school (such as attendance registers and punishment books). Such material allows the researcher to compare different accounts and sources of information. None is sufficient in isolation, but together they can reveal a detailed and critical picture of the processes at work in a school.

The City Road study

For two years I carried out intensive ethnographic field work in City Road Comprehensive, a large (1,000 pupil) multi-ethnic inner-city school situated a few minutes' walk from the centre of a Midlands city. During 1984 and 1985 I visited the school at least three times a week, focusing on pupils in three (later two) mixed ability forms as they moved from their third-year option choices, through their fourth year and into the final year of their compulsory schooling.[4]

The school's pupil intake was almost entirely working-class: of the two forms which I studied throughout the fieldwork only 13 per cent were from non-manual backgrounds (compared with approximately 30 per cent of children under sixteen in the entire county and 20 per cent of children under sixteen in the city district according to the 1981 Census).

Of the 211 pupils in the age-group which I studied (sometimes referred to as 'the research age-group'), nineteen were Afro-Caribbean (9 per cent of the age-group); fourteen were South Asian (7 per cent) and ten (5 per cent) were of mixed race. The remaining white European group included 168 pupils (80 per cent). Despite the numerical dominance of the last group, the ethnic minority pupils were a significant part of the pupil population; both teachers and pupils (of all ethnic origins) usually overestimated the proportion of ethnic minority pupils in the age-group. City Road was considered a multi-ethnic school by its teachers and pupils, and known as such throughout the city.

Although the school had gained something of a tough reputation it was not thought to have any special problems. For instance, unlike some local schools, City Road was not subject to accusations of racial discrimination from a local Afro-Caribbean pressure group which was protesting at the rate of suspensions and expulsions of ethnic minority pupils.

Like most schools, the positions of responsibility in City Road were dominated by male teachers. When I began the research thirty-nine of the sixty-five full-time teachers in the school were male (60 per cent); however, four of the five senior management team were male (80 per cent), as were fifteen of the twenty-one heads of department (71 per cent) and all five of the pastoral heads of year. During the fieldwork only one Afro-Caribbean teacher worked in City Road (as part of the Special Needs department). She had no contact with Afro-Caribbean pupils in my case study forms and was a rather peripheral member of staff. In addition, two LEA peripatetic teachers of South Asian ethnic origin worked in the school for a small part of each week. The school was, therefore, dominated by the perspectives of white male teachers.

City Road operated a system of mixed ability teaching in most subjects, although some 'setting by ability' was introduced in mathematics, science and English lessons prior to the fourth year. Following subject option specialization, some additional subjects were able to introduce setting in the upper school (that is, the fourth and fifth years) but most subjects remained mixed ability throughout.

The organization of the book

For the sake of clarity I have organized the book into two closely related parts. Each chapter deals with a particular issue or theme which develops both the overall picture of life in multi-ethnic schools and the account of key research on issues of controversy and debate in the field. The two parts are separated so as to signpost their different emphases clearly.

The chapters in Part One focus on the day-to-day interaction of teachers and pupils in multi-ethnic settings; they explore teachers' perceptions of order and indiscipline (chapter 2); and the ways in which pupils of Afro-Caribbean (chapter 3) and South Asian ethnic origin (chapter 4) responded to their very different experiences of comprehensive education.

Each chapter in the second part of the book explores a particular issue which has aroused considerable controversy in the field as a whole. This section begins by considering the problem of defining and measuring 'opportunity' in a multi-ethnic society, and includes a review of recent research on the associations between educational achievement and ethnicity, social class and gender (chapter 5). The development of different curriculum responses is examined in the light of the controversy surrounding multicultural and anti-racist approaches (chapter 6). This also highlights the importance of recent reforms of state education, including the establishment of the national curriculum and a national system of assessment and testing. These developments have particular consequences for the use and development of ethnic minority community languages (chapter 7).

The two parts of the book, therefore, are not discrete: their content and conclusions complement each other to reveal the complexity of the field.

PART ONE

City Road – Teaching and learning in a multi-ethnic comprehensive

Chapter 2

Discipline and control

The myth of an Afro-Caribbean challenge to authority

Research in multi-ethnic schools consistently indicates that, as a group, pupils of Afro-Caribbean ethnic origin experience more conflictual teacher–pupil relationships than their peers of other ethnic origins. For example, when a sample of second- and third-year pupils in four Local Education Authorities (LEAs) were asked whether they had been praised or criticized by a teacher in the previous week, it was found that 'West Indian' children 'receive distinctly more criticism than those originating from the UK and much more than those of south Asian origin' (Smith and Tomlinson, 1989, p. 96). Concern about the level of suspensions and expulsions of Afro-Caribbean pupils is becoming a familiar feature of the educational world. When the now abolished Inner London Education Authority (ILEA) first collected data on the ethnic background of suspended and expelled pupils (for the year 1986/7), Caribbean students of both sexes were over-represented in the figures: 14 per cent of pupils in the authority were of Caribbean origin, yet they accounted for more than 30 per cent of all suspensions (*Times Educational Supplement*, 9 September 1988).

Such findings are clearly of importance. In isolation, however, statistics offer a very simple and incomplete picture. To understand the dynamics of life in multi-ethnic schools, researchers must venture through the school gates and into the classroom.

19

Inside multi-ethnic classrooms

Until recently the multi-ethnic classroom remained an unex-
plored area. The first research to gain widespread recognition
in this field was conducted by Peter Green (1983a, 1983b).
Green observed seventy white teachers (twenty-eight male and
forty-two female) in primary and middle school classrooms. His
observations and analysis were structured by a modified
version of the Flanders schedule (Flanders, 1970), a system in
which an observer records the nature of classroom talk at
frequent regular points throughout a lesson.[1] The system has
been criticized for inflexibility and its inability to take account
of non-verbal communications. Green's findings therefore relate
to only a part of classroom life – teacher and pupil talk. Despite
this limitation, Green's findings were very important because
they revealed that pupils who share the same classroom can
have very different experiences of education; differences which
may relate in part to the gender of the teacher and pupil, but
which also reflect the students' ethnic origin. As he put it, 'boys
and girls of different ethnic origins taught in the same multi-
ethnic classroom by the same teacher are likely to receive
widely different educational experiences' (Green, 1985, p. 53).

Green found that the teachers gave most individual attention
to pupils of their own gender; this was most pronounced
among male teachers. He also discovered differences according
to the pupils' ethnic origin. While Asian pupils experienced
generally positive attention (praise), 'West Indian' boys'
classroom experience was much more negative, being subject
to more than twice the amount of criticism predicted by their
size in the pupil sample (Green, 1983b, p. 5). This pattern was
not repeated for Afro-Caribbean girls, who received less
individual attention from male teachers than their size in the
sample would have predicted.

> The girl of West Indian origin, whilst she is relatively ignored
> by her male teacher, appears to receive a more positive style
> of teaching than her male counterpart who must, at times,
> wonder if there is anything more to classroom activity for
> him than criticism, questions and directives. (Green, 1983b,
> p. 5)

Similarly, the women teachers also 'spent a considerable

20

amount of their time criticizing boys of West Indian origin and giving them directives' (Green, 1983b, p. 6).

Overall Green's findings indicated that both Afro-Caribbean boys and girls received more criticism than their Asian and European peers of the same sex, regardless of the teacher's gender (Green, 1983a, p. 93). Green's results suggest, therefore, that Afro-Caribbean pupils (especially boys) suffer relatively more authoritarian and negative relationships with their teachers than their Asian and white European classmates.

It must be remembered, however, that Green's data can only indicate broad distinctions within the life of certain primary and middle school classes; his work reveals nothing of the processes behind the teacher–pupil relationships. It might, for instance, simply be argued that the Afro-Caribbean males merited criticism by their behaviour in the classroom. It is in the generation of qualitative insights into the life of multi-ethnic schools that ethnographic methodologies offer a critical avenue of research into the position of Afro-Caribbean pupils in the English comprehensive school.

Teacher–pupil conflict and the stereotyping of Afro-Caribbean pupils

Over recent years an increasing amount of ethnographic work has been conducted in multi-ethnic schools. There is no room to discuss every publication in this field, but a consistent pattern has begun to emerge. To date, the most influential ethnography of teacher–pupil relations in multi-ethnic English schools is that conducted by Cecile Wright as part of a wider investigation into the educational and vocational experiences of young people of ethnic minority groups (Eggleston, Dunn and Anjali, 1984, 1986). Wright studied two schools in a single Midlands authority.[2] In 'Upton' school pupils of Afro-Caribbean and Asian origin made up approximately 25 per cent of the pupil population, whereas in 'Landley' school they accounted for more than 60 per cent. Wright reported a conflictual relationship between Afro-Caribbean pupils and their teachers in both research schools, and argued that this led teachers to assign pupils of Afro-Caribbean ethnic origin to the lower streams and bands in the upper school.

In Landley there was a feeling among staff that the school

21

was being 'swamped' by ethnic minority pupils, while at Upton great resentment was caused by crude racist jokes which were made by some members of staff during lessons. One teacher remarked:

> I was down at Lower School, I had a black girl in my class, she did something or another. I said to her, if you're not careful I'll send you back to the chocolate factory. She went home and told her parents, her dad came up to school, and decided to take the matter to the Commission for Racial Equality. It was only said in good fun, nothing malicious. (Wright, 1985a, p. 11)

Like Peter Green, Wright reported that interactions between Afro-Caribbean pupils and their white teachers 'very frequently took the form of enforcing discipline rather than encouragement or praise' (Wright, 1985a, p. 12). Furthermore, Wright argued that the conflictual nature of the Afro-Caribbean pupil–white teacher relationship clouded all official dealings with pupils of Afro-Caribbean ethnic origin.

In sum, the case study indicates that the relationships between teachers and pupils of West Indian origin in both schools was often antagonistic. The teacher–pupil relationship influenced the teachers' professional judgement of the pupils' ability and some West Indian pupils may have been placed in inappropriate ability groups and examination sets, so restricting their educational opportunities. (Wright, 1985b, p. 22)

This conclusion is similar to that reached by Geoffrey Driver in an earlier ethnography of a multi-ethnic school. Driver is best known for his research in which he argued that 'West Indian' pupils were not underachieving to the degree suggested by previous work (Driver, 1980a, 1980b). Both his methodology and findings have been very strongly criticized (cf. Taylor, 1983, pp. 113–22) and, as a result, his earlier ethnographic study of a multi-ethnic secondary modern school (Driver, 1977, 1979) has often been neglected. Driver himself must take some responsibility for this state of affairs, as his published accounts of the earlier study are brief, rather vague and inconsistent in the use of certain key terms. In addition, in

22

trying to defend his later work, Driver has further confused the situation by failing to distinguish between the different research projects (Driver, 1984). Despite these problems, the earlier work does offer some significant material.

Driver's study of 'West Midlands School' was carried out in the early 1970s and examined the factors which influenced the perspectives of a group of 'West Indian' pupils and their teachers. The study was inconclusive but of value in pointing to the complexity of interactions in a multi-ethnic school. In particular, Driver noted the problems which white teachers experienced when trying to interpret the behaviour of their West Indian pupils. He argued that the teachers did not have the 'cultural competence' (1977) to identify correctly the meanings which pupils were conveying in their actions, and that this 'confusion' (1979) led the teachers to see 'West Indians' as difficult, problem pupils. Such perceptions were subsequently institutionalized through the pupils' placement in non-academic streams: a decision which teachers based upon behavioural rather than academic characteristics.

> Faced with the limitations of their own cultural competence
> . . . teachers often felt that the only way forward was a power-based insistence that these pupils act according to the standards which they [the teachers] stipulated for them. This tended to intensify an already conflictual situation and to heighten the ethnic awareness of those involved. (Driver, 1977, p. 356)

In his later article Driver offered some examples of the teachers' 'confusion' in multi-ethnic classrooms. Firstly, he stated that white teachers were often unable to distinguish between the West Indian pupils, although they had long since learnt the separate identities of their white pupils. Further examples of 'confusion' referred to a failure to interpret meaningful behaviour correctly, whether it was respectful or derogatory, and noted the teachers' negative responses to pupils' use of patois (Driver, 1977, pp. 136–8).

Driver's view that white teachers were unable to distinguish between behavioural and academic evaluations of 'West Indian' pupils was subsequently supported by Cecile Wright's work and by Barrie Middleton's (1983) study of 'Valley View High' (a northern comprehensive) where teachers also saw Afro-

23

Caribbean pupils as a source of trouble who could be best contained in the non-academic classes of the upper school (known as the 'B' band). The following quotation concerns the fate of an Afro-Caribbean girl who was officially judged to be on the borderline between the academic and non-academic bands:

> Take Maxine last year, I had her name pencilled in for the A band. What happened? It turned out that there were two girls to choose from; one was Maxine, a noisy West Indian girl, and the other, a quiet white girl. Guess who got the vote? Mr S. said Maxine didn't deserve to get the A band. I saw her work recently and she's gone backwards. (Middleton, 1983, p. 88)

Middleton's work therefore offers support for both Driver (1977, 1979) and Wright's argument concerning the importance which teachers' attach to their Afro-Caribbean pupils' behavioural (rather than academic) performance. Unlike Driver, however, Middleton did not question the teachers' perception that Afro-Caribbean pupils were a greater behavioural problem. In fact, he stated: 'It is not denied in this study that the black boy is clearly more demanding, or badly behaved, than his white counterpart' (Middleton, 1983, p. 117). In contrast, Driver queried the accuracy of teachers' perceptions. In his notion of 'cultural competence'/'confusion', Driver began to explore the importance of teachers' definitions of order and disorder in an ethnically mixed environment. Cecile Wright acknowledged the potential of this work as 'a partial explanation' but went on to state that:

> it is difficult to accept 'confusion' as sufficient cause for misallocation in banding and setting. How, for example, is it possible to 'confuse' a mark of 82% ... in allocating a child to a CSE set? And how is it possible to 'confuse' an internal report which gives an attainment score of 6 ... indicating that all subjects were graded A or B – and still allocate the child to the bottom of three bands? (Wright, 1985b, p. 22)

In answer to her questions Wright continued, 'Another possible explanation is provided by a teacher reporting on a West Indian pupil who is favourably placed. The teacher's comment: *No trouble as yet this year, can be a little loud.*' (Wright,

1985b, p. 22; original emphasis). This comment embodies the assumption that the pupil not only has the potential, but is also likely to cause trouble in the future. Such views are strikingly similar to those which I found in City Road Comprehensive; views which reflected and reinforced the staff's belief that Afro-Caribbean pupils represented a greater challenge to their authority than any other group in the school. After two years' research in City Road I concluded that the teachers' belief was not an accurate picture of their Afro-Caribbean pupils. Nevertheless this myth had massive consequences for inter-actions between white teachers and Afro-Caribbean pupils. In order to understand the origins, dynamics and consequences of the myth it is necessary to examine the day-to-day interaction of Afro-Caribbean pupils and white teachers. In so doing it will become clear that Driver and Wright's analyses have much more in common than is at first apparent.

Ethnocentrism and teacher–pupil interactions in City Road

When considering conflictual teacher–pupil interactions, we must begin by considering teachers' definitions of what constitutes appropriate pupil behaviour.

Certain styles of behaviour, dress and demeanour were generally required of all City Road pupils. In public gatherings such as school assemblies, and in various school handbooks which were given to all pupils, the headteacher and senior staff made it clear that all pupils (regardless of age, gender, 'ability' or social background) were expected to meet a series of demands concerning their attitude and behaviour in (and around) the school. All pupils were encouraged to attend school regularly and punctually, to be smartly dressed in school uniform, to be polite and obedient around members of staff, and always to try their hardest in any academic or sporting endeavour.

In addition to these consciously defined official requirements, City Road teachers also operated a series of less clearly articulated, unofficial requirements concerning the pupil role. Previous work by writers such as Howard Becker (1951, 1952) and, more recently, Sharp and Green (1975) has suggested that teachers differentiate between pupils according to how closely

25

they meet certain notions of the 'ideal client', a construction
which is drawn primarily from the lifestyle and culture of the
teacher concerned.

> Professionals depend on their environing society to provide
> them with clients who meet the standards of their image of
> the ideal client. Social class cultures, *among other factors*,
> may operate to produce many clients who, in
> one way or another, fail to meet these specifications and
> therefore aggravate one or another of the basic problems of
> the worker–client relation ... (Becker, 1952, reprinted in
> Becker, 1970, p. 149; emphasis added)

As Becker suggested, social class factors are not the only ones
reflected in teachers' 'specifications' of the ideal client; in City
Road, ethnic differences also influenced the ways in which
teachers' perceived their pupils.

The notion that human beings often interpret 'strangeness' as
in some way threatening is not a new one (cf. Schutz, 1964);
we are often suspicious of things which we do not understand.
However, in their institutional role, teachers in multi-ethnic
schools are required to perceive and respond to a variety of
traits which may seem alien to them. The most obviously
'strange' behaviour in City Road often reflected beliefs and
practices associated with Asian pupils who, for religious
reasons, were sometimes required to dress and eat differently
to their white peers. City Road teachers had some understanding of the cultural basis of such differences and (to their credit)
routinely accepted that, for instance, Asian girls would not be
subject to the same uniform rules as their peers of other ethnic
origins (Asian girls were the only female pupils exempt from
wearing skirts to school).

Despite the apparent similarities in their linguistic and
religious backgrounds, pupils of Afro-Caribbean origin also
exhibited cultural traits which were not familiar to their white
teachers. Although these styles were not as obviously 'foreign'
as Asian languages or dress customs, their origins nevertheless
lay outside the white cultural experience of the teachers. This
fundamental point went unrecognized by staff who imposed
their own ethnocentric interpretations upon Afro-Caribbean
pupils' behaviour, that is, they judged the pupils' actions in
terms of a set of understandings and expectations rooted in

their own white experience and culture.

In the year group which I studied, all but three of the nineteen Afro-Caribbean pupils had been born in the United Kingdom. This does not mean that they had therefore been part of the same cultural experience as their white peers. Many of the Afro-Caribbean pupils were to some extent living within two cultures; firstly, the culture of their home and social life, which often reflected key elements of an Afro-Caribbean experience and tradition, and secondly, the 'white' culture of the school. In addition to the influence of their parents and guardians, most of whom had emigrated to this country from the Caribbean, these pupils seemed to gain a heightened awareness of their cultural 'difference' – their ethnicity – from the media and from their contacts with a large Afro-Caribbean community centred around another part of the city. Television programmes which dealt with the black experience in Britain were especially popular among the Afro-Caribbean pupils in my case study forms; a current affairs show and a situation comedy were particular favourites. The latter focused upon a group of black teenagers in London and reflected many of the styles of language and demeanour which the pupils could encounter in a local district ('Cityside') and which I sometimes observed among Afro-Caribbean pupils in the school.

Cityside was the main centre of Asian and Afro-Caribbean settlement in the city and, although it was a bus ride away from City Road, almost all of the Afro-Caribbean pupils had some contact with the life of the area; a few had lived there for a time, while others had close family or friends there. This second group included pupils who had been attracted to the area as somewhere to go when they were at a loose end and who had subsequently made contacts with other Afro-Caribbean youths and post-school-age teenagers in Cityside.

In interviews and informal conversations with Afro-Caribbean pupils it became clear that they frequently adopted different styles of language and demeanour when they were in the 'separate' worlds of the school and their social life outside. These styles, however, were not always exclusive to one setting and elements of a wider Afro-Caribbean youth culture were sometimes seen within the school. For example, a particular style of walking (with seemingly exaggerated swinging of the shoulders and a spring in the step) was occasionally used by some Afro-Caribbean males in the school. My observations suggested that the style was exclusive to Afro-Caribbean males and that it was always interpreted as in some way inappropriate by members of staff. It is worth examining the teachers' views in more detail since, although the style of walking did not contravene school rules, it frequently led to pupils being criticized.

Teachers' reactions to the style of walking could range from initial amusement, with members of staff exchanging grins behind the pupil's back, to more or less disguised hostility. Frequently the style resulted in the pupil being told to 'get a move on', and on one occasion I saw Charley Thompson (a member of one of my case study forms) called out from a line of pupils entering the assembly hall and ordered to 'Stand up straight' and 'Walk properly'.

Although, in my experience, the staff seemed always to regard this style of walking as inappropriate, its meaning was not fixed for the pupils concerned. When I asked Charley about the incident described above he told me:

> I always walk – well, its not my usual walk sir[3] but you know that most black people *do* walk like that [smiles] don't they? Have you ever noticed that, you know with springs in their foot and things like that. [He laughs] I just can't help it, it's the way – it's the people I hang 'round with, and they walk like that, so you just pick it up . . .

This style of walking, therefore, often reflected nothing more than a 'good feeling' – something which was usually lost in the face of staff responses to it. However, on rare occasions the style did have more symbolic importance. During one lesson which I observed, for instance, Charley was ordered out of the room as punishment for speaking with a friend. The whole class fell silent and all eyes turned to watch him. Charley stood, slowly placed his pen on the desk and left the room in the same relaxed walking style described above. On this occasion his walk did not express a feeling of well-being, rather, it allowed Charley to salvage some dignity from the situation, acting as a sign of his independence: he did not leave with his head bowed in embarrassment.

It is impossible to say whether the teachers' negative interpretation of the style of walking was either a response to, or a catalyst for, its occasional use as a strategy of resistance.

Indeed, the question is unimportant. What should be noted is that a behavioural style, rooted in the ethnicity of Afro-Caribbean pupils, was without exception interpreted by their white teachers as being inappropriate to school. This reflected a more general tendency among the staff to devalue anything which did not conform to their own (white) expectations and experience.

I have examined teachers' interpretation of the style of walking in detail because it was a behavioural trait whose control by staff could not be justified by reference to any educational rationale. For example, teachers often displayed similar attitudes towards types of dress and speech which reflected Afro-Caribbean ethnicity, yet it could be argued that these were clearly in conflict with certain of the school's stated policies. Thus teachers would remind pupils that school rules forbade the wearing of badges and caps or berets and that everyone should try to speak 'correctly'. Consequently the official policy that (as the headteacher put it in assembly one morning) 'No one has the right to expect any different treatment to anyone else' meant that certain displays of ethnicity were, in fact, labelled as 'deviant'.

I am not suggesting that the teachers used school rules as an excuse to harass Afro-Caribbean pupils. The vast majority of staff I spoke with seemed genuinely to believe that 'treating everyone the same' was the best way to deal with the ethnic diversity of the school's pupil population. Unfortunately, one consequence of this perspective was that in the day-to-day life of the school almost any display of Afro-Caribbean ethnicity was deemed inappropriate and was controlled, either officially (in the case of non-uniform dress) or informally (in the case of speech and the style of walking noted above).

Clearly the situation was complex, but the interaction of the factors noted above was very important, for it meant that relationships between Afro-Caribbean pupils and white teachers were set within a wider school context where the pupils' ethnicity was devalued and became a potential source of conflict.

The control and criticism of Afro-Caribbean pupils

Earlier I noted that Peter Green's research (1983a) in primary and middle school classrooms had suggested that 'West Indian'

29

pupils received disproportionately high amounts of control and criticism from their white teachers. A similar pattern of interaction was apparent in City Road Comprehensive during the pupils' final years of compulsory schooling.

As the research age-group began their final year I observed several lessons (in both core and optional subjects) which involved members of my case study forms. As part of my observations I noted the number of criticisms and controlling statements which the teacher directed at each pupil. I discovered that whenever Afro-Caribbean pupils were present they were always among the most criticized and controlled pupils in the group. Perhaps even more significant than the frequency of critical and controlling statements which Afro-Caribbean pupils received, was the fact that they were often singled out for criticism even though several pupils, of different ethnic origins, were engaged in the same behaviour. This was potentially even more harmful to teacher–pupil relations. In sum, Afro-Caribbean pupils were not only criticized more often than their white peers, but the same behaviour in a white pupil might not bring about criticism at all.

A frequent recipient of such control was Paul Dixon, an Afro-Caribbean pupil in one of my case study forms. Paul achieved highly in written examinations but his form tutor told me that he had received complaints concerning Paul's 'silly behaviour in some lessons'. Paul was a member of the top English set (whom teachers expected to achieve highly in external examinations), where he sat with a group of boys, mainly white, who would often whisper comments to each other during lessons. Paul took a full part in such exchanges, but was by no means the only pupil to speak. However, it was usually Paul whom the teacher told to be quiet, and during my observations of the set he was the single most criticized pupil.

A tendency specifically to control Afro-Caribbean pupils, even when members of other ethnic groups were also involved in the 'deviant' act, was sometimes quite startling. On one occasion both Paul Dixon (Afro-Caribbean) and Arif Aslam (Asian) arrived seven minutes late for a mixed ability lesson which I observed. They apologized for the delay but explained that they had been with the head of guidance. Almost half an hour into the lesson most of the group were working steadily and, like the majority of their peers, Paul and Arif were holding a conversation while they worked. The teacher looked up from the pupil he was dealing with and shouted across the room: 'Paul. Look, you come in late, now you have the audacity to waste not only your time but his [Arif's] as well.' The fact that both Paul *and* Arif had arrived late, and that the conversation was a two-way affair, was not reflected in the teacher's statement which explicitly criticized the Afro-Caribbean pupil while implying that his Asian friend was a blameless victim.

Teachers were often unaware of their disproportionate criticism of Afro-Caribbean pupils and most of the incidents which I witnessed were not as clear-cut as the one above. Yet the pattern of teacher–pupil interactions did not go unnoticed among the pupils. During their fifth year I asked pupils in my two case study forms to answer some sentence completion items. Pupils of Afro-Caribbean origin accounted for approximately 10 per cent of the age group, yet in response to the item, '. . . . . is picked on by some teachers', half of the pupils nominated were of Afro-Caribbean origin.

During our conversations many Afro-Caribbean pupils complained about unfair treatment; their views were often confirmed by their white peers, who, some would say, offered more persuasive evidence since they had nothing to gain by characterizing white teacher–Afro-Caribbean pupil relations in this way.

DG	Do you think the teachers particularly like or dislike some people?
James Murray (white)	I think some are racialist.
DG	In what ways would you *see* that?
James	Sometimes they pick on the blacks. Sometimes the whites are let off. When there's a black and a white person, probably just pick on the black person.

His teachers saw James as a pupil of average ability and (unlike some of his more alienated peers) he could not be accused of having any vested interest in portraying teachers in a negative way. Pupils whom I identified as highly committed to the official school value system (who might be labelled 'pro-school')[4] also reported that some of their Afro-Caribbean peers were subject to frequent and sometimes 'unfair' criticism. However, such pupils often had quite close relationships with

31

staff and they did not use their particular observations as a basis from which to generalize that there was victimization of Afro-Caribbean pupils *per se*.

DG	Do you think that any groups of pupils are treated differently?
Julie Bexson (white)	Some people who've got a bad reputation, you know, they get picked on more (. . .) Like if you're messing around in class sometimes, then the teacher will always presume that it's *you* who's messing around. If anything goes wrong, it's you that gets it . . . I can't really explain.
DG	You can't think of any, say in your form, that might get –
Julie	[interrupting] *Charley* [Afro-Caribbean]. Yeah, definitely. If there's any messing around it's always Charley that's done [punished] for it . . .

And, in a different interview:

DG	Do the teachers treat any groups of pupils differently?
Anthony Clarke (white)	I know Mr Dean used to shout at Wayne and Charley a lot [both are Afro-Caribbean], but I mean, all the coloureds reckon that teachers are prejudiced against them . . . I think that's a load of *crap*.

It is clear, therefore, that an awareness of teachers' frequent criticism and control of Afro-Caribbean pupils was not restricted to the Afro-Caribbean pupils themselves or to their more 'disaffected' white peers. Furthermore, as I have already noted, the pupils' reports were supported by my own classroom observation. Yet, the disproportionate criticism which these pupils experienced in class was not the only dimension to the conflict which so often characterized their interaction with teachers. A further, critical dimension concerned the application of the school's official disciplinary procedures.

Afro-Caribbean pupils and school-wide sanctions

Interactionist analyses of 'deviance', such as those outlined by Becker (1963) and Hargreaves, Hester and Mellor (1975), do not (as they are often accused, for instance by Blackledge and Hunt, 1985, pp. 304–5) suggest that once a person is 'labelled' s/he will automatically internalize that judgement and commit further acts of deviance (cf. Hargreaves, 1976; Syer, 1982). For example, Howard Becker identified several factors which *may* lead to the development of a 'deviant career'. Among the most important potential influences is the reinforcement of negative judgements in subsequent interactions with actors in positions of institutional authority, such as police or teachers (Becker, 1963, pp. 36–9). Furthermore, it is reasonable to suppose that negative labels attain even greater significance where they are no longer the preserve of separate teacher–pupil relationships but carry the force of institution-wide sanctions.

Comprehensive schools have evolved many different systems of reward and punishment (cf. Gillborn, Nixon and Rudduck, 1989, pp. 259–68). City Road operated a number of disciplinary procedures ranging from the opportunity for any teacher to keep a pupil back after school ('a personal detention'), to the mechanisms for permanent exclusion from the school roll ('expulsion'). The former were very frequent, carried little official weight and were not recorded by the school. The latter represented the most serious sanction which the school (in conjunction with the LEA) could apply to a pupil. However, during my research too few pupils were expelled for any clear pattern to emerge concerning their ethnic origins. Between these extremes lay a variety of official sanctions, two of which were centrally recorded by the school and whose application may be more fully analysed. The first was the system of individualized report cards and the second, senior management detentions.

Report cards were a formalized means of monitoring a pupil's behaviour. The pupil was given a printed card which included spaces for subject teachers to confirm the pupil's attendance and to comment on their behaviour. To take one example, a card given to Wayne Johnson (an Afro-Caribbean boy in one of my case study forms) requested subject teachers' comments on his 'punctuality, attitude and behaviour'. Pupils were required to hand this card to each of their subject teachers and finally present it to their form tutors at the end of the school day. Each card included enough space for a week's comments. In some cases pupils were given several cards consecutively. Indeed, during the first term of her fifth year, one of my case study pupils (an Afro-Caribbean girl) was told that she would receive report cards for the remainder of her school career.

The importance of report cards was twofold. Firstly, they indicated that the pupil's behaviour was considered enough of a problem to warrant official action beyond informal word-of-mouth reporting. Secondly, they represented a likely source of reinforcement of 'deviant' labels. The official requirement to take note of, and record, the behaviour of a particular pupil drew teachers' attention to a potential source of trouble and could lead to actions which might inflame the situation further, such as forcing the pupil to change his or her seat. In such circumstances pupils often felt that they were being victimized:

> Wayne Johnson   You just walk in a room, sit down. They
> (Afro-Caribbean)   say 'Get up and move over there'. And all
>   I did was walked in the room.

In view of these factors it was significant that during their secondary school careers a much greater proportion of Afro-Caribbean pupils in the age-group received at least one report card: 37 per cent of Afro-Caribbeans (N=7) compared to 6 per cent of pupils of all other ethnic origins (N=12).[5] Given the greater control and criticism of pupils of Afro-Caribbean origin, their proportionately greater receipt of report cards was in the predicted direction. It must be said that the absolute number of pupils who received report cards was very small and the figures must therefore be treated with extreme caution. A more broadly based comparison may be made by examining the receipt of senior management detentions by pupils of different ethnic origins.

These detentions took their title from the level of staff who supervized the after-school sessions. Being instructed to stay after the normal school day, to be supervized by a senior teacher, represented a serious statement about the recipients' behaviour: a teacher giving senior management detentions had to record a 'reason for detention' in the school punishment book and an explanatory letter was sent to the pupil's home, requiring written acknowledgement by a parent or guardian.

I studied the school's punishment books and noted each senior management detention which involved a pupil in my research age-group at any time between the beginning of their third year and the end of the autumn term in their fifth year (when my intensive fieldwork ended). The figures lent further support to my belief, based upon observational and interview data, that Afro-Caribbean pupils were subject to proportionately greater degrees of control and criticism than their peers of other ethnic origins. A majority of Afro-Caribbean pupils (68 per cent, N=13) received at least one senior management detention during my research. The pattern was true for both sexes and unique to pupils of Afro-Caribbean origin. Furthermore, a majority of Afro-Caribbean pupils who appeared in the punishment books went on to total four or more such detentions. Once again this pattern was true for both sexes and unique to pupils of Afro-Caribbean origin. A full breakdown of the data by gender and ethnic origin is presented in Table 2.1.

The proportionately greater receipt of report cards and senior management detentions among pupils of Afro-Caribbean origin was indicative of the conflictual nature of their interactions with teachers in City Road. Pupils of other ethnic origins were sometimes subject to the same controls as their Afro-Caribbean peers, but the frequency of the control and criticism of Afro-Caribbean pupils was significantly greater. This served to reinforce both the existing conflicts between staff and pupils, and the simplistic notions which each sometimes held concerning the other; specifically, the pupils' sense of victimization and the teachers' perception of Afro-Caribbean pupils as a likely source of trouble.

The myth of an Afro-Caribbean challenge to authority

So far I have discussed the tendency among white teachers in City Road to control and criticize disproportionately their pupils of Afro-Caribbean ethnic origin. I have shown how both white and Afro-Caribbean pupils were aware of this, and how the conflict was reinforced through the use of official school disciplinary procedures. I now wish to examine the way in which both sides interpreted the conflict as being 'racially' motivated. Both the teachers and their Afro-Caribbean pupils

Table 2.1 The frequency of detentions per pupil detained during the third, fourth and fifth years* in City Road Comprehensive (by gender and ethnic origin)

| | Detentions per pupil detained at least once | | | | | | | | | | |
| | 1 only | | 2 to 3 | | 4 to 5 | | 6 to 10 | | 11 or more | | Total | |
	%	N	%	N	%	N	%	N	%	N	%	N
MALE												
White	53	23	35	15	7	3	2	1	2	1	99	43
A-Caribbean	0	0	29	2	43	3	29	2	0	0	101	7
South Asian	50	3	50	3	0	0	0	0	0	0	100	6
Mixed race	33	1	33	1	0	0	33	1	0	0	99	3
ALL MALES	46	27	36	21	10	6	7	4	2	1	101	59
FEMALE												
White	45	10	18	4	18	4	14	3	5	1	100	22
A-Caribbean	17	1	0	0	67	4	17	1	0	0	101	6
South Asian	100	1	0	0	0	0	0	0	0	0	100	1
Mixed race	100	1	0	0	0	0	0	0	0	0	100	1
ALL FEMALE	43	13	13	4	27	8	13	4	3	1	99	30
ALL PUPILS												
White	51	33	29	19	11	7	6	4	3	2	100	65
A-Caribbean	8	1	15	2	54	7	23	3	0	0	100	13
South Asian	57	4	43	3	0	0	0	0	0	0	100	7
Mixed race	50	2	25	1	0	0	25	1	0	0	100	4
TOTAL	45	40	28	25	16	14	9	8	2	2	100	89

* Fifth year: autumn term only.
Note: Percentages are rounded to the nearest whole number.

frequently described the conflict between them not merely as teacher versus pupil, but as white versus black.

Of particular importance was a tendency among members of staff to generalize that a pupil's behaviour signified a more deep-seated challenge to the authority of the school: specifically, an Afro-Caribbean challenge to white authority. I was present at a fourth-year parents' evening, for example, when Paul Dixon's father reported that his son had complained to him about racial victimization by staff. After the meeting I spoke with Paul's form tutor who told me:

I think he [Paul]'s got it in for white (...)
When you're talking to him he's going [looks away from me,
feigning apparent lack of interest].
You know, you can see him thinking, 'What right have you
got – a white – to tell *me* off'.   (field notes)

As I have already stated, Geoffrey Driver (1977, 1979) has
questioned white teachers' 'competence' to interpret accurately 'West Indian' behaviour. As an example of 'confusion' on the
teachers' part Driver noted:

Turning the eyes away was observed on many occasions to
be made by a West Indian pupil as a sign of deference and
respect to a teacher, yet it was received and interpreted by
the teacher as an expression of guilt or bad manners. (Driver,
1979, p. 137)

Whether the incident involving Paul Dixon was an example of
this kind of 'confusion' cannot be assumed. It was clear,
however, (from the evidence of white teachers and their Afro-
Caribbean pupils in City Road) that some teachers' readiness to
identify a racially based threat to their authority in their
dealings with Afro-Caribbean pupils could only add to the
existing conflicts.

Michael Cooper (mixed race)	... I got caught [playing truant] once, [a teacher] he asked me why I was doing it, but I couldn't give him a reason. So he started going *barmy* at me, saying, 'Oh, all 'cause you're a different colour from me, you can't answer me' and all this.

I wish to stress that the imputation of a deliberate challenge
to authority – typified by the phrase 'you can see him thinking'
(Paul Dixon's form tutor) – was not a crude stereotype held by
obviously prejudiced teachers. Rather, it was a way of thinking
which was rooted in the ethnocentric assumptions of teachers
and their responses to the day-to-day demands made upon
them within the school. The vast majority of teachers whom I
met in City Road (and all those quoted in this chapter) seemed
genuinely committed to ideals of equality of educational
opportunity, yet in order to carry out their job they had to

37

control pupils. The teachers' insistence that all pupils should be 'treated alike', plus the range of demands upon their time and energies, led them into a disproportionate amount of conflict with Afro-Caribbean pupils. This was a simple fact of life for many teachers and reinforced their belief in an Afro-Caribbean challenge to authority, a myth which seemed impervious to the complaints of pupils and parents. Many teachers had personal experience of 'trouble' with pupils of Afro-Caribbean origin and they often generalized this image onto the group as a whole.

A female member of staff	I've never been assaulted by a white kid. I've been thrown against a wall by a pupil and it was a black kid. I've been called a 'Fucking slag' but I've only ever been *hit* by a black kid. (field notes)

This statement reflects the view, common among City Road staff, that, as a group, pupils of Afro-Caribbean origin presented a greater disciplinary problem than their peers of other ethnic origins. Indeed, the statement (from a dedicated and normally compassionate teacher) seems to imply that the Afro-Caribbean threat was qualitatively, as well as quantitatively, more serious.

The detention data (in Table 2.1) certainly supported the claim that Afro-Caribbean pupils were frequently in trouble. The question now arises as to why pupils of Afro-Caribbean origin appeared so often in the school detention books; was it that they simply broke school rules more often than their peers? I have argued that much of the pupils' so-called deviance depended upon their teachers' interpretation of unfamiliar behaviour and an imputation of an Afro-Caribbean challenge to authority. These questions may be explored further by returning to the information available in the school detention books.

In addition to examining the number of detentions given by staff, it was possible to use the teachers' brief comments on the reason for detention (recorded at the time the detention was given) as the basis for a tentative breakdown by the type of explanation offered. In particular I focused on the nature of the recorded offence(s) as situated either in the 'routine' agreements and rules governing behaviour in the school, or in the 'interpretation' of pupil action by the member of staff who gave the detention.

I classified as 'routine' all detentions where the reasons given in the punishment book referred only to the pupils' transgression of some school rule for which the appropriate punishment was always felt to be a senior management detention. For example, 'Smoking', 'Truancy' and 'Shop at breaktime', were staff entries which referred only to the particular rule which had been broken.

I counted as 'interpretative' all staff entries where teachers justified detentions by reference to their own interpretation of pupils' behaviour, as opposed to simply observing which rule was judged to have been broken. If the member of staff, in officially recording his/her reason for giving a detention, felt it necessary to include a comment on the attitude of the pupil then I classified that detention as interpretative. For example:

- Persistent disruptive behaviour and rudeness when challenged.
- Nuisance on the stairs, denial, lies.
- Rudeness and attitude towards apology.

The classification was an attempt to examine the extent to which detentions were earned by breaking clearly defined school rules as opposed to offending teachers' less explicit expectations of acceptable behaviour. Clearly, all detentions relied upon teacher interpretation to some extent, however, the distinction is a reasonable one: in my experience during two years of fieldwork in City Road, any pupil discovered truanting or smoking on the school premises would receive a detention. In contrast, teachers' perceptions of 'misbehaviour', 'rudeness' and 'attitude' could vary dramatically.

In applying the routine/interpretative classification I sought to represent the teachers' own justifications as closely as possible. In so doing, it is likely that I underestimated the true incidence of interpretative detentions. One form tutor, for example, gave three girls (two of them were Afro-Caribbean) a total of nine detentions over just three days − all for 'persistent lateness'. These entries represented a teacher's conscious decision to 'clamp down' on a particular group of girls. The detentions were, therefore, closer to the type which I have defined as interpretative. However, since I have no way of knowing whether any other apparently routine detentions are based on similar clampdowns I have decided to apply my classification consistently, based purely on the official entry in the punishment book. Similarly, where a pupil failed to attend a detention s/he automatically received another to replace the one which had been missed. These were known as repeat detentions and in my analysis I counted them as routine because, although the original offence may have been inter-pretative, there was no element of interpretation involved in the carrying over of a repeat detention. Thus I restricted my own interpretation of the detention data to a single criterion, that is, the teacher's written reason for detention. If I had introduced my personal knowledge of particular cases it might be argued that I had biased the analysis in some way, for instance, because I knew a greater proportion of the Afro-Caribbean pupils in the age-group.

Table 2.2 applies the routine/interpretative distinction to all detentions received by pupils in the research age-group during my fieldwork. The data suggest that the offences of Afro-Caribbean pupils tended to be of a different nature to those of other ethnic groups. The majority of all detentions given during the research (for both sexes and all ethnic origins) were categorized as routine (67 per cent); less than a third of all detention offences were described by the teacher in interpret-ative terms (30 per cent). This distribution was reproduced almost identically for pupils of either gender: 67 per cent of all male and 68 per cent of all female detentions were classified as routine, with 30 per cent and 31 per cent respectively as interpretative. It would appear, therefore, that there was little or no significant difference in the incidence of types of detention offence between male and female pupils.

However, some important differences were discernible in relation to pupils' ethnic origin. For all white and Asian pupils detained, routine violations appeared twice as often as interpretative ones. In contrast, pupils of Afro-Caribbean origin had an almost equal division between routine and interpretat-ive descriptions.[6]

In comparison to white and Asian pupils, therefore, a greater proportion of the detentions given to Afro-Caribbean pupils appear to have been based upon offences whose identification rested primarily in the teachers' interpretation of pupil attitude or intent. The same also appears to be true for male pupils of mixed race (where one parent was of Afro-Caribbean origin).

Despite my qualifications concerning the definition and application of the detention offence categories, therefore, the patterns which emerged are in the predicted direction. Hence the data support the hypothesis that City Road teachers tended to perceive a disproportionate challenge to their authority in the behaviour of Afro-Caribbean pupils. Pupils of Afro-Caribbean origin did not simply break clearly defined school rules more often than their peers.

Table 2.2 'Reason for detention' given during the third, fourth and fifth years* in City Road Comprehensive (by gender and ethnic origin)

| | Reason for detention | | | | | | | |
| | Routine | | Interpretative | | Other** | | Total | |
	%	N	%	N	%	N	%	N
MALE								
White	77	72	22	21	1	1	100	94
Afro-Caribbean	45	14	45	14	10	3	100	31
South Asian	73	8	27	3	0	0	100	11
Mixed race	43	6	50	7	7	1	100	14
ALL MALE ENTRIES	67	100	30	45	3	5	100	150
FEMALE								
White	75	54	25	18	0	0	100	72
Afro-Caribbean	50	12	46	11	4	1	100	24
South Asian	0	0	100	1	0	0	100	1
Mixed race	100	1	0	0	0	0	100	1
ALL FEMALE ENTRIES	68	67	31	30	1	1	100	98
ALL PUPILS								
White	76	126	23	39	1	1	100	166
Afro-Caribbean	47	26	45	25	7	4	99	55
South Asian	67	8	33	4	0	0	100	12
Mixed race	47	7	47	7	7	1	101	15
ALL DETENTIONS	67	167	30	75	2	6	99	248

* Fifth year: autumn term only.
** Other detentions: where staff comment was absent or illegible.
Note: Percentages are rounded to the nearest whole number.

THE MYTH AND TEACHERS' REJECTION OF AFRO-CARIBBEAN PROTESTS

There is evidence, therefore, that as a group pupils of Afro-Caribbean origin were disproportionately subject to negative sanctions within City Road and that a relatively greater proportion of their 'offences' reflected an important degree of teacher interpretation. In addition to pupils' accounts of classroom interaction, I have given examples of this from my own observations (for instance, concerning Charley's walk and Paul Dixon's conversation with Arif) as well as providing secondary analysis of official school punishment records. Teachers' frequent interpretation of a 'bad attitude' was one aspect of what I have termed the myth of an Afro-Caribbean challenge to authority: the belief that, as a group, Afro-Caribbean pupils presented a threat which was both quantitatively and qualitatively greater than any other group of their peers. This myth remained largely unspoken, but was an important part of staff culture in City Road. The teachers were not overtly racist, yet their ethnocentrism had racist consequences. The teachers believed that Afro-Caribbean pupils were a likely source of trouble. This belief influenced their perception of Afro-Caribbean pupils so that any 'inappropriate' behaviour might be interpreted as a serious challenge which called for clear (negative, critical) action.

An important consequence of the myth was the lack of sympathy, and even suspicion, which greeted any complaints against the school concerning behaviour which pupils or parents considered to be racially prejudiced. At one parents' evening I saw staff laugh at a white parent's suggestion that one of their colleagues (whom they described as 'a very experienced teacher') had insulted a pupil of mixed race. Most complaints were not dismissed quite so lightly, for the majority of staff recognized that 'race' could be a very sensitive issue and tried to deal with grievances rationally. Yet on each occasion that 'race' was raised the school's response was to deny the validity of the accusation. This did not entail teachers openly accusing students of having lied, rather it would be implied that they had imagined the victimization. As one teacher told me, 'it [prejudice] mainly exists in their minds.' This view was not always expressed so simply, but whenever staff spoke of such accusations they always denied their accuracy. For instance, a member of the senior management team told me of an occasion when an Afro-Caribbean pupil was given detention:

42

it just happened that we decided that night that detention
would be cleaning up the yard, picking up litter. But they
[Afro-Caribbean pupils] saw it as picking on him, 'It's not
right, making him pick up litter just 'cause he's black.'
(field notes)

City Road teachers used anecdotes such as this to support
their view that accusations of prejudice were, at the very least,
likely to be over-reactions. Indeed, there was a widespread,
although less often stated, feeling that accusations of victimization were frequently used as a smokescreen to divert attention
from the pupils' own actions. As one example, during the
fieldwork a local Afro-Caribbean pressure group received a
great deal of publicity concerning its accusation of racial
discrimination in some schools' suspension procedures. During
a conversation in the staffroom, a City Road teacher offered a
very different reason for the over-representation of Afro-
Caribbean pupils in the figures:

They're the ones who are causing most trouble.

This view received widespread support among the teachers
who were present. The consequences of teachers' ethnocentric
interpretations of pupils' actions, plus the operation of the
myth of an Afro-Caribbean challenge, help to explain how such
a view can become a part of staff culture that is taken for
granted.

Conclusions

In this chapter I have presented a variety of data in an attempt
to highlight the complexity of the factors which lay behind the
often conflictual relationships between pupils of Afro-Caribbean
origin and their white teachers in City Road Comprehensive. I
have shown that, as a group, Afro-Caribbean pupils experienced
a disproportionate amount of punishment, and that they were
sometimes exclusively criticized even when peers of other
ethnic origins shared in the offence. This pattern supports the
findings of some previous work in multi-ethnic schools.
    More importantly, I have presented evidence that Afro-
Caribbean pupils' very sense (and display) of their own
ethnicity could lead them into conflict with teachers who

43

perceived some actions to be indicative of a more deeply rooted challenge to their authority. This builds upon the work of Geoffrey Driver (1977, 1979) and Cecile Wright (1985a, 1985b, 1987) who have both written critically about white teachers' perceptions and expectations of West Indian/Afro-Caribbean pupils as a source of disruptive behaviour. I have argued that the myth of an Afro-Caribbean challenge to authority had very great strength and resulted in a situation where any Afro-Caribbean pupil or parent's claim of injustice would be rejected as misguided, or even malicious.

The City Road teachers were not, therefore, overtly racist — the vast majority would reject all notions of innate differences between 'races' and they genuinely tried to treat all pupils fairly. However, the teachers' ethnocentric perceptions led to actions which were racist in their consequences: as a group, Afro-Caribbean pupils experienced more conflictual relationships with teachers; they were disproportionately subject to the school's reporting and detention systems; they were denied any legitimate voice of complaint.

Given the Afro-Caribbean pupils' greater experience of conflict with their teachers, the question arises as to how the pupils responded. In particular, how was it that some Afro-Caribbean pupils managed to succeed academically despite this situation? These questions are addressed in the following chapter.

Chapter 3

Resistance and accommodation

Afro-Caribbean pupils in City Road

The previous chapter outlined the processes which lay behind the often conflictual relationships between white teachers and Afro-Caribbean pupils in City Road Comprehensive. The patterns of control and criticism were reminiscent of previous work and support the notion that, as a group, Afro-Caribbean pupils generally experience school in a way which is qualitatively different from that of their peers of other ethnic origins. As a result of the teacher–pupil conflict, pupils of Afro-Caribbean origin are in a relatively disadvantaged position within the pupil population.

Because of the myth of an Afro-Caribbean challenge to authority, any complaints of racial prejudice (by pupils or parents alike) fell on unsympathetic ears. Given this situation, Afro-Caribbean pupils knew that avenues of formal response were of little use; when I asked if she had ever complained about a member of staff, an Afro-Caribbean pupil told me: 'There's no point – they always stick together.' Although this statement simplifies the processes involved, it accurately represents the staff's response to any accusations of unfairness or prejudice along 'racial' lines. Because the formal means of response were known to be ineffective, the pupils' informal response became all the more important. In this chapter I focus on some of the different ways in which Afro-Caribbean pupils have responded to their disadvantaged position within the school.

The chapter begins by clarifying the concept of subculture, a

45

term which has often been used inconsistently in relation to this area. I then consider how Afro-Caribbean pupils in City Road responded to their conflictual experience of teacher–pupil interactions. In particular I highlight the difficulty of the situation by examining the processes which led one group of males into increasing conflict with the school's authority system (culminating in educational failure), while a peer in the same year group managed his relationships with staff so as to avoid further conflict and achieve highly in academic terms. This information is then compared with previous research to illustrate something of the range and complexity of the responses of Afro-Caribbean pupils. The chapter ends with a note on the interrelations between gender and ethnicity as factors which influence pupil experience and subculture.

Pupil adaptations as subculture

Within any social interaction there are as many ways of adapting to the situation as there are actors. It is, however, useful to distinguish between a multitude of unrelated individual adaptations and a series of attitudes and types of behaviour which are shared and reinforced through interaction between members of a social group. In much sociological and educational literature, the latter has come to be known as 'subculture'.

There is no universally accepted definition of subculture. The term often appears in articles and books with little or no explanation. In much sociological work, however, there is a common thread to the use of the term which can be captured by reference to the understanding applied in studies of student culture by Howard Becker and his colleagues (Hughes, Becker and Geer, 1958; Becker and Geer, 1960; Becker *et al.*, 1961). These writers isolated several elements which constituted a subculture; a group of two or more people interacting extensively and sharing a common situation (role or problem) which served as the basis for the development of 'a body of collective understandings' (Becker *et al.*, 1961, pp. 46–7). These understandings and agreements included shared goals and values (often taken for granted by members of the group and seen as a natural outlook) and 'modes of co-operation'. That is to say, rules develop which govern interaction within the group, and between the group and non-members (Hughes, Becker and Geer, 1958). This view is summarized below:

- **Intensive interaction** of people who share a
- **Common situation** (role or problem) and develop
- **A body of collective understandings and agreements** including
    shared goals and values (a group perspective)
    modes of co-operation (group norms/rules of behaviour)

Source: Adapted from Hughes, Becker and Geer, 1958; Becker and Geer, 1960; Becker *et al.*, 1961.

The group's shared understandings and agreements represent a *sub*culture in the sense that they are not handed down to the actors, but are created within the demands and confines of the institution and may sometimes stand in opposition to certain elements of its official culture. Sociologists and educationists, therefore, do not use the term to denote a necessarily inferior culture (as a lay audience might assume).

Becker's definition retains the core of an earlier approach which characterized gang delinquency as a 'shared frame of reference' which is 'continually being created, re-created and modified' (Cohen, 1955, p. 65). The approach of Howard Becker and his colleagues is particularly useful because it isolates certain defining characteristics which might serve as the basis for the identification and study of different subcultures in the real world of the school classroom and playground, through the recognition of both an attitudinal (shared goals and values) and a behavioural element (modes of co-operation).

The adaptations of Afro-Caribbean pupils in City Road Comprehensive

A great deal of the existing work on the educational experiences and achievements of Afro-Caribbean and South Asian pupils has concerned itself with how the pupils adapt to their situation as members of an ethnic minority in a society and school system where the dominant images, traditions and assumptions reflect an ethnocentric concern with white experience and culture (cf. Taylor, 1983; Taylor with Hegarty, 1985). Consequently, much of the work which I draw upon in the second part of this book will have significance in relation to this area. In this section, however, I want to focus specifically upon the ways in which the Afro-Caribbean pupils in my research age-group adapted to the conflict and criticism which was a fundamental part of their educational experience.

Afro-Caribbean pupils adapted to their situation in a variety of ways which cannot all be considered in detail; at this point I will concentrate upon the adaptations which seemed to represent two extreme forms of response at either end of a range of different adaptational styles and subcultures. Both examples concern male pupils (I shall turn to the interrelations of gender and ethnicity later in this chapter). My reason for presenting the cases is that they clearly demonstrate the importance of displays of Afro-Caribbean ethnicity, highlighting the size of the task which faced academically ambitious Afro-Caribbean pupils in a school dominated by white teachers and their ethnocentric perspectives. Both cases concern pupils whom staff described as 'able', yet failing to achieve because of their 'attitude'. In each case I will outline the pupils' adaptations and consider their consequences in terms of academic achievement.

A *subculture of resistance*

A group of three Afro-Caribbean males in City Road established a dominant reputation within the age-group. As one teacher told me, 'They're *the* stand-out group in that year' (field notes). The three pupils (Wayne Johnson, Barry Clayton and Roger Haynes) were widely seen by staff as being intelligent yet determined to cause trouble. While most teachers knew that these pupils 'hung around' together, few recognized the strength of the bond between them. In fact, they developed a coherent subculture glorifying those elements of their identities within the school which were frequently devalued (their ethnicity) and subject to control (their physical prowess).

The importance of the informal group

Afro-Caribbean pupils in City Road regularly faced certain problems during their day-to-day experience of school. Recurring conflicts with their white teachers was a particular example. However, such experiences were not sufficient to lead most of the pupils to the adaptational responses which this clique exhibited. The extensive interaction of the three pupils at an earlier point in their careers seemed crucial in shaping the responses which set them apart from their peers.

Wayne, Barry and Roger were Afro-Caribbean males who not only shared a similar sense of ethnicity but also interacted on a frequent and intense basis. Barry and Roger were members of the same form group throughout their secondary school careers. Wayne joined City Road as a second-year pupil and was the only Afro-Caribbean male in his form. Wayne seemed to have met and become friendly with Barry and Roger through contacts in lessons and particularly during sporting events and practises which were held after the school day. All three became prominent members of the school's sporting teams during their second year.

The three pupils seemed to have formed a closely knit group very quickly and by the time my fieldwork began (early in their third year) they could always be seen together at breaktimes and even during assemblies (where members of different forms were supposed to sit apart). Further evidence of their closeness was found in Wayne's responses to questionnaires which I administered; following a disciplinary meeting Wayne had been moved to a new form within City Road, yet his only friendship choices outside his new form were Barry and Roger: he indicated no friendship links with his previous form.

Outside school the three pupils also spent a great deal of time together. They would structure much of their free time around group activities, such as hanging around the city centre, 'loafing'. They also shared social contacts in the wider youth culture of the Cityside district, the main area of Afro-Caribbean and Asian settlement in the city. Such contacts led them into larger social networks involving post-school-age Afro-Caribbeans. It was within these larger networks that Wayne, Barry and Roger would sometimes attend dances and meet in local bars.

Goals and values

All three members of the clique were seen to engage in displays of ethnicity which owed much to a media presentation of 'blackness' and to their own contact with the larger Afro-Caribbean community in Cityside. All three members occasionally wore badges featuring the colours of Ethiopia and used Creole expressions and styles of speech. I also saw Wayne and Barry use the relaxed style of walking which was exclusive to Afro-Caribbean males in the school (see chapter 2). The clique members were not unique in their displays of ethnicity, but the importance of these symbols within the group was very great. Their shared ethnicity was crucial to the group, the three mixed only with Afro-Caribbeans outside the school and identified their ethnic origin as the single most important factor in their experience of schooling. Displays of ethnicity (through styles of walking, speech and dress) often led to conflict with staff and this in turn led to further conflicts as the clique reinforced its reputation, among staff and pupils alike, as a 'hard', physically powerful unit.

The members of the clique revelled in their physical prowess. The three had established an image as a very threatening force within the school and, like the working-class white 'lads' described by Paul Willis (1977), they were proud of their reputation.

Wayne   No [pupil] in [City Road] has ever come out with an insult to us three, *never*.
DG   Why do you think that is?
Wayne   'Cause they *know* me you see. 'Cause they know us. They know us *good*. They know us too well to say anything back to us. Because Clayton ... they know not to mess with him (...)
DG   So you think you've got the kind of reputation where people will –
Wayne– Shut up and keep their mouths shut.

This extract may sound like empty boasting, but there is good reason to suppose that the claims were well founded. For example, in a sentence completion questionnaire, administered to my two case study forms during their fifth year, I included the item, '......... picks on other pupils.' In response, nineteen of the twenty-two nominations made by male pupils cited either Barry or Roger (by that time Wayne had been expelled).[1] Similarly, some pupils referred to the clique during individual interviews with me, and even those who had themselves been disciplined for fighting in the past felt the need to stress the confidentiality of their statements. The following warning is taken from an interview with a white pupil who had been suspended for fighting earlier in his career at City Road.

> ... but don't let that out. They [Barry and Roger] are about the two hardest in the school, so my neck'll be gone if anybody finds out I've said that.

Like Willis' lads (1977, pp. 35–6) the clique's tough reputation was not always tested to the point of physical conflict. In fact they had developed several intimidatory strategies which would usually avoid the need for violence. As Barry put it, 'You just *brace yourself* on 'em.'

DG   If you have [an argument] with a pupil, does
                it *usually* end up with a fight?
Barry Clayton   No, we just probably argue, and they just go
                about their business (...)
                Tony Moakes, he took my pen. In chemis-
                try he took my pen and he wouldn't give it
                me back. I was arguing with him ... I kinda
                just took off my blazer... He just gave it me
                back. I sat down. (...) You just keep a
                serious face.

Such strategies were necessary, not only because fights always involve some element of risk, but also because such trouble would bring about severe conflicts with staff, conflicts which the pupils knew from experience could lead to formal suspensions and even expulsion from the school.

It was clear that the clique was founded upon a very strong informal group; however, it would be wrong to assume that the clique existed in complete isolation from the rest of the pupil body. Although Wayne, Barry and Roger recognized a set of strong mutual obligations, most of their time in school was spent in uneventful and even friendly contact with non-clique members, including white pupils.

Modes of co-operation

The clique was characterized by an intense loyalty and sense of equality among its members. Teachers typically saw Wayne Johnson as 'the biggest problem' and assumed that he acted as leader to the other pupils. On one occasion the year head described Wayne to me as follows:

> He likes to steal the show, you know, he's *very arrogant*, will take advantage of the slightest possibility (...) He likes to drag people in with him. He likes to be the *showman*, the big guy, 'Look at me,' you know. 'I can do this, I can do that'.

In conversations with the group members, however, it became clear that there were no clear authority distinctions within the group:

> Wayne   ...we ain't got no leader. They [teachers] reckon I'm the leader, but I'm not the leader of nothing.

The lack of any group leader may have been related to the very small size of the clique. Certainly this was a factor which seemed to heighten the sense of loyalty and mutual obligation which the members displayed. In a very real sense the three pupils felt themselves to be 'one':

> Wayne   Us three, we stick together you see. Anything happens to one, anything happens to *one*, they've got the other two to deal with (...) It's just us three, nobody else.

This is not to say that the three pupils spent their time exclusively in each others' company. They had not consulted each other over their third-year subject choices and consequently there was no optional lesson where the three were together during their fourth and fifth years. In lessons and form periods the clique members had routine contacts with other pupils, many of whom were white. Outside the group their closest contacts were with other Afro-Caribbean males within the school, some of whom cited Wayne, Barry or Roger as close friends in response to my questionnaires. In the eyes of the clique, however, these contacts were not of the same importance as the three-man grouping itself, which not only came together at every opportunity during the school day, but also structured much of their free time after school.

It should be noted, therefore, that although the clique recognized strong bonds of mutual obligation it did not exist in social isolation – the young men's relationship with other actors in the school was more complex than might at first appear. Paul Willis (1977) has described the 'counter-culture' of a group of white working-class lads who seemed to see non-group members as at best inferior (the 'ear'oles' and 'the Jamaicans'), and at worst as prey (the Asians). In contrast, the members of this Afro-Caribbean group glorified their position and were conscious of their group identity, yet they existed within a wider and more complex network of social contacts within the school. Their social contacts reflected their ethnicity and gender (the strongest ties being recognized by other Afro-Caribbean males in the school). However, they did not define any group of pupils as natural enemies: being of Afro-Caribbean or mixed race background may have saved a pupil from the clique's physical attentions, but being white or Asian did not define a pupil as a target. Rather than setting out to create trouble with their peers or teachers, the clique generally seemed to respond to hints of trouble from other actors. Any such hint of trouble would not be ignored, however, indeed, the assumptions and values of the clique (stressing the ethnicity and physical prowess of the three) meant that *any* perceived threat or victimization was likely to be met head on, sometimes with dire consequences.

The consequences of the subculture

The clique's glorification of its members' ethnicity and physical prowess acted as a basis for power within the pupil body and offered an independent standpoint which distanced them from the potentially demoralizing effects of the criticism faced by Afro-Caribbean pupils in the school. The three pupils were subject to much criticism and control but remained convinced of their own worth and potential. Nevertheless, a spiral of increasing control and response seems to have developed. The clique's reputation meant that staff expected trouble from the three; for instance, when I asked Barry and Roger's form teacher for permission to speak with them she replied: 'Yeah sure, have they been prats again?' (field notes). This image of the clique (as being frequently at odds with authority) may have led staff to increased control of the pupils. Certainly this seemed to be the case when I saw the three together about the school and watched Wayne in class. Whenever a teacher sought to control a member of the clique, the pupils, in view of their reputation as being 'hard' and their belief that they were often victimized, were unlikely to accept the judgement quietly. This is illustrated in the following discussion about Mr Flint (a particularly authoritarian teacher):

Wayne   Everybody else goes, 'Don't stand up to him'. I stood up to him (. . .)

DG   [What about] Barry and Roger?

Wayne   *They won't back off nobody.* Shit, I know them two wouldn't (. . .) Sometimes I'll just put my head down [and work], if I don't walk into a room and they start picking on me. I'll just get on with my work. But if they start picking on me – say I'm talking to somebody, just pick on me. But if somebody else is talking to somebody they don't pick on them – that's not right. They should pick on the other people as well, and I don't like that.

DG   Apart from you individually, do you think there are any other people that they pick on?

Wayne   Yeah, Barry and Roger.

It should be emphasized that both sides of the relationship faced a situation which seemed to offer them little room for manoeuvre: in order to teach, the staff had to maintain control, yet the group's reputation and perception of their position could not allow them to let control or criticism go unchallenged. This situation led to heightened conflict with staff and an increased sense of victimization and group identity among the clique members. Indeed, the clique's experience of conflict with the staff was such that they asserted that, as a whole, the school was a racist institution.

Barry   If me and somebody else is late . . . it's *me* who's in trouble (. . .) Most of 'em [teachers] are prejudiced.

Wayne   [The teachers] are after all the coloureds in that school.

This claim of racial victimization was only made with reference to Afro-Caribbean and some mixed race pupils. Wayne stated that 'I've never seen *no* Asian pupils get done yet.'

Almost every other Afro-Caribbean pupil with whom I spoke in City Road stated that one or more teachers were biased against their ethnic group, yet they saw such teachers as the exception rather than the rule. The clique's reversal of this assessment seemed to reflect its history of very serious conflict with the school. For example, each member received several senior management detentions and two were given report cards (see chapter 2). Also, Wayne and Barry were each suspended from the school on more than one occasion.

It is important to realize that the clique's assessment of the teachers as prejudiced was not a simple blanket accusation, used to divert attention from their crimes (as many of the teachers would argue). When, for instance, I asked Barry about his most recent suspension he told me that the teachers' actions had been justified.

Barry   I brought a knife to school (...) Just carried it in my pocket, to peel an orange (...) They took the knife off me, sent me home, said 'Don't come back until your parents come.'

DG   Then what happened?

Barry   They come up, sorted it all out and I was allowed back in.

DG   Do you think the school was justified in doing that or were they over-reacting?

Barry   No, they *should* have done that (...) I think they would have sent anybody home what they seen with a knife.

Similarly, the group listed a number of teachers whom they felt were fair with them, teachers who 'got on' instead of seeking to impose their authority.

Wayne   [Good teachers] *They get on*, they talk the same language I do. They get on (...) They muck in. They do the same things [we] do. If you're quiet, they're quiet. If you shout, they shout.

This assessment of good classroom practice was echoed by one of the teachers whom the clique described as being fair with them:

Mr Finch   I just treat them as I find them. They know how far to go with me. If they give me any trouble,

> they know they'll get the same back, but usually
> they're alright (...)
> If you're straight with them, they're okay.
> (field notes)

Mr Finch's view was not, however, typical of official assessments of the clique. As I have shown, the three were not 'anti-school' in the sense that some have used the term (cf. Lacey, 1970; Ball, 1981). Wayne, Barry and Roger each accepted the need to gain qualifications and had relatively clear visions of their post-school careers. The clique members did not reject the aims of schooling – theirs was not a *'counter-culture'* (cf. Willis, 1977) – yet they did clash with some of the techniques employed by their teachers. Given the general belief in the myth of an Afro-Caribbean challenge, the pupils' history of conflict with teachers was widely interpreted as signifying a deliberate rejection of the school's authority. As early as March of his second year, Barry was suspended from City Road and a change of school was suggested. In the suspension report the headteacher wrote: 'There is a general feeling that Barry is preoccupied with flouting authority and that he will seek any opportunity to undermine it.'

A senior member of staff also described Roger Haynes to me as a pupil who 'flouted authority'. Similar views were held concerning Wayne Johnson and it is revealing to examine briefly some of the staff comments concerning Wayne's eventual expulsion from the school.

Wayne's expulsion from City Road

When I began my fieldwork, during the age-group's third year, the year head told me that Wayne was on the verge of expulsion; 'he really is at the end of the road'. In fact Wayne survived the third year but unofficially he was not expected to complete his education in City Road.

A senior teacher	If he lasts through the fourth year – I mean what we're waiting for now, is for him to do one more thing and he'll be expelled.

This vision of the most likely end to Wayne's career in City Road was based upon his record of suspensions since he joined

the school as a second-year pupil. The LEA operated a
hierarchy of suspension 'types' culminating in a 'C' suspension,
which almost always meant expulsion. Wayne's career was
exceptional in that he remained in City Road despite two 'C'
suspensions.

> The year head ... he had a 'C' suspension about last April
> [ten months ago], which is the final one, and
> we had him back with a final warning. And
> then we had *another* 'C' suspension after
> that. You know, this is how incredible it
> was.

The fact that Wayne had survived as long as he did was seen by
his teachers as evidence of the school's fairness. One of them
stated that: 'if he'd have been *white* he would have gone a *long*
time ago (...) we have to appear to be more than fair.'

There was no doubt that Wayne had received several 'final
warnings'; however, his accumulated warnings and suspensions
must be seen within the overall context of Afro-Caribbean
pupil–white teacher relationships in the school as whole. Of
particular importance was the myth of an Afro-Caribbean
challenge – the teachers' widespread belief that, both as
individuals and as a group, Afro-Caribbean pupils were
especially prone to threatening teachers' authority. Wayne had
not committed any single offence so serious that it would
normally have brought about expulsion: he was suspended and
eventually expelled for a series of more minor incidents. It was
the cumulative nature of Wayne's deviancy which his teachers
stressed. The following quotation is taken from an interview
during Wayne's third year:

> The year head I have him for [one lesson], for instance, and
> I don't hear a word out of him, he just gets
> on with the work. But there are other areas
> of the school where, if you give him half an
> inch, he'll take a mile (...) You name it, he's
> done it. Short of hitting a member of staff.
> Very, very insulting to members of staff.
> Theft. Disobedience. Undermining the mem-
> bers of staff's authority. Told kids not to
> listen to members of staff. Refused to leave

the room when requested. Just generally, he's done everything he could possibly do to get expelled. Short of, there's been no incident of him hitting anybody.

After Wayne's expulsion it was the cumulative nature of his offences which was again stressed by staff:

DG	Why's he been expelled, what did he do?
Wayne's form teacher	Well, nothing really – nothing serious, but it's, you know, it's just the latest in a long line ... (field notes)
The year head	It was just two or three incidents on top of what had already gone off, you know, in the year, and really he just had to go.
Headteacher	Well, it was just the final straw ... It was this attitude. *He would not back down*. He was in a fight and the member of staff tried to separate them, and he just would not let it go – screaming and shouting obscenities ... (field notes)

The staff's emphasis upon the cumulative nature of Wayne's deviance was particularly significant because there was some evidence that the timescale of his offences was shortened in the teachers' recollections. The following quotation, taken from an interview prior to Wayne's expulsion, illustrates this:

DG	When was his last suspension?
Teacher	Last month. [i.e. January]
DG	Last month, what was that one about?
Teacher	(...)[Having consulted a record] No, 7th of November.

Clearly such errors would be unlikely during official suspension meetings when all documentation should be to hand. However, if such a mistake had been repeated informally it could have led to increased official action much sooner, by amplifying the teachers' belief that Wayne was bent on challenging the school's authority – an accusation which was levelled against many Afro-Caribbean pupils.

Wayne's form teacher	Wayne Johnson was just somebody who we tried and tried and tried with ... School wasn't the place for him with his *inner drive*, as I saw it, to always appear to be number one, and unbowed by any authority ... Our institution just couldn't brook that kind of continual challenge ...

Teachers' perspectives concerning the myth of an Afro-Caribbean challenge operated in such a way that any offence by an Afro-Caribbean pupil could be interpreted as indicative of a more general 'attitude' (an 'inner drive'). In the case of this Afro-Caribbean male clique, who rejoiced in both the ethnicity and the physical independence of its members, the processes were amplified until the school took very serious official action against the three in the form of suspensions and even an expulsion. As a result of these processes Wayne did not complete his secondary education in City Road Comprehensive and neither Barry nor Roger gained any pass grades in their external examinations.[2]

The clique of Afro-Caribbean males described here shares certain similarities with pupil subcultures which have been analysed before. I have already noted that an emphasis upon toughness seems to be a common feature of many working-class male subcultures (cf. Willis, 1977). Rather than simply transferring elements of an existing class or ethnic culture into their school life, however, the City Road clique seemed to glorify the physical prowess of its members as the one element of the staff's image of them which they could exploit to enhance their position within the pupil population. The clique represents one form of response to the situation which was encountered within the school; a situation where the ethnicity of the three was routinely devalued and where, as a group, Afro-Caribbean pupils were subject to disproportionate amounts of control and criticism. The clique's subculture reflected both ethnicity and gender, but the former may have been the more crucial factor since, as the research progressed, a parallel grouping of Afro-Caribbean girls emerged as an important part of the pupil population (see below).

Farrukh Dhondy (1974) has argued that a culture of resistance, similar in many ways to that which I have described above, will come to typify the black response to the educational system in this country. However, as I have already stressed, the subculture described here was an extreme response to the Afro-Caribbeans' situation in City Road; a response which, although rooted in the pupils' day-to-day experience of the school, was by no means inevitable.

Adaptations as accommodation: the case of Paul Dixon

Like the clique members described above, Paul Dixon was an Afro-Caribbean pupil at City Road Comprehensive who was described by teachers as 'intelligent' yet 'underachieving'. Paul had a poor reputation which could result in additional control in the classroom. Indeed, his reputation was such that teachers sometimes drew attention to his good efforts in class as being uncharacteristic of his general attitude. The following account of classroom interaction, which illustrates this, is taken from an interview with Vicky Mitchell, a white girl in one of my case study forms, who was very highly committed to many aspects of the official school value system.

> DG   Do you think that any groups of pupils are treated differently in the school?
>
> Vicky   Yeah, I mean Paul Dixon (...) I could cause trouble as well as him, if something went wrong while the teacher wasn't there, they'd probably try and blame him, when it could've been *me*.
> (...) Paul and people like that, you know, if they really do settle down to their work then the teacher'll say, 'Oh, what's wrong with you, *you're working!*' And taking it out of them then *'cause they are working*. And I suppose he thinks 'Why bother ... they're always getting at me'. I feel sorry for him in a way.

During his fifth year I observed Paul in both 'set' and mixed ability teaching groups. In both, Paul was frequently criticized by staff even though his 'offences' were usually shared by white and Asian peers who frequently went unpunished. Paul was acutely aware that he was subject to more criticism than some of his peers and (like Wayne, Barry and Roger) he interpreted the control as racially motivated. His father mentioned this to

Paul's form teacher at a parents' evening and Paul first told me of his thoughts during an interview in his third year. In particular Paul stressed conflict with his form teacher (Mr Palmer):

> ... he's prejudiced. You've been in our class right, now ain't you (...) He's always on about my colour sir, whenever I'm getting done he says 'You're only doing this 'cause you're black' and all that ...

Paul's disproportionate experience of criticism and control was typical of Afro-Caribbean pupils in the school, yet his response was very different to that of the clique noted above. Paul consciously sought to counter his reputation and promote an image of academic effort. During my observations of the top ('O' level) English set in City Road, in addition to being the most frequently criticized member of the group, Paul was also the pupil who volunteered most answers to the teacher's questions. He acted in ways which publicly emphasized his commitment to academic achievement. In the English set he would shout across at a relatively noisy group of girls to be quiet and he was always among the last pupils to pack away their work at the end of lessons.

Paul not only sought to counter his 'troublesome' image by emphasizing his dedication to academic achievement, he also tried to avoid any further conflict with members of staff. This policy meant that when a teacher criticized him, Paul would quickly accept the criticism with 'Yes sir' or 'Sorry sir'. Unlike many of his Afro-Caribbean peers, Paul did not comment on the fact that other pupils were committing the same 'offence' without punishment. Paul's apologies had the effect of quickly moving the interaction on beyond the criticism and avoiding any further problems which might arise if he was seen to question the teacher's view openly.

Similarly, Paul would try to minimize contact with members of staff with whom he felt he was most likely to conflict. For example, in a fourth-year interview I asked Paul how he got on with his teachers (remembering that in the third year he had accused his form teacher of prejudice):

Paul   They're all alright.
DG   Any that you particularly like?

61

Paul   Not really.
DG   Any that you *dislike*, you don't get on with?
Paul   No ... Mr Palmer's alright now (...)
DG   You say Mr Palmer's alright *now*, how has he changed?
Paul   He hasn't *changed* really, it's just that I don't talk to
        him that much – I only answer the register.

The most significant fact about Paul's career in the fourth and
fifth years at City Road was that he successfully resisted those
elements of his school experience which might have led him
into further conflict with the school. Rather than argue with his
form teacher or seek a change of form group, he simply
minimized his contact with that teacher. As the extract above
illustrates, although Paul did not have close relationships with
any member of staff, neither did he generalize from his
experience to assert that the majority of staff were racist. He
identified the conflicts which threatened his academic performance and did what he could to avoid them.

It is also significant that (unlike the clique discussed earlier)
Paul did not emphasize his ethnicity through any displays of
dress or demeanour, for instance, in styles of walking or
speech. This undoubtedly avoided further conflict with staff.
Unlike his approach to teacher–pupil interactions in class,
however, this may not have been a conscious strategy.

Paul's efforts to avoid trouble and concentrate on his work
also led to qualitative changes in his social relations with peers.
He maintained contacts with pupils of differing academic levels
within the school, but it became apparent that as the age-group
moved through the upper school, he was no longer seen as the
leader of a form-based 'gang' of lads.

When I first met Paul's form there was an obviously exclusive
group of boys who sat around the same desk and were referred
to by their teachers and classmates alike as 'Dixon's gang'. Paul
was one of two Afro-Caribbeans in the gang, the other members
being two white boys, an Asian and a pupil of mixed race.
During their third year Dixon's gang was described by the year
head as a source of trouble which led to the underachievement
of all concerned. In my working notes I identified the gang as
an interesting group whom I should try to understand in more
detail. However, during the fourth and fifth years something of
a split occurred within the group. As usual, the same pupils sat
together in form periods and they continued to have some

contact outside school hours. Yet the gang was no longer a single unit; Paul and Arif Aslam (the Asian member) took no part in the pre-arranged truancy of other gang members and often spent form periods revising for tests together while the others discussed television or football. The split within the friendship group was by no means total, but it was clear that they no longer shared similar adaptations to the demands of school. The importance of this development was as an indicator of the strength of Paul's determination to resist the image which many teachers held of him as a potential troublemaker. Paul distanced himself not only from certain members of staff, but also from some of his closest friends within the school.

Like the members of the clique discussed earlier, Paul Dixon recognized and rejected the negative image which some staff held of him. Rather than reacting through a glorification of that image within a culture of resistance, however, Paul channelled his energies into succeeding against the odds by avoiding trouble when he could and minimizing the conflicts which he experienced with his teachers. Although he maintained friendships among his peers, Paul's strategy, of accommodating conflictual teacher–pupil interactions and moving beyond the criticism, was carried out in isolation: it was an individual adaptation, rather than a subcultural one.

Paul completed his secondary education at City Road by gaining 'O' level and equivalent pass grades in six separate subjects: the highest achievement of any Afro-Caribbean male in the school that year.

The complexity and range of Afro-Caribbean pupils' adaptations

So far I have examined two contrasting examples of how Afro-Caribbean males in City Road adapted to their position within the school. The pupils shared many similar experiences: each was described by staff as being intelligent yet troublesome; each was subject to disproportionate amounts of control and criticism, which they interpreted as being racially motivated. However, the pupils' responses to their situation were very different. The clique members revelled in their ethnicity and physical prowess, and would respond angrily to occasions where they felt themselves to be treated unfairly. In direct contrast, Paul Dixon consciously sought to counter the staff's negative image of him. He minimized contact with those teachers he expected most trouble from and when faced with a conflictual situation Paul quickly accepted the criticism without complaint.

These cases represent extreme forms of response (many pupils' adaptations fell somewhere between the two) but they were not unique – there were parallel examples of female pupils' adaptations which shared the same fundamental features (see below). Before considering the issue of gender, however, it is useful to comment on the similarities between the responses noted above and those revealed in previous school-based research. Although the details may vary, the general patterns of resistance and accommodation seem to be a recurring feature in Afro-Caribbean pupils' responses to schooling.

In her analysis of the pupil–teacher interaction in two Midlands schools, Cecile Wright (1985a, 1985b, 1986, 1987) frequently refers to David Hargreaves' study of 'Lumley' Secondary Modern school (Hargreaves, 1967). In particular, Wright draws parallels between Hargreaves' account of the delinquent subculture of some working-class (white) males and her own observations of Afro-Caribbean boys and girls:

[Hargreaves] found that pupils in the lower streams were deprived of status and subsequently developed an anti-school culture which was used to gain status . . . How then did [the] estranged relationship between the Afro-Caribbean pupils and their teachers affect the pupils' behaviour? As in the Hargreaves case, these pupils have developed a sub-cultural adolescent group within the school which is not only anti-school, but is also somewhat anti-white. (Wright, 1986, pp. 132, 134)

Wright briefly considers the actions of an 'all-black' group of 30 or more boys and girls who moved around the school together and acted to assert their 'blackness' through various verbal and non-verbal means, most obviously through the use of patois (Wright, 1986, pp. 134–5). Wright presents this group as an extreme example of Afro-Caribbean pupils' response to their disadvantaged position in teacher–pupil interactions. However, she goes on to present data from both her research schools which suggest that the pupils' basic analysis – that they were caught in 'stimulus–response situation' (Wright, 1986, p. 135) – held true for the majority of Afro-Caribbean pupils in the schools. For instance:

Researcher	You have all said that you feel that you are treated unfairly in the school. How do you feel this makes you behave?
Delroy	Bad!
Researcher	When you say 'bad' what exactly do you mean by this?
Paul	It means that we turn around and make trouble for them.
Delroy	Yeah, we try to get our own back on them. We behave ignorantly towards them, and when the teachers talk to us and tell us to do something we don't do it, because we think about how they treated us. (Wright, 1986, p. 136)

Wright does not state her position in simple terms, but the thrust of her analysis seems to indicate that overall she feels that the Afro-Caribbean pupils tended towards a response which emphasized disruption as resistance to their negative experience of school:

From conversations, it appeared that they [Afro-Caribbean pupils] were not against education *per se*; in fact a number of them had left school to go to further education. However in school their energy was not always tapped so was sometimes directed towards disrupting the school or, as one pupil said: 'to get our own back on them for the way they have treated us'. (Wright, 1986, p. 146)

Wright therefore emphasizes pupil adaptations of resistance through negative responses to the school's poor assessment of them. Her observations share many elements with those presented above (concerning the male clique in City Road) and with Mac an Ghaill's description of a group of 'anti-school' Afro-Caribbean males ('the Rasta Heads') whose concern with elements of Rastafarianism helped them reject 'the model of white society presented by teachers, and resist institutional incorporation into white cultural identities' (Mac an Ghaill, 1988, p. 110).

Yet, as Paul Dixon's case has illustrated, despite their disadvantaged position within the classroom some Afro-Caribbean pupils can and do succeed (more on this below). The crucial point is that the success of a few does not prove that the situation is really alright for all; rather, the manner of their success (involving strategies of accommodation and personal sacrifice above and beyond mere academic effort and achievement) is further evidence of the disadvantaged position of pupils of Afro-Caribbean ethnicity.

Gender and ethnicity

Much social science research has concentrated upon the experience of male pupils only. For the most part, this pattern has been reproduced in qualitative studies of pupil experiences and adaptations (for instance, Hargreaves, 1967; Lacey, 1970; Willis, 1977). Despite some notable exceptions (Lambart, 1976; McRobbie, 1978; Meyenn, 1980; Griffin, 1985), around half of the pupil population has remained almost absent from detailed study. When we consider research on gender *and* ethnicity, therefore, it is hardly surprising that to date very little work has been published. Some valuable accounts do exist, however, especially in the work of Sharpe (1976), Fuller (1980), Weis (1985) and Mac an Ghaill (1988, 1989).[3]

Because so few studies have focused on issues of gender and ethnicity the picture is unclear. Some have suggested that factors associated with gender have a particular influence upon the adaptations of Afro-Caribbean males and females – given previous work on pupil subculture it would be surprising if this were not the case (cf. Woods, 1980b). However, it has been argued that the adaptations of the genders may be fundamentally different; Mary Fuller, for example, presented a study of a small group of 'black' girls which contrasts their 'pro-education' strategies with their male peers' anti-school and anti-white responses.

> [A] sub-culture emerged from the girls' positive acceptance of the fact of being both black and female. Its particular flavour stemmed from their critical rejection of the meanings with which those categorizations are commonly endowed. Their consequent anger and frustration, unlike that of their

black male peers, was not turned against themselves or translated into an automatic general dislike of whites or the opposite sex. Rather their feelings and understandings gave particular meanings to achievement through the acquisition of educational qualifications. (Fuller, 1980, p. 81)

The girls' desire to prove their worth, and to have some element of independence and control over their lives, led them to value academic success as a means to an end. Fuller described the girls as 'pro-education' but not 'pro-school', where the latter is taken to imply a high degree of conformity with the official goals and values of the institution (cf. Lacey, 1970; Ball, 1981; Hammersley, 1985). In fact the girls seemed to act deliberately in ways which distanced them from the 'good pupil' role and allowed them to minimize friction with peers of the same ethnic origin who did not share their commitment to academic success. On the other hand, their deviance was well measured so as to avoid serious conflict with members of staff.

Mac an Ghaill (1988) has described a group of Afro-Caribbean and Asian young women who responded in much the same way as Fuller's girls. The 'Black Sisters' (as Mac an Ghaill calls them) showed the same kinds of limited resistance which was carefully measured so as to avoid open conflict with teachers (Mac an Ghaill, 1988, p. 27). In contrast, however, the Black Sisters were less successful in avoiding conflict with their ethnic minority peers whose resistance was more overt. The following quotation gives some impression of the sacrifices which such a course of action can entail:

Joanne (Afro-Caribbean) I didn't get the full impact 'till third year. I noticed they didn't want to be near me. 'Coz they sort of associated getting on in school with what white people did and if you got on in school, you must be a choc-ice [a derogative name meaning black on the outside and white on the inside]. (Mac an Ghaill, 1988, p. 31)

The studies by Fuller and Mac an Ghaill are of great

importance. They highlight the variety of responses which are possible given the rejection which many Afro-Caribbean pupils experience in their relationships with white teachers. The academic success of Fuller's girls (each gaining an average of around seven examination 'passes' at sixteen-plus) demonstrates the complexity of life in schools. Unlike Paul Dixon, Fuller's girls were able to maintain a strong sense of pride in their ethnicity; although he did not reject his colour, Paul did nothing to highlight his ethnicity – a strategy similar to that of 'racelessness' which has been recently described among some American high school students of both sexes (Fordham, 1988a, 1988b). However, there are also clear similarities between Paul's actions and those of Fuller's girls, in that both recognized the importance of teacher–pupil relations in as much as they carefully managed their interactions with staff so as to avoid the conflict which some of their peers experienced, and which could lead to academic failure.

The differences and similarities between the strategies of an academically successful male (in City Road) and a group of similarly successful females in 'Torville' school (Fuller, 1980) hold important lessons in relation to the influence of gender and ethnicity.

Firstly, it would appear that success and failure are not dependent on gender: we now have studies of Afro-Caribbean pupils of both genders who have succeeded despite facing teachers' negative expectations. It would seem that, in terms of their experience of schooling, for Afro-Caribbean pupils of both sexes it is their ethnicity which is most important.

Secondly, the form of response (as characterized by resistance or accommodation) is not determined by gender. Just as both male and female pupils have found inventive and successful means of achieving academically despite their teachers' negative views, so members of both sexes have responded in a way which is clearly characterized by a high degree of resistance and conflict. I have already noted Cecile Wright's work on the responses of Afro-Caribbean pupils, in two schools, who in the main responded negatively (by causing disruption) to their teachers' assessments of them. Although much of Wright's work seems to refer specifically to male pupils, she has clearly stated that both male and female students were involved in some of these acts (Wright, 1986, pp. 134–5) and has presented her analysis as true of the Afro-

68

Caribbean pupils *per se*. Further evidence on this point is available from my work in City Road Comprehensive. Although I have examined the adaptations of resistance and accommodation through the detailed description and analysis of male pupils' responses, there were parallel cases among the Afro-Caribbean females in City Road. For reasons of sample selection, gender and the absence of key informants[4] I was unable to study these pupils in anything like the detail which was possible in the male cases detailed above. I did, however, spend time in class talking with and observing some of the girls who were involved, and the parallels with the male adaptations became very clear. Of particular interest was a group of Afro-Caribbean girls (including members of both the fourth and fifth years) which was built around a core of four fifth-year girls.

The group spent a great deal of time together around the school, especially during lunch-breaks, and occasionally truanted together at pre-arranged times. Like Wayne, Barry and Roger, the girls came to take on a highly visible group identity. They adopted the role of 'protectors' of younger Afro-Caribbean pupils (of both sexes) in the school: if they saw any argument or fight involving a young Afro-Caribbean pupil and a peer of another ethnic origin, they would intervene – often in a physically aggressive way – to ensure the safety of the former. This role also extended to arguing with staff if a young Afro-Caribbean was being reprimanded. In addition to their identity as a highly visible informal grouping, therefore, the girls also displayed a distinctive set of values and assumptions about their role in the school. Hence their group had all the hallmarks of a subcultural response.

The development of this subculture had been clearly influenced by both their ethnicity and their gender. The former was clear in some of the styles of dress and language which the girls used, especially in conversations with each other; the latter was apparent in the girls' assumptions about their likely post-school roles and in their evaluations of some of the teaching staff. When they left school, for example, they hoped to be involved in 'caring for others'. For some this meant nursing or primary teaching, for others it meant raising their own children or looking after an elderly guardian. Similarly, when it came to commenting on their teachers, the girls not only criticized staff for racism (as did Wayne, Barry and Roger) but also for characteristics related to their gender. Hence, a male member of staff was criticized as being both racist and 'creepy' – in comments such as 'He likes to use his hands too much,' or 'He's always touching you.' A female teacher was dismissed with, 'She'll *never* get a man, have you seen her legs? Like tree trunks, no ankles!' The girls' humour and their experience of harassment as both Afro-Caribbeans and young women clearly illustrated the importance of both their ethnicity and gender, central factors in their subcultural stance as protectors of younger Afro-Caribbean pupils.

Conclusion: resistance, accommodation, negotiation

In this chapter I have examined some of the ways in which Afro-Caribbean pupils have responded to their greater experience of criticism and control within schools dominated by the perceptions, values and expectations of white teachers. The data from my study of City Road Comprehensive showed many important similarities with previous research, especially that by Mary Fuller and Cecile Wright. The City Road cases indicated two extremes of a range of responses; from the open resistance and high level of teacher–pupil conflict inherent in Wayne, Barry and Roger's response, to the conscious management and accommodation of conflict which characterized Paul Dixon's approach.

I have presented examples which clearly illustrate the range of possible responses. In so doing my aim has been to highlight the processes which led a group of able Afro-Caribbean males into increased conflict with teachers and, ultimately, to academic failure. In contrast, Paul Dixon's case illustrated the very great demands which academically ambitious Afro-Caribbean pupils must meet if they are to succeed despite teacher ethnocentrism: 'mere' ability and dedication to hard work are not enough, they must also adapt to their disadvantaged position in such a way that they do not reinforce the widespread belief that they represent a threat to the teachers' authority.[5]

In presenting this information I have sought to recognize the complex nature of the processes at work. For example, it should be remembered that (unlike other groups which have been studied, such as 'the Rasta Heads' in Mac an Ghaill, 1988) neither Wayne, Barry nor Roger were 'anti-school', yet their teachers perceived them to be bent on rejection of school and white authority. As Signithia Fordham's work in a Washington high school (Fordham, 1988a, 1988b) has emphasized, there is no clear dichotomy in the responses of Afro-Caribbean pupils; it is not an either/or question of 'resist' or 'accommodate'. Rather, there is a spectrum of possible responses. Hence, building upon the work of Genovese (1972) and Anyon (1983), Mac an Ghaill (1988) has written of 'resistance *within* accommodation' (emphasis added). The essential point is that pupil adaptations are complex and negotiated – as Colin Lacey noted, twenty years ago, in relation to white working-class male subcultures, a degree of flexibility is a basic requirement of any pupil in the mainstream of state education:

> Anyone consistently unwilling or unable to co-operate with the school in a wide variety of situations could not be retained ... On the other hand, a boy consistently unwilling or unable to operate the norms of the anti-group sub-culture would be bullied or pilloried by his peers beyond normal endurance. (Lacey, 1970, p. 87)

Elements of resistance and accommodation are likely to be present in the adaptational responses of all pupils. In the case of Afro-Caribbean pupils, however, the categories become all the more powerful because of the processes which make accommodation such a demanding strategy, given the teachers' myth of an Afro-Caribbean challenge. The importance and complexity of teachers' stereotypes of different ethnic groups can be further explored in relation to the situation of pupils of South Asian origin. This is the focus of the next chapter.

Chapter 4

South Asian pupils

Differentiation and polarization in a multi-ethnic setting

If there was this 'racism' in schools – operating to the extent that has been suggested – one would expect that Asian children too would suffer from it ... The fact of the matter is that Asian children not only behave *better* than white children and black children ... they also *achieve* better than white children and black children. So why are they immune if there's this underlying racist tendency so strongly in our schools?

This statement illustrates perhaps the two most common beliefs which are held concerning pupils of South Asian ethnic origin: that they both behave and achieve more positively than their Afro-Caribbean peers. In this case the quotation is from a radio interview with the Labour chair of City Road's local education committee. Both survey and ethnographic research has revealed the strength of these same stereotypes among English schoolteachers (cf. Brittan, 1976b; Mac an Ghaill, 1988).

There was a tendency for Asian male students to be seen by the teachers as technically of 'high ability' and socially as conformist. Afro-Caribbean male students tended to be seen as having 'low ability' and potential discipline problems. (Mac an Ghaill, 1988, p. 64)

In the following chapter I will consider the available

evidence concerning the academic achievement of pupils of different ethnic origins. In this chapter I concentrate on the experiences and adaptational responses of South Asian pupils in City Road. In particular I focus on the ways in which their ethnicity was reflected in the pupils' relationships with their peers and teachers. Through an analysis of the academic differentiation to which Asian pupils were subject, the data highlight crucial differences between the experiences of South Asian and Afro-Caribbean pupils, differences which demonstrate the complexity of life in multi-ethnic schools and warn against the simplistic assumption that all ethnic minority pupils will experience stereotyping in similar ways.

Pupil–pupil relationships

A variety of approaches has been used to investigate friendship patterns among school pupils of different ethnic origins. Although much of the research is now somewhat dated, there is a great deal of evidence to indicate that as pupils move through successive age-groups they tend to become more strongly involved in friendship patterns which reflect their ethnic origin. This has generally been found to be the case for both Afro-Caribbean and South Asian pupils (cf. Rowley, 1968; Kawwa, 1968; Jelinek and Brittan, 1975).

Unfortunately, this is a particularly difficult area to generalize about; studies have used samples of very different sizes and have not always been clear or consistent in their classification of 'racial' and ethnic groups. Several studies have shown smaller, or even no marked preference for own-group friendship choices (cf. Cohen and Manion, 1983, pp. 113–15). The most recent work in this field indicates that among white, Afro-Caribbean and Asian pupils 'there is a fairly strong tendency for children to choose friends within their own group' (Smith and Tomlinson, 1989, p. 101).

The variation between studies may partly reflect differences in the structure and interpretation of the research instruments. Cohen and Manion (1983), for example, have listed several factors which might influence the degree of own-group choices revealed by questionnaires; they include the amount of contact with members of other ethnic groups, teacher attitudes, language, pupil gender and social class background.

73

Questionnaire responses are best interpreted where additional data sources are available as a test of their validity (Moreno, 1953). Consequently, when qualitative researchers have used such measures they tend to give primacy to the more detailed and sensitive observational and interview data which they are able to generate (cf. Lacey, 1970; Ball, 1973, 1981).

Ethnicity and the friendship network

During my fieldwork in City Road there were never more than three Asian girls in the age group which I studied. In the following analysis, therefore, I concentrate on the experiences of the eleven Asian males who were present throughout the entire period of the fieldwork.[1] The majority of these pupils were British-born Muslims whose parents had emigrated to this country from Pakistan. However, school records were often incomplete and it was not always known (even by the pupil) whether they had always lived in this country. In addition, three male pupils' parents had emigrated from India; of these pupils two (Parminder and Surrinder) were Sikh, the other (Dhilip) was Hindu.[2]

In the previous chapter I noted that for some Afro-Caribbean pupils in City Road their shared sense of a common situation served as the basis for a subcultural response to conflictual teacher–pupil relationships. However, this was not the case for all Afro-Caribbean pupils and even in the more extreme cases the pupils did not exist in a social world based exclusively upon their ethnicity. The members of Wayne Johnson's clique, for instance, continued to have generally uneventful (even good-natured) interactions with non-Afro-Caribbean pupils throughout most of their secondary school careers. As in the case of Afro-Caribbean pupils, a sense of their shared experiences and culture was a central feature in the lives of South Asian pupils in City Road.

Ethnicity played a major role in the social relations of the Asian students in the age-group, so that all except the two Sikh boys were connected via a complex network of shared friendships. These contacts were often based upon experiences which took place outside City Road; some friendships existed between pupils who never met during the routine of the school day.

Rafiq   Well I know Mansur and Amjad very well, but not too
bad Aziz (...) I knew Mansur when I was small, and I
knew Amjad when I was small. At nursery I used to
know Amjad. And Mansur I used to know when I used
to go to read [the Koran], I used to meet him down
[at the mosque]. (...) Aziz reads [at the same mosque]
but he don't live 'round my area.

Shared ethnicity could sometimes act as a very powerful
unifying force; for example, during the fast of Ramadan some of
the Muslim lads became particularly close as daily they came
together at the mosque and shared in the problems of satisfying
the (sometimes conflicting) demands of the school day,
homework etc., and their duties of religious study, prayer and
observing the fast.[3]

Ethnicity and racial harassment

The shared ethnicity of the Asian males also united them in
other ways within the school, such as through contact in
lessons or coming together to defend someone from a racist
attack by a peer. One pupil in particular acted as something of a
guardian to other Asian males.

Within City Road, Asian pupils were frequently subject to
attacks from their white peers. Usually this took the form of
racist name-calling but I also observed physical assaults, an
experience which is not confined to school pupils – a 1981
Home Office report stated that Asians were 50 times more
likely than whites to be the victims of racially motivated attacks
(cf. Home Office, 1981; CRE, 1987).

The following examples are taken from my field notes
concerning the lowest of the fifth-year English sets, a small
group specifically designed to house those with no examination
prospects. There were two Asian pupils in the set, Rafiq and
Sadiq (both Muslims, born in the UK of Pakistani parents).

field notes: racist name-calling

Several pupils are waiting in the corridor outside the room.
The teacher is late.

The four white boys present begin amusing themselves by
insulting Rafiq [an Asian male who, although not physically
strong, usually takes a full part in the 'messing about' and

75

verbal sparring which typifies pupil–pupil relationships in this group].

Rafiq is the subject of various taunts; Barry Flemming, for example, thinks it's funny to simply repeat 'Chapatti' over and over again.

When Rafiq tries a counter-insult Jimmy Bailey responds by shouting, 'Curry breath' at him across the corridor.

Two more white males are also laughing at Rafiq now and in an attempt to salvage some status in the boys' eyes Rafiq insults a passing third-year girl: *'Hey, fatty.'*

The girl keeps walking and so, looking for a similarly passive response, Rafiq insults the next girl to pass by, a fifth-year who immediately delivers an insult along identical lines to those which Rafiq has endured for the last five minutes:

Rafiq: 'Hey there's Bailey's girlfriend.'

Passing girl: 'Shut it Rafiq, you curry man.'[4]

Field notes: pupil–pupil aggression

There is a sophisticated system of unspoken 'rules' which structure and contain the pupil–pupil aggression in this set. Although there is a lot of aggressively threatening language and behaviour, the 'rules' ensure that conflict is usually managed without escalation into real physical violence. The only exceptions to this have both involved Ian Taylor [a white boy known as 'the best fighter' in the group] and the two Asian boys in the set.

Last week, Taylor grabbed Rafiq and held him in an arm-lock for more than 20 seconds; today, Taylor turned his attention to Sadiq.

At the end of the lesson, Taylor was collecting the pupils' exercise books when he moved around behind Sadiq, put his left hand on the back of Sadiq's head and tried to force the Asian pupil's face onto his desk.

Sadiq took no other action than to brace himself and resist the pressure: he did not actually try to stop Taylor.

The teacher saw what was happening and immediately ended the incident with a sarcastic, *'Ian* ... Collect the papers, don't bang Sadiq on the desk – he's small enough as it is.'

This kind of victimization was a common experience for many of the Asian boys in City Road. Racist name-calling was a regular, almost daily, experience for pupils such as Rafiq and

Sadiq, and although physical attacks were less frequent they were by no means uncommon.

Ian Taylor	[Rafiq]'s always mouthing ... Like when sir tells him to do something he's always [mimicks in a childish drawl] 'Wa, wa, wa...', every time he's talking. So me and Barry beat him up (...) I like beating him up.
DG	Why?
Ian	I don't know ... He just gets on your nerves.

Some teachers, schools and LEAs consistently underestimate the significance of the racial harassment which many ethnic minority pupils endure. Both the Swann Committee and a recent report by the Commission for Racial Equality (CRE) have called on teachers and lecturers to recognize the 'extra-crippling dimension brought to [name-calling and bullying] by a racist motivation' (CRE, 1988, p. 18). The reports cite several cases which graphically illustrate the seriousness of the situation; the following extract is taken from an essay by an Asian fifth-former:

I attended a middle school where approximately 90% of the pupils were white ... The Asians were constantly in fear of being attacked by the several gangs of white boys. As we ran towards the staff room a teacher would come out and disperse the white gang, throw us back into the playground and then walk back in as if nothing had happened. The teachers had no idea of what we were experiencing. (Swann, 1985, p. 34)

Racist name-calling insults not only the individuals who are victimized, but also their families, their culture – everything with which they identify. As the report *Learning in Terror* (CRE, 1988) vividly highlighted, teachers frequently fail to appreciate the seriousness of such attacks:

A seven-year old girl at a school in the North-West was subjected to persistent name-calling by a white child of the same age, whose older sister also beat her up. The abuse escalated and the families became involved. The mother went to the school to discuss the problem when she saw that her child was becoming increasingly disturbed, to the point of bed-wetting and attempting to bleach her skin. The child's reports to the teacher had no effect. (CRE, 1988, p. 11)

Within City Road, racist name-calling was almost totally restricted to white–Asian pupil interactions; generally, Afro-Caribbean pupils were neither subject to nor the perpetrators of such attacks. By contrast, racist attacks (usually, but not always, verbal) were a regular fact of life for most Asian pupils and this clearly influenced the strength of their friendships with other Asians in the school.

Rafiq   They [Mansur, Amjad and Aziz] are good friends. You see, they keep me with them and they don't fight me, you know, or beat me up like that. Other [pupils] start picking on me and causing trouble . . .

Contacts with their Asian peers outside the school (at the mosque and/or living in the same neighbourhood) and within City Road itself (in lessons or as a defence against white attackers) were, therefore, an important factor which served to link all but the two Sikh boys in a complex friendship network which extended across the age-group. That is to say that in interviews and responses to friendship questionnaires, Dhilip (a Hindu) and each of the eight Muslim males in the year group cited at least one Asian peer as a close or best friend; taken together these friendships joined the pupils in an extended network so that, for example, although Rafiq did not count Jabar as a close friend, he knew him and if necessary could call upon his assistance via Amjad, one of Rafiq's best friends who was also close to Jabar.

A shared sense of ethnicity was, therefore, an important factor in the Asian boys' friendships. Asian males in City Road did not form a single, exclusive friendship group, however. Indeed, none of these pupils were involved in networks based *solely* upon shared ethnicity. The pupils' questionnaire responses indicated that many Asian males were part of ethnically mixed friendship networks which seemed to be built upon school-based contacts in form groups or lessons. Therefore, while their ethnicity linked the Asian males socially to a greater degree than was true for pupils of other ethnic origins, they were also part of much larger ethnically mixed networks.

78

Hence ethnicity did not act as the basis for the development of any exclusively Asian group. There was no Asian equivalent of the Afro-Caribbean clique described in the previous chapter.

Teacher–pupil relationships

Just as they did in relation to Afro-Caribbean pupils, City Road staff often held generalized images of South Asian cultures. Although some were sensitive to variation within the Asian community, on the whole teachers' views seemed to reflect a mixture of popular misconceptions and white media images of South Asian peoples. For instance, many teachers saw their Asian pupils as suffering through over-strict, sometimes 'destructive' traditions within their communities. The following extract from my field notes illustrates some of the most common teacher perceptions of South Asian communities:

A senior member of staff has just argued with a South Asian lad. The teacher turns to me and asks,
'Did you see *Panorama* about the Asians?'
His question refers to a television programme, screened the previous evening, which focused on disputes in Bradford concerning the availability of Halal meat in schools and a recent *Salisbury Review* article by a local headteacher, Ray Honeyford.
The programme had interviewed Asian and white parents; the latter objected to what they saw as 'special treatment' for 'immigrants' and they often repeated the phrase, 'When in Rome do as the Romans do'.
The teacher explains that what he dislikes is the way that 'the Asians' are increasingly making demands without any sense of compromise. He goes on to discuss the role of Asian women and notes the conflict which he assumes girls must experience between school ('they're free when they're here') and home; 'There was one bit where a man said that if he was to forbid his wife to touch a cup of coffee, she wouldn't ever drink coffee unless he said she could.'

However, teachers' images of South Asian pupils and parents were not always negative. On one occasion, I was told by a pastoral head of year that one pupil came from a 'very supportive, caring family. Typical Indian family really.' This notion of a typically supportive family extended to all South Asian pupils in the age-group, and was in direct contrast to the teachers' tendency to doubt the concern of Afro-Caribbean parents whom they had met.

Humanities teacher	[An Afro-Caribbean pupil's] father gives the impression that he probably gives him a good hiding now and again – I don't know.
	I've got a feeling that the father is just supporting on the surface, you know. I don't feel there's a great deal of *real backing* there when it really matters.

This quotation is typical of official assessments of Afro-Caribbean parents; even those who were seen as well-intentioned were usually judged to be ineffective.

In marked contrast to the myth of Afro-Caribbean pupils as a threat to authority, there was a general feeling among City Road teachers that Asian pupils were 'quiet' and certainly not 'troublemakers'. This belief survived despite the fact that teachers sometimes saw fit to discipline Asian pupils. At one point a deputy head informed me (with great confidence) that no Asian pupils had been detained in the recent past, yet an examination of the school records revealed that more than half of the Asian males had received at least one detention during the fieldwork period (see Tables 2.1 and 2.2). This is not to say that Asian pupils always experienced good relationships with their teachers. In their day-to-day dealings with Asian pupils, however, teachers did not hold any notions of them as being particularly troublesome; in fact, quite the reverse was true.

Classroom observation indicated that Asian pupils experienced teacher–pupil relations which were generally similar to those of their white peers of similar degrees of academic involvement. Hence teachers' expectations of Asian pupils seemed to owe more to their identity as a member of a particular set or friendship group than to their ethnic origin. In order to explore this further, it is necessary to consider the nature of teacher–pupil interactions and pupil adaptations more generally among the white and Asian pupils in City Road.

Before examining detailed evidence from the school, it is helpful to locate the arguments within the wider context of previous work on academic differentiation and subcultural polarization.

Academic differentiation and subcultural polarization in City Road

A note on the theory of differentiation and polarization

A great deal of the sociological literature on pupils' experience of schooling has focused on the development of contrasting adaptations to the demands of school, adaptations which may be crudely summarized as the 'pro-school' and 'anti-school' subcultures. Although the 'bi-polar' model (Brown, 1987) has attracted a good deal of criticism it continues to offer an attractive framework which is taken up by critical theorists and classroom teachers alike. Martyn Hammersley (1985) has used the work of Hargreaves (1967), Lacey (1970) and Ball (1981) as the basis for a 'rational reconstruction' of their findings into a theory of differentiation–polarization.

This theory claims that if pupils are *differentiated* according to an academic-behavioural standard, for example by being streamed or banded, their attitudes to that standard will become *polarized*. In particular, those given the lowest rankings will reject it and the values it embodies. (Hammersley, 1985, p. 247; emphasis added)

As part of a co-ordinated research project, based in the University of Manchester, Colin Lacey and David Hargreaves set about analysing individual schools as social systems (Hammersley, 1985, p. 245).[5] Lacey studied a boys' grammar school ('Hightown') and Hargreaves a secondary modern ('Lumley'). Both noted a gradual polarization in the pupils' attitudes towards the official school value systems. They argued that teachers routinely differentiated between pupils on certain grounds, especially achievement and behaviour (Lacey, 1970, pp. 57–8). Such differences were institutionalized and amplified by streaming systems which grouped together pupils who shared similar experiences of academic success or failure. Thus, ideal conditions for the generation of subcultures were created

81

by the school (see chapter 3). One subculture, centred around the high streams, accepted the official goals of the institution and strove towards academic success. Another subculture, identified within the lower status classes, rejected the school's value system and substituted an oppositional culture. These orientations were referred to as 'academic' and 'delinquescent' by Hargreaves (1967, p. 162) and as 'pro-school' and 'anti-school' by Lacey (1970, p. 187). Both writers used these conceptions as 'ideal types' (cf. Weber, 1904) that is, they were simplifications of reality, abstracted for the purposes of sociological analysis.

Many writers have criticized the pro/anti-school model, usually by arguing that it offers too simplistic an account of classroom life (cf. Furlong, 1976; Bird, 1980; Hammersley and Turner, 1980). My own analysis confirms the significance of these observations. However, the criticisms do not fundamentally undermine the main elements of the differentiation–polarization model. Indeed, it provides a useful (though imperfect) framework for the interpretation of Asian and white pupils' adaptations to life in the fourth and fifth years in City Road.

Staff attempts to combat subcultural polarization

Teachers told me that 'the options could be the making' of certain pupils. On the other hand, a number of pupils were expected to 'turn off' at this point. The teachers offered several reasons why pupils might develop so well (or so poorly) following their subject option choices. The most frequent explanations concerned the amount of differentiation in the upper school achieved by increased use of 'setting by ability'. A humanities teacher, for instance, stated that 'with the option system they might start to work because there's a certain amount of grading now, and the brighter kids go together.'

If the increased differentiation in the fourth year could 'make' a pupil, surely it might also 'break' one? It was interesting to note that while the staff accepted that school processes (option choice and the limited increase in setting) might lead some pupils to improved efforts, they were not so quick to accept the possible corollary, that the same processes might lead others to reduced efforts. Although an increase in 'trouble' was expected, it was usually seen as an unavoidable consequence of academic failure rather than a reflection of the school's treatment of the pupil. The increasing 'disillusionment' (as the staff referred to it) was something which the school sought to minimize by emphasizing that it was in the interests of all pupils to do their best during their time at school.

Several writers have questioned the notion that a single set of school values and expectations are consistently presented to pupils (cf. Bird, 1980; Hammersley and Turner, 1980). I have already shown that teachers' expectations and treatment of pupils could vary dramatically even where the pupils had committed the same offence (see chapter 2). Despite the variability of teacher expectations in particular classroom situations, however, overall the school did in fact present a relatively consistent set of expectations concerning appropriate pupil behaviour and attitudes. In gatherings such as form periods and assemblies, the pupils were consistently presented with models of how they should act if they hoped to succeed within the school (and in society). During tutorial periods, for example, form teachers would sometimes address their tutees on the importance of continued effort and respect for staff. It was in assemblies (when an entire year group was addressed at once) that the most formal attempts at motivation were made.

Throughout my time in City Road the pupils were encouraged to adopt an approach to school which included a number of central features concerning both effort and demeanour: they should work to the best of their ability, be punctual, polite, and dressed in school uniform. Whatever their ability, pupils were expected to defer to the authority of teachers. These were not the sum of the school's requirements and their day-to-day interpretation and enforcement by staff was by no means universal and unproblematic, but in addresses to the year group as a whole these expectations concerning 'the right way' were continually repeated by staff.

These expectations represented an officially communicated school value system. The following example is taken from the headteacher's address to the first assembly of the age-group's fifth (and final) year in City Road. The head used the occasion to highlight the characteristics which he identified as indicators of future success or failure.

I'll tell you what some of the signs are.

Those people who keep coming to school, simple and straightforward and uncomplicated. They see they are

83

dressed as they should be, they see they arrive on time. They come to school except when it's just impossible because they're too ill. They're the ones that succeed.

Those people who are *sloppy* in the way they present themselves (...) who are only too happy to find some excuse or another to get out of that day – a bit of a cold and they don't come. They will not succeed (...) there have been times when it's been more important to [some] to waste time, to try and bend the rules. I'm thinking particularly of dress rules. They'd rather let themselves down. *Because they're the ones that have to pay for it.* It's nothing more than irritating to the rest who are working hard.

The headteacher's speech outlined two alternative approaches to the demands of the school: one was in accordance with the official requirements concerning demeanour and effort (the 'ideal client': Becker, 1952), the other was in conflict with the norms and values of the school. The elements of each are familiar as those which formed the basis for the pro/anti-school model of pupil subcultures outlined in previous works. The head's aim was to identify for pupils the 'correct' way of behaving and to hold out the promise of future success. He concluded, 'If anyone's sitting in here thinking to themselves, "I've left it too late". *Don't.*' The head's speech was exceptional in the clarity with which it distinguished between the 'right' and 'wrong' approaches to the demands of school, but its message was repeated throughout the fourth and fifth years. By encouraging pupils to believe that success was possible, and at the same time issuing threats of the consequences if they clashed with the school authorities, staff continually attempted to minimize what they perceived as the increasingly deviant behaviour of some pupils in the fourth and fifth years.

It is clear, therefore, that the school anticipated, and attempted to contain, subcultural polarization in the post-option years. Some evidence in support of the teachers' expectation of increased trouble in the upper school was found in the school punishment books, where an increasing proportion of the age-group received senior management detentions. A comparison between the three terms of the third year and three terms taken from the upper-school years showed that the proportion of the age-group appearing at least once increased from 16 per cent (twenty-six pupils) to 27 percent (forty-four pupils) – a pattern which was true for both boys and girls.[6]

Although the receipt of senior management detentions is, at best, a crude guide to the quality of teacher–pupil relationships, the data indicate that during the fourth and fifth years an increasing proportion of pupils was identified as acting in conflict with important aspects of the school's official expectations.

The teachers' anticipation of increasing trouble, their attempts to combat it, and the increased proportion of pupils appearing in the detention records would seem to indicate that some form of subcultural polarization occurred following the increased differentiation and selection in the upper-school years at City Road. The precise nature of that polarization cannot be assumed; rather, we need to look closely at the detail of how white and Asian pupils experienced and adapted to life in the fourth and fifth years.

Case studies of differentiation and polarization

Very little research has examined the ways in which Asian pupils have experienced and responded to schooling in this country. There are some excellent anthropological studies of South Asian communities but remarkably little attempt to continue the studies in multi-ethnic classrooms (cf. Ballard and Ballard, 1977; Saifullah Khan, 1977, 1979; Bhachu, 1985). Furthermore, although Asian pupils appear in Cecile Wright's quantitative data, they are conspicuous by their absence from her qualitative accounts of pupil adaptations in multi-ethnic schools (Wright, 1985a, 1985b, 1986).

As I noted earlier, several writers have commented on the relatively positive nature of teachers' stereotypes of Asian students when compared with Afro-Caribbean pupils (cf. Brittan, 1976a, 1976b; Tomlinson, 1981, 1983). To date, the most detailed published account arises from Mac an Ghaill's work on a boys' comprehensive school. In order 'to challenge the teacher stereotype of the "high-achieving, conformist" Asian student' Mac an Ghaill presented a detailed study of 'The Warriors' – an anti-school group of pupils born in England of Indian or Pakistani parents (Mac an Ghaill, 1988, p. 138). The study offers an important corrective to simplistic teacher stereotypes, but, by concentrating upon 'anti-school' pupils, Mac an Ghaill does not fully explore the complexity and range of Asian pupils' adaptations and experiences of school. It is hoped that the following data from City Road will add to our understanding of this important field.

As the age-group completed the fourth year of their secondary education I conducted a series of in-depth interviews with each pupil in two of my original case-study forms. I saw each pupil individually and the interview followed a relatively structured schedule of questions which investigated a wide variety of issues. I sought information on how the pupil perceived his/her experiences of City Road to that date (including the options process) and probed certain perspectives and actions which might place them in harmony or conflict with elements of the officially communicated school value system. For example, I asked about the pupils' attitudes to external examinations and wondered whether the school had got any better or worse during the fourth year. Was City Road 'too strict'? Had they ever truanted? I also asked about the pupils' relationships with staff: did they particularly like or dislike any teachers; if so, why? Did they feel that any pupils were 'treated differently'?

The interviews generated a great deal of data and, in conjunction with my observations around the school, I had anticipated that I would be able roughly to categorize the pupils in relation to a revised version of the pro/anti-school model (cf. Woods, 1979). However, this proved impossible for most pupils: there seemed as many different adaptations as there were pupils. Although some seemed to approximate the pro- and anti-school typologies, the complexity of their adaptations often led to striking contradictions between their general orientations and specific attitudes and types of behaviour. These contradictory elements were often of such a dramatic nature that the labels 'pro-' and 'anti-school' were simply not adequate.

The complexity of the pupils' adaptations is best demonstrated by drawing upon interview and observational data to examine the cases of two Asian pupils. It should be emphasized that I could just as easily have used white pupils as the basis for these case studies; although (as I have shown) their ethnicity was a major factor in their experience of school, in terms of their day-to-day relations with staff the Asian students seemed to experience patterns of differentiation and adaptational response which were similar to those of their white peers. I have chosen to focus on these pupils in order to illustrate specifically the complexity of the Asian pupils' adaptations to school, and thereby contrast their experiences with those of the Afro-Caribbean pupils already considered in the previous chapter.

Case study 1: Arif Aslam: commitment, academic success and truancy

During Arif Aslam's third year the pastoral head of year told me that Arif was 'underachieving' because he fooled around in class and was too talkative. Mr Palmer, Arif's form tutor, also told me that he had received several complaints from staff who were unhappy with his behaviour in lessons. In the fourth year, however, Arif began to attract very favourable reports and Mr Palmer cited him as a perfect example of the changes in attitude which could result from the differentiation of the subject options process. The following quotation is taken from an interview with Mr Palmer at the end of Arif's fourth year.

> Arif's an *outstanding change*, there's no doubt about that (...) Both Paul Martin [head of year] and I have found that Arif has changed completely. Now last year he was in a gang, with Paul [Dixon], Michael [Cooper] and Ben [Watson], who spent all their time acting and messing around ... *Now, he's changed completely*, he really has. I mean his reports explain it, he's got double A's and B's [for effort and achievement] all over the place. And every member of staff has commented on it. *Every one.* That's a *vast* change in Arif from his attitude last year.

Such a description seems to indicate that, by his final year of compulsory education, in the eyes of staff Arif had become something of an ideal (pro-school) pupil, yet the complexity of his adaptations went far beyond such a label.

ARIF'S EXPERIENCES OF ACADEMIC SELECTION AND DIFFERENTIATION: In City Road each pupil's subject option choices were supposed to be made at a meeting between the pupil, his or her parents, form tutor and a member of the school's senior staff or guidance team.[7] Although the options process was presented as a time of choice, in the vast majority of cases the staff made sure that pupils followed options which were 'suited' to their ability. This was possible because of a variety of strategies which allowed teachers to dominate the option meetings (cf. Gillborn, 1987, pp. 109–20). Arif's option meeting was one of only two occasions where staff domination broke down; when he left school Arif wanted 'to be a vet' and he had carefully researched the consequences of this aspiration. Arif controlled his option meeting by virtue of his precise knowledge of the examination subjects which he needed to pass at sixteen- and eighteen-plus in order to compete for a place in one of the few relevant higher education courses. Arif's studious preparation was typical of his approach to school and evidenced his acceptance of the teachers' advice that all pupils should think carefully about their subject choices.

In his fourth and fifth years Arif studied towards a total of eight external examinations (all of which he passed) in seven different subject departments. Four of these departments operated some form of setting by ability in the upper school and in each case Arif was placed in the 'top' set. These groups were left in no doubt about the academic demands which they faced and were constantly reminded of work schedules and the requirements of their courses of study. The following quotation, from the teacher's address at the beginning of a 'top' set English lesson, illustrates the degree of forward planning and sense of urgency which the academic requirements of the subject fostered in the pupils:

> I'll just explain about the assignments. You've got two to hand in, obviously I want those as soon as possible, they're overdue now ... The poetry and the Shakespeare (...) I explained why it was important to do the Shakespeare if you'd not done as well as you might expect first time. You do in fact *have* to submit an essay on Shakespeare for your course, so therefore it's doubly important that you did well second time around.

ARIF'S INTERACTIONS WITH STAFF AND PEERS: Arif was a confident pupil who enjoyed good relationships with his teachers. Staff described him as being one of the most intelligent pupils in his age-group and in lessons he always made a great effort to complete his work and be friendly and courteous to teachers. I observed many fifth-year lessons in City Road and noticed that Arif always gave a great deal of attention to his work and never clashed with teachers; this was the case whether he was in the selective 'top' English set or a mixed ability option where pupils who represented the full range of ability in the school were taught together simply because they had chosen the subject from the same timetable block.

In the mixed ability class Arif sat with a small group of close friends (including both Asian and Afro-Caribbean pupils) who would hold competitions to see who could get the highest marks for their work and who could be first to complete different sections of the syllabus. Like other pupils in the class, this group of friends held conversations during lessons, but almost always at a noise level which was acceptable to the teacher – the exceptions were when an Afro-Caribbean member of the group (such as Paul Dixon) was singled out for criticism (see chapter 3).

In the top English set Arif sat with another Asian male (Mohammed Abid) who had a reputation for writing extraordinarily long and detailed essays; once again, Arif would vie with his friend to get the highest marks. Arif was no less talkative in English lessons but like the majority of the set he structured his conversations around the organization of the lesson itself. Pupils in the top set generally spoke when there were natural breaks in the lesson, for example, when the teacher gave out paper, left the room without leaving them work to do, or signalled that it was time to start 'packing away'. It was not that pupils in the 'top' set did not gossip, but that they confined their gossiping to points where they were not in competition with the teacher. I analysed a tape recording of one top set lesson and discovered that about a quarter of the 55-minute lesson was taken up with pupil–pupil talk – yet because the noise had taken its cue from the structure of the lesson itself, the overall impression was of a very orderly, even quiet, group of pupils.

It might appear, therefore, that Arif's time in City Road had all the hallmarks of the creation of a classic pro-school pupil: his experience of selection and differentiation was very positive; he gained access to all the subject options which he wanted and, where setting occurred, he was always placed in the top set. In addition, Arif enjoyed good teacher–pupil relationships and worked extremely hard. In certain key respects, however, Arif acted in direct conflict with the goals and values which the school consciously promoted in assemblies and form periods.

ARIF'S CONFLICT WITH THE SCHOOL VALUE SYSTEM: Despite a strong commitment to academic success and his general deference to teachers' advice (on matters such as the need for careful options preparations) Arif did not simply mirror all aspects of the school's value system. In interviews with me Arif criticized teachers who expected too little of pupils and noted that his Afro-Caribbean peers received less favourable treatment from some staff. In particular Arif accused individual teachers of being 'racialist' in their disproportionate criticism of his friend Paul Dixon (see chapter 3). His readiness to question teachers' actions was not, however, the most striking conflict between Arif and the school's portrayal of conduct which would lead to future success.

Occasionally, when he felt that the situation warranted it, Arif would truant from school, something which went directly against the school's emphasis upon attendance at all costs (see for instance the headteacher's speech noted earlier).

DG Do you ever take time off from school when you're not ill?

Arif Yeah. [he laughs]

DG You do ... how regularly?

Arif Not *that* regularly, I only do it when I'm in *desperate* trouble, like I have to hand in a literature essay. Like, *Tuesday mornings* is my most favourite day for taking days off 'cause we've only got *games* and careers [guidance] and technical graphics. Technical graphics I can catch up on, and I'm not really bothered about games and careers.

Clearly this kind of act seriously conflicted with the officially communicated school value system, yet in certain respects it reflected how deeply Arif was committed to other official expectations; specifically, that work should be in on time and completed to each pupil's best ability. Despite his occasional truancy, in general Arif showed a very high degree of involvement in the school value system. Indeed, the style of his truancy was further evidence of his commitment to academic success: he timed his absences to coincide with subjects of little or no academic status in the school. Only one of the lessons (technical graphics) led to an external examination and he was sure he could 'catch up on' any work he missed. Furthermore, Arif emphasized that he would only truant in order to spend time on other school work for subjects of higher academic status (such as an essay on English literature). His truancy was always an individual enterprise; he never pre-arranged absences with friends. Sometimes Arif went to a local library to work, on other occasions he simply stayed in his bedroom without his parents' knowledge.

> I don't nick off for the sake of nicking off (...) Twice I've done it on a Tuesday morning when I just stayed in my room all morning ... My Dad was at work and my Mum didn't realize all morning.

Case study 2: Rafiq Ali: cooling out, conflict and academic goals

Rafiq Ali and Arif Aslam had a great deal in common. Both were male pupils born in the UK of Pakistani parents, were Muslim, spoke Urdu at home and were members of the same mixed ability tutorial group throughout their time in City Road Comprehensive. However, the two were not close friends. Although they shared some common friendships among the other Asian males in their age-group, Arif had little contact with Rafiq, whom he described to me as 'the dumbo in our class'. This judgement of Rafiq's academic ability was shared by City Road teachers who saw him as one of the least able pupils in the age-group.

RAFIQ'S EXPERIENCES OF ACADEMIC SELECTION AND DIFFERENTIATION: During the subject options process Rafiq was 'channelled' (cf. Woods, 1976, 1977; Tomlinson, 1987) into the very lowest status subjects. City Road pupils were required to choose four options (including at least one science and one humanity) from a selection within separate timetable blocks. In addition to a craft subject, Rafiq initially listed biology, religious education and history as his favoured choices; he eventually emerged from the options process with none of these subjects.

Rafiq's choices were altered during a combination of several informal negotiations with subject teachers and guidance staff, and a more formal options meeting. Rafiq's experiences were a

91

clear example of 'cooling out' (cf. Goffman, 1952; Ball, 1981, p. 135) – a process whereby 'over-aspiring' pupils are made to lower their sights and accept more 'realistic' choices in line with teachers' perceptions of their relative lack of ability. Rafiq found himself following an upper-school curriculum which was specifically reserved for those of the very lowest ability; for his science option he studied applied science, a mode III CSE course which focused on 'practical' aspects of science. This was a limited grade course where even the highest grade possible (CSE grade 3) was not equivalent to an 'O' level pass. In the humanities area, rather than following two separate subjects, Rafiq was admitted to the double community studies course; again a CSE mode III course which was written and examined within the school (with external moderation). Community studies was a low status option which involved a certain amount of work outside the school, such as helping out at local nurseries or visiting 'old folks' homes'. The double option involved a small number of pupils having twice the normal amount of time in the lesson (accounting for a quarter of Rafiq's entire timetable) and had been introduced as a conscious attempt to fill up the timetable of pupils whose lack of ability and/or discipline meant that they were judged unsuitable for more mainstream subject areas.

A senior member of the 'guidance' team.
Really you don't want any more than twelve in that group. When you look at some of the characters in there you could do with a single, one-to-one approach (...) [Double community studies] was hopefully going to cater for the less able child who wanted a more practical approach (...) I mean we've got some bright kids who don't know what to *leave out* [of their options], you've got a certain amount of less able kids who don't know what to pick. So in each area we've tried to create something for them.

Entry to double community studies was closely guarded by the school's senior staff who ensured that only the 'least able' finally took the option. Together, the applied science and double community studies courses represented the very lowest status curriculum which City Road pupils could receive – they were the 'sink' courses, designed specifically for pupils for whom academic failure had become a way of life (cf. Ball, 1981).

Rafiq studied four subjects in addition to applied science and double community studies; two were craft options which did not set by ability, the other two (English and mathematics) each placed Rafiq in the lowest (non-examination) set. The following quotation from the head of the English Department concerns the criteria which had decided membership of the 'bottom' English set:

> We considered *very* carefully who we placed in the bottom group. Because some had done *badly* enough on the exam to merit inclusion in the bottom group but we felt it would not be sufficiently challenging for them, and they would be demoralized by removal from the mainstream. So only exceptional cases, mainly very poor behaviour, attitude ... truancy or just inability to cope with *any* simple work.

Rafiq's English set were, therefore, seen as 'no-hopers'. The school's low academic and behavioural expectations of these pupils were reflected in many ways; for instance, in contrast to Arif's top English set (where work was scheduled weeks, even months, in advance) there was little or no continuity of work from one lesson to another. Examination requirements did not concern the bottom set; indeed, even the school's attendance requirements were seen as having less meaning in a group where truancy was a frequent, almost routine event.

Teacher	[Taking the register] Bailey?
Jim Bailey	Sir.
Teacher	Blimey, look what the wind blew in.
	Careful Jim, you're in danger of being a regular attender (...)
	Where's Flemming – he's not often away. Not like Harper, you don't expect him to turn up.

RAFIQ'S INTERACTIONS WITH STAFF AND PEERS: During his fourth year Rafiq's subject teachers increasingly began to report instances of aggressive behaviour in lessons. Conflict was a frequent occurrence in 'sink' lessons, between teacher and pupils (often seen in shouted exchanges concerning a pupil's lack of work) as well as between classmates. This was reflected in the senior staff's decision to limit the number of pupils in 'sink' courses (see the guidance teacher's comment above). The level of pupil aggression was one of the most striking features of the bottom English set. Indeed, the group's aggressive manner was commented upon by every teacher who came into contact with them; unfamiliar teachers would be quizzed about a variety of personal details ranging from length of teaching experience to their marital status and, in the case of male staff, which football team they supported. Once the pupils had gained such information it would be used as ammunition to challenge the teacher's right to be telling them what to do or even to query the teacher's sanity.

With the exception of physical attacks by a white pupil upon each of the Asian males in the group (see above), aggression in the set was always verbal. The threatening behaviour was not as chaotic as first appeared, however, as the pupils had developed a variety of 'fronts' (cf. Goffman, 1959) which ranged from the 'hard men' at one extreme (who tried to maintain an image of aggressive toughness) to the 'wimps' (who were purely victims) at the other end of the spectrum. These fronts shaped a great deal of pupil–pupil and teacher–pupil interaction in the set and often led Rafiq into further conflict with his teachers and peers. Rafiq tried to align himself with the hard men; he frequently shouted at his teachers and did what he could to irritate the other pupils in the group. This last attribute was part of a battery of strategies which Rafiq had developed in order to 'mess about' and thereby avoid work.

In the bottom English set 'work' was loosely understood to be anything which the teacher had asked to be done. In the case of putting together display materials this was acceptable, but anything which involved writing was to be avoided at all costs. The following extract from my field notes describes Rafiq's expertise in this field.

Of all the pupils, Rafiq is the most adept at avoiding 'work'. He uses a variety of strategies which include:
- *copying from his neighbour*;
- *talking and joking* with the teacher and/or other members of the set;
- *insulting another pupil* – often picking an argument so that the defence of his honour takes up more time;
- *daydreaming* – staring into space, yawning etc.;
- *asking questions* – having spent time involved in any of the above strategies, Rafiq often waits until the teacher is

busy and then puts his hand in the air for help. He then calls out to the teacher and is told to wait. This seems to give him licence to move away from his desk and chat to other pupils until the teacher is free. When the teacher is finally free to help him, Rafiq announces 'Sir, I don't understand sir.' The teacher carefully explains the task, Rafiq nods and looks at his paper as if to start writing. Once the teacher has moved away, Rafiq turns to his neighbour and begins a conversation.

In many respects, therefore, Rafiq's time in City Road appears to have been a clear example of differentiation and polarization resulting in anti-school behaviour; certainly his love of messing about in lessons and his aggressive style of interaction with teachers and peers were in conflict with the kinds of behaviour which the school attempted to promote through motivational speeches in assemblies and form periods. In fact Rafiq's responses to school were much more complex than might initially be apparent, and he showed a high degree of commitment to some aspects of the official school value system.

RAFIQ'S COMMITMENT TO ASPECTS OF THE SCHOOL VALUE SYSTEM: Despite the creative effort which Rafiq put into avoiding 'work' during lessons, he continued to value academic success as a goal. When I first interviewed Rafiq (as a third-year pupil) he already realized that any examinations he was entered for were likely to be the lower status CSE rather than GCE 'O' level examinations; yet despite his negative experiences of selection in the school, Rafiq continued to value examination success. The following is from an interview at the end of Rafiq's fourth year:

> GCE is a bit harder, its O *level*. I'm not really bothered [about whether it's GCE or CSE] as long as I can get an exam (...) It's important 'cause say if you're gonna get a job right, they'll need to know what you got for your grades won't they. They'll need grades, then they can find out if they want the person or not − if you haven't got one they can say, [dismissively] 'You can go.'

Although Rafiq's desire for certification did not find expression in his written work in class, there were clear signs that he genuinely wanted to experience some form of educational success. For example, in the bottom English set one of the quickest ways to attract the hard men's aggressive attention was to volunteer an answer to one of the teacher's questions. Despite this risk Rafiq consistently volunteered answers – on occasions, he was the only pupil to offer answers during the entire lesson. Similarly, as the following extract from my field notes shows, he was the first pupil to show any enthusiasm when the possibility of examination entry was raised:

Teacher	Do any of you *really* feel you want to be put in for the English exam? CSE?
Rafiq	*Yeah*. Me.
Teacher	You do Rafiq?
Rafiq	Yeah. [several seconds pause] Why, is it hard or will it be easy?
Teacher	Be hard for you.
Rafiq	[Disappointed] Tut.
Teacher	Anybody else?
Phillip	I will sir.
Gary	[Hand in the air] Yeah, I will sir.
Teacher	[To Phillip] It'll take you a long while to answer your papers *the speed you're producing that letter* – come on, get a move on. [Phillip starts writing]
Rafiq	Sir, when's the exam?
Teacher	After next Easter.
Rafiq	Sir I won't be here.
Teacher	You leaving at Easter?
Rafiq	Yeah.
Teacher	When's your birthday? [checking Rafiq's eligibility]
Rafiq	October ... 23rd.
Teacher	What will we do without you?
Rafiq	I'll come back for the exam.

Further evidence of Rafiq's commitment to certain aspects of the school value system was seen in his attendance record. Unlike Arif, and in contrast to almost every other member of his English set, Rafiq *never* truanted from school. In addition, he always wore full school uniform and in interview he complained (like Arif) that some teachers were not strict enough, but felt that overall City Road staff were 'good teachers'.

Despite their apparent similarity in terms of ethnic origin, religion, gender and form group, Arif and Rafiq experienced two very different types of pupil career in City Road. Following entry to his desired option choices and selection to the highest sets, Arif maintained a very high degree of academic commitment and was successful in external examinations (he gained eight 'O' level passes). In contrast, Rafiq was 'cooled out' during the options process and took a full part in the conflictual peer and teacher interactions which characterized life in the 'sink' subjects and bottom sets. Rafiq gained no educational qualifications. To a degree, therefore, Arif and Rafiq can be taken as representative of the process of academic differentiation and consequent subcultural polarization: a process which could be seen at work in the school careers of many white and Asian pupils, of either sex, in City Road.

However, existing characterizations in terms of a bipolar model of pupil adaptations do not capture the complexity of life in schools – to argue at the level of ideal types alone can only perpetuate existing confusions about the meaning of certain key terms. Arif described some teachers as 'racialist' and occasionally truanted from lessons (hardly typical of a pro-school position), while Rafiq risked verbal and physical abuse to answer teachers' questions and continued to value the goal of academic success throughout his time in City Road (not characteristics of an anti-school position). Clearly the situation is a complex one. In the following section I will briefly outline a revised model which allows for the complexity of pupil adaptations to the school value system.

Refining the pro/anti model as a continuum of involvement

Both Peter Woods (1979, 1983) and Stephen Ball (1981, pp. 116–21) have tried to accommodate the variety of pupil adaptations by adding additional categories to Hargreaves' and Lacey's pro/anti-school typology. Yet each attempt remains at the level of an ideal type and seems artificially static in its conceptualization of a pupil's potential to move in any direction (as regards harmony or conflict with the official value system) on any issue and in any action throughout the school day. In order to accommodate this complexity the analysis of pupil adaptations has to be conceptualized in broader terms. One possible solution may be found in Amitai Etzioni's work on the nature of compliance in complex organizations (1961). As Percy Cohen (1968) has noted, an important aspect of Etzioni's analysis is the recognition that 'compliance has two aspects: the *internal motivation* of the actor, and the *external pressure* exercised by other actors, and by the system in which the actors participate' (P. S. Cohen, 1968, p. 138; emphasis added). In different instances either of the internal or external aspects of compliance may become more or less important, but an element of both will always be present to some degree. This is an important point and offers a strong basis for the character-ization of pupil adaptations. Such a conception allows a role for the actor both as an individual personality with decision-making potential and as a participant in a social context (for instance, in relation to teacher and peer expectations). Etzioni's characterization of 'involvement' is especially important.

> Organizations must continually recruit means if they are to realize their goals. One of the most important of these means is the positive orientation of the participants to the organizational power. *Involvement* refers to the cathectic-evaluative orientation of an actor to an object, characterized in terms of intensity and direction.
>
> The intensity of involvement ranges from high to low. The direction is either positive or negative. We refer to positive involvement as *commitment* and to negative involvement as *alienation*. (The advantage of having a third term, *involve-ment*, is that it enables us to refer to the continuum in a neutral way.) (Etzioni, 1961, pp. 8–9; original emphasis)

As critics of the bipolar model of differentiation and polarization have emphasized, no pupil action or attitude should be seen as *determined* by some general orientation to school. The school day, indeed the entire pupil career, is made up of countless decisions concerning possible choices of action and possible positions on questions such as the value of school achievement and conformity with official expectations (Hammersley and Turner, 1980). Yet despite the variety of possible choices of action, some pupils do hold certain attitudes, and act in certain ways, which place them largely in harmony or conflict with the official school value system.

98

A pupil might move between different degrees of involvement on different occasions and on different issues, yet overall his/her views and actions (attitudes and behaviours) may tend to reflect broadly similar levels of involvement. Hence it is possible to conceive of a pupil who has a generally high degree of involvement (is committed to key elements of the school value system) yet on occasions acts in conflict with the school's expectations. Arif's truancy is a good example. Similarly a pupil may often act in ways which conflict with the school value system and have no realistic chance of educational success – such pupils have a low degree of involvement in the school value system – yet on occasions they might act in accordance or harmony with the school's expectations, sometimes in quite a dramatic fashion. Rafiq is an example of such a pupil.

Rather than trying to characterize pupils' adaptations within a dichotomous bipolar model of pro/anti-school positions, therefore, it is more realistic to view pupils' involvement in relation to a continuum ranging from relative commitment through to alienation from the school value system. The model of a continuum allows for the variety and complexity of pupil adaptations while retaining important elements of previous work which have shown the potential of differentiation–polarization analyses.

Conclusions

the debate is led astray by two false assumptions, namely that all West Indian children fail and all Asian children succeed ... thanks to these assumptions, some have argued that the reasons for West Indian children's underachievement cannot be found in the factors they share in common with the Asians ... thus racism, either in the society at large or in the school, is dismissed as an important factor on the ground that otherwise we would not be able to explain Asian success (Bhikhu Parekh, quoted in Swann, 1985, p. 69).

In this chapter I have examined the experiences of male pupils of South Asian ethnic origin in City Road Comprehensive. By highlighting the complexity of life in multi-ethnic schools, the chapter has confirmed the truth of Bhikhu Parekh's analysis of the fallacies which often underlie the debate concerning the existence of racism in schools. Despite the generic label 'ethnic minority pupils', students of Afro-Caribbean and South Asian ethnic origins experience school in very different ways, some of which I have been able to highlight in this and the previous two chapters. In both cases the pupils' ethnicity influenced their choice of friends and their experience of teacher expectations, which often reflected 'racial' stereotypes. However, teacher stereotypes of Asian culture and traditions did not mean that all of their assumptions operated against the pupils' interests. In direct contrast to the Afro-Caribbean case, for example, staff tended to assume that Asians were well-disciplined, hard-working students who came from stable families where educational success was highly valued.

The differences in teachers' expectations of Afro-Caribbean and South Asian pupils were such that the students responded to school in different ways. Asian pupils experienced school differently to white pupils (witness the acts of racial harassment), but their relationships with teachers more closely mirrored those of their white, not their Afro-Caribbean, peers. Some South Asians, such as Arif, experienced very positive teacher–pupil relationships of a kind unknown to Afro-Caribbean pupils in the age-group.

As a group, Afro-Caribbean pupils faced negative teacher expectations which transcended individual judgements concerning their 'ability'. Wayne Johnson and Paul Dixon (whose cases I detailed in chapter 3), for example, were both judged to be 'able' pupils. Yet, neither experienced the positive teacher–pupil relationships which Arif enjoyed. Consequently, ethnicity and teacher stereotypes did not place Asian and Afro-Caribbean pupils in positions of equal disadvantage; in terms of their academic careers the Asian males in City Road experienced school in ways which resembled the careers of their white, rather than their Afro-Caribbean, peers. In examining the adaptations of Afro-Caribbean pupils (see chapter 3) ethnicity was the central factor; teachers' ethnocentric judgements were the prime obstacle to be negotiated if the pupil hoped to succeed academically. In contrast, although their ethnicity was an important factor in their school experience, the Asian males seemed to follow academic careers which displayed some of the characteristics of differentiation and subcultural polarization which were also apparent in the careers of white pupils of both sexes. Although the 'bipolar' model was found to be too simplistic, a revised version (in terms of a continuum of involvement) does seem to be of use in understanding the cases of Arif and Rafiq, Asian pupils who shared the same gender and ethnicity yet followed divergent paths in the upper school.

PART TWO

Beyond City Road – Issues for education in a multi-ethnic society

Chapter 5

Achievement and opportunity

Controversies in the measurement and meaning of educational achievement

Equality of opportunity was the dominant educational issue of the 1960s and 1970s. In the 1980s, however, successive Conservative governments redefined policy objectives so that the criteria of efficiency and 'cost-effectiveness' came to dominate the language of official statements and initiatives (cf. Bell, 1988). In the 1980s education was often perceived in terms of an industrial/economic paradigm (Gillborn, 1989). As in the USA, policy was framed according to what Richard Elmore has described as the 'batch processing' model of schooling:

> That is, the 'materials' (students) are assembled into standard batches (classes) and are processed (taught) according to predictable steps or stages, within well-defined constraints of time and space. This is the most efficient, predictable, and reliable way to handle the large volume of clients that public schools are forced to accommodate. (Elmore, 1987, p. 63)

The batch processing model was dramatically reflected in the prescriptions of the Education Reform Act 1988 which established a national curriculum involving externally defined programmes of study and the imposition of testing at 'key' ages.

Yet, despite its relegation from the prominence enjoyed during the 1970s, the concept of equality of opportunity continues to lie at the heart of much educational controversy and debate. This reflects the political importance of the concept as a tool in the analysis, critique and practice of education in this country.

The purpose of this chapter is to examine critically the concept of equality of opportunity and to summarize research data on the academic achievements of different ethnic groups. Before examining some of the contemporary debates, however, it is necessary to locate the development of the concept within its historical context.

Equality of opportunity

There is no single definition of equality of opportunity. Within the educational world, Halsey, Heath and Ridge (1980) have identified three related but separate understandings. The first approach is concerned with the formal opportunities for *access* and *participation* which are open to members of different social groups. In this minimal sense equality of educational opportunity already exists in this country; unlike South Africa, for example, access to certain institutions of higher education is not officially (and legally) restricted to members of particular social or ethnic groups.

A second understanding of the concept emerged prior to the 1944 Education Act when debate increasingly focused upon inequalities of *circumstance* which (despite formal opportunity) might present real barriers to some individuals. The provision for free education for all (in the 1944 Act) was an important move towards greater equality of opportunity in terms of this second definition. However, in relation even to this basic understanding, genuine equality of educational opportunity has not been achieved in this country – witness the fact that, in addition to the existence of an important (and growing) private sector, there are still no statutory rights to financial support to enable students to bridge the gap between the end of compulsory schooling and entry to higher education. Differences in financial circumstance still influence educational opportunity in 1990s Britain.

During the 1960s, in both Britain and the USA, a third definition of equality of opportunity achieved prominence:

the third definition of equality of opportunity ... is one

106

which compares the relative chances of access to schools and qualifications which were, *substantively* as distinct from *formally*, open to the children of different social classes. In effect, taking the word 'equality' to have its normal meaning in common speech, the definition now shifts from equality of opportunity to equality of outcome. (Halsey, Heath and Ridge, 1980, p. 202 original emphasis)

In Britain the third definition of equality of opportunity (focusing on outcome) came to prominence during the debates concerning selection at eleven-plus (cf. Evetts, 1973) and has continued to enjoy widespread support. The Committee of Inquiry into the Education of Children from Ethnic Minority Groups (Rampton, 1981; Swann, 1985), for instance, used this understanding in their analysis of rates of achievement. Consequently, it is the third definition of equality of opportunity which lies at the heart of recent debates and controversies concerning associations between ethnicity and educational achievement. The notion of 'underachievement' emerged as a central concept in these debates.

Underachievement

The third definition of equality of opportunity, therefore, uses measures of achievement (outcome) as indicators of opportunity. This approach assumes that 'the distribution of talent is random in the population and, in addition, the distribution of talent is random in different groups within the population' (Evetts, 1970, p. 428). Consequently, the degree to which equality of opportunity is achieved is signalled by the extent to which different groups (based on social class, gender, ethnicity or whatever ascribed characteristic) achieve equal success rates. It is in this sense that we can speak of a group underachieving in relation to the performance of other groups within the population. As Andrew Dorn (1985) has observed, this approach is an advance on previous notions of equality of opportunity because it goes beyond questions of individual intent:

> it rests on collectivist and impersonal notions of justice and equality and is concerned with the structural exclusion of racial groups. It is concerned to look beneath the surface of formal treatment and identify the discriminatory effects of institutional practices. (Dorn, 1985, p. 21)

Table 5.1 Sixteen-plus examination results by ethnic origin: six surveys compared (percentages)

Study, location & year of exam*	No exams taken	No graded passes	1+ CSE 4/5	1+ CSE 2/3	'O' level passes** 1–4	5+	Total	Number of cases
AFRO-CARIBBEAN								
1) London, 1972	(—	17 —)	18	44	20	0	99	250
2) Inner London, 1976	11	7	20	40	21	2	101	2,382
3) 6 LEAs, 1979	(—	17 —)	(—	80	—)	3	100	718
4) 5 LEAs, 1982	(—	19 —)	(—	75	—)	6	100	653
5) Inner London, 1985	14	3	13	38	27	5	100	2,981
6) YCS, 1985	6	9	7	40	31	7	100	244

ASIAN

Sample						Not available		N
1) London, 1972	14	3	8	29	27	17	98	389
2) Inner London, 1976	(—	20	—)	(—	63 —)	17	100	466
3) 6 LEAs, 1979	(—	19	—)	(—	64 —)	17	100	571
4) 5 LEAs, 1982	16	2	8	26	30	18	100	1,124
5) Inner London, 1985	8	4	8	29	32	19	100	435

TOTAL SAMPLE (all pupils)***

Sample						Not available		N
1) London, 1972	(— 30	—)	12	31	23	3	99	2,018
2) Inner London, 1976	19	8	11	27	26	10	101	24,398
3) 6 LEAs, 1979	(—	21	—)	(—	64 —)	15	100	6,196
4) 5 LEAs, 1982	(—	19	—)	(—	63 —)	18	100	5,942
5) Inner London, 1985	19	3	9	29	30	10	100	17,058
6) YCS, 1985	10	5	5	28	31	20	99	14,429

* Reported in (1) Maughan and Rutter, 1986; (2) Mabey, 1986; (3) and (4) Swann, 1985; (5) Kysel, 1988; (6) Drew and Gray, 1989.

** Includes GCE grades A–C and CSE grade 1.

*** Includes Afro-Caribbean, Asian, white and all other ethnic groups.

Source: Adapted from Drew and Gray, 1989, Table 7.

In order to examine the opportunities which are substantively available to pupils from different ethnic minority groups, many researchers have examined students' performance in examinations at the age of sixteen-plus. Table 5.1 details examination results broken down by ethnic origin as found in six of the most important surveys carried out during the last two decades.

The surveys summarized in this table present a relatively stable picture of the associations between ethnic origin and educational achievement in this country.[1] As a group, Afro-Caribbean pupils appear to underachieve in relation to the proportion of students who reach the highest levels of examination achievement. DES data generated for the Swann report (survey number 4 in Table 5.1), for example, showed that while 6 per cent of 'West Indian' pupils gained five or more higher passes in 'O' level (and equivalent) examinations, 17 per cent of 'Asian' and 19 per cent of 'all other leavers' achieved the same success; overall, 18 per cent of pupils in the sample gained five or more pass grades (Swann, 1985, p. 114). On the basis of such material the Committee of Inquiry concluded that Afro-Caribbean children *as a group* are underachieving in our education system' (Rampton, 1981, p. 10; original emphasis). This conclusion was repeated in the Committee's full report (Swann, 1985, p. 63).

Great caution should be applied when interpreting survey results such as those summarized in Table 5.1. By collapsing 'Asian' scores into a single category, for example, significant variations between different South Asian groups may be obscured. Data on sixteen-year-olds in inner London in 1985, for instance, revealed that, in terms of their average examination performance, 'both the highest- and lowest-achieving group in the study would have been classified as "Asian" in previous studies' (Kysel, 1988, p. 83).

Table 5.2 reproduces some of the 1985 ILEA data. The contrasting achievements of Indian and Bangladeshi pupils dramatically highlight the problems of aggregating different subgroups into larger more simple categories: by lumping all South Asian groups together important differences in socio-political backgrounds and educational experience are lost. Although Kysel's analysis gains considerably from the ability to identify different 'Asian' groups, the study suffers from a limitation which is common to many statistical surveys, namely

Table 5.2 Sixteen-year-olds' examination achievements in ILEA (1985) by ethnic origin

Ethnic origin	5 or more 'O' levels %	Average exam performance Av. score*	Number of cases
African	10.3	16.9	426
African Asian	24.7	22.7	162
Arab	6.6	14.0	91
Bangladeshi	4.2	8.7	333
Caribbean	4.6	13.6	2,981
English, Scottish, Welsh, Irish	10.3	15.2	10,685
Greek	11.5	17.6	243
Indian	26.4	24.5	398
Pakistani	17.7	21.3	231
SE Asian	17.0	19.1	300
Turkish	2.6	11.9	268
Other	18.0	21.3	940

* Formula for ILEA exam score is based on a scoring system first developed by Byford and Mortimore, 1985. GCE grades receive the following points: A = 7, B = 6, C = 5, D = 4, E = 3. CSE grades: grade 1 = 5, grade 2 = 4, grade 3 = 3, grade 4 = 2, grade 5 = 1. Ungraded results in both exams are scored as zero.
Source: Adapted from Kysel, 1988, Tables 1 and 2, pp. 84–5.

the inability to take account of socioeconomic (social class) factors which are known to be strongly associated with educational achievement. Hence, although the English, Scottish, Welsh and Irish (ESWI) group appears to have achieved relatively poorly, this may be a result of their lower social class position – as Nuttall and his colleagues have observed:

> It should be recognised that the ESWI population of inner London is not representative, socially or economically, of the total ESWI population of the United Kingdom and Eire, and

there could be confounding of the ethnic differences with socio-economic differences. (Nuttall *et al.*, 1989, p. 774)

Similarly, the sixth survey in Table 5.1 shows the highest proportions of academically successful Afro-Caribbean young people to date; this may reflect a real improvement in performance and/or the fact that the Youth Cohort Study (YCS), reported by Drew and Gray, is the first nationally representative survey in this field (more on these points below). These qualifications notwithstanding, Table 5.1 seems to indicate that in terms of the highest levels of examination performance, Afro-Caribbean pupils, as a group, have suffered relative underachievement which 'would not appear to have changed very much over this thirteen-year period' (Drew and Gray, 1989, p. 12).

Despite the fairly stable picture which apparently emerges from many surveys of achievement, however, both the concept of equal opportunity and the notion of underachievement have been criticized by writers from a broad range of educational and political thought. Before considering research evidence in further detail it is, therefore, necessary to examine the range of criticism which has been levelled against both the concept and evidence of underachievement.

The 'liberal' critique: equal opportunity as a conservative goal

In his book *Ethnic Minorities and Education* (1984), Robert Jeffcoate describes his perspective as 'liberal, egalitarian and integrationist' (p. xi). His treatment of equality of opportunity begins by noting that the concept stresses individual perform-ance and gain 'at the expense of the spirit of altruism and cooperation' (Jeffcoate, 1984, p. 53). Similarly, the 'gross disparities in wealth, power and status' which characterize our society remain unchallenged. As a goal, equality of opportunity merely refers to how disparities are achieved: it is 'a meritocratic creed rather than an egalitarian one' (p. 53).

Jeffcoate is especially critical of the way in which the concept accepts the education system's own definition of worth and success, so that the ideal of equality of opportunity is 'perverted into a preoccupation with the academic destinies of an intellectual elite' (p. 73). He goes on to attack the 'prevailing obsession' with results in sixteen-plus and eighteen-plus examinations, which are poor predictors of future success in higher education or employment, and in which the majority of students are labelled as 'failures'.

As a corrective to what he sees as a narrow and elitist version of equality of opportunity, Jeffcoate argues for 'a fresh, and genuine, commitment to the aim of developing *all* the "talents and abilities" of *all* children "to the full"' (p. 73; original emphasis). He is especially critical of the 'academic snobberies' which depreciate the value of those areas of the school curriculum (and public life) where Afro-Caribbean young people have been particularly successful, such as sport, music and dance. As Jeffcoate insists, there is 'no intrinsic reason for sporting and artistic success being less meritorious than academic success. After all, they also require discipline and determination as much as innate ability' (p. 74).

Jeffcoate's critique has much to recommend it. He rightly identifies both a narrow concern with traditional notions of academic success and an emphasis on examination results which define the majority as failures. While Jeffcoate's observations are valid, however, they are not sufficient cause to reject the definition of equal opportunity which focuses upon achievement. There are two principal reasons for this: first, the complex and problematic status of sporting and artistic ability, and second, the very real importance of educational certification in the youth labour market.

SPORT AS A SIDETRACK: As Jeffcoate himself acknowledges, the view that Afro-Caribbean pupils may have special 'talent' for artistic or sporting activities smacks of nineteenth-century racialist theories of genetic difference and the crude stereotypes which were used to excuse the slave trade. Although pupils' achievements in all parts of the curriculum should be acknowledged and valued, research evidence suggests that white teachers sometimes use sport 'as a side-track' (Carrington, 1983), a means of social control which maintains the pupils' investment in the school while simultaneously reflecting and reinforcing crude stereotypes of Afro-Caribbean pupils as more suited to physical/manual tasks than to academic/non-manual activities.

West Indian pupils seem to be more muscular, more physically developed and have better physical skills than

113

white children of the same age. Only rarely does one see a weak, flabby or poorly co-ordinated West Indian child. They have a raw talent (PE teacher)

Whereas they're not successful in the classroom they can show their abilities on the sports field (Humanities teacher). (Carrington, 1983, p. 52)

EDUCATIONAL ACHIEVEMENT AND THE LABOUR MARKET: Research commissioned in the early 1980s by the now-abolished Schools Council highlighted the crucial role of examination results in post-sixteen selection within both the education and labour markets. The study revealed that qualifications in English and mathematics had influence well beyond their proper scope, a finding which held true for selection to institutions of higher and further education as well as in the post-school labour market. It stated: "For each group of users [English and mathematics] appeared as essential factors among the selection criteria ... many users take performance in these subjects as a sufficient basis upon which to judge "general ability"' (Goacher, 1984, pp. 64, 66). This finding supports the emphasis which the Rampton/Swann Committee of Inquiry gave to English and mathematics qualifications in both their interim and full reports.

Given the history of racism and prejudice in this country it would, of course, be foolish to imagine that educational certification is sufficient to guarantee Afro-Caribbean and South Asian school-leavers the jobs and higher education places which their achievement warrants. Qualifications alone are not sufficient to gain access to education or employment, but they are frequently a necessary condition: without them access may not even be a possibility. Consequently the importance of educational certification for ethnic minority pupils should not be minimized.

Studies of the experiences of young people in Sheffield and Bradford have shown that 'black' (that is, 'Asian, Afro-Caribbean and African') young people were more likely to be unemployed than their white peers with similar educational qualifications. This suggests that black young people meet racism in the youth labour market, even when they have qualifications. However, black young people with educational certification fared significantly better than their black peers with fewer qualifications

114

(Clough and Drew, 1985). Consequently, although qualifications guarantee nothing they can make employment success a possibility. As Brian Goacher concluded, '16+ examinations retain their power to affect the lives of the majority of school leavers' and 'remain the most potent reflection of a pupil's educational experience at the end of the period of compulsory schooling' (Goacher, 1984, p. 64).

Although Jeffcoate rightly identifies equal opportunity as an essentially conservative goal – one which accepts the system's definitions of success, emphasizes personal gain and fails to challenge gross inequalities of power and prestige – the concept remains of crucial importance. It focuses upon the outcomes of educational experience which have vital consequences for the future life-chances of all school-leavers.

The 'new right' critique: equal opportunity as revolution

While Jeffcoate has criticized equal opportunity as a narrow, elitist and conservative concept, others have described it as the tool of revolutionaries. Antony Flew has been particularly vocal in his attacks. In 1984 Flew's pamphlet, *Education, Race and Revolution*, was published by the Centre for Policy Studies (CPS), a right-wing organization whose members came to enjoy considerable influence over the thinking and policy-making of the Thatcher government (cf. Oldman, 1987; Quicke, 1988). The pamphlet's main arguments were repeated (word-for-word) in Flew's contribution to a collection of new right essays on 'anti-racism' (Palmer, 1986).[2] In that collection, Flew's paper sets itself the task of 'clarifying the concepts' and therefore represents an important statement of new right criticisms of the equal opportunity philosophy.

Flew's basic proposition is that perspectives which link substantive achievement with equal opportunity are politically motivated attempts to attack 'White British Society'. He speaks of the (now abolished) Inner London Education Authority (ILEA) as representing 'the full-frontal, hardcore version of Benno-Bolshevism' and identifies any concern with equality of outcome as 'Neo-Marxist'.

Flew's attack is couched in language which Peter Newsam has described as 'the intellectual equivalent of foaming at the mouth' (Newsam, 1984). His style should not, however, obscure the importance of his views (in CPS publications and thinking) and the ingenuity with which he selects examples and analogies to suit his purposes. In the following commentary I will outline Flew's main arguments while highlighting the assumptions and linguistic sleights of hand which he attempts.

Flew's tactics are simple. First, he systematically misrepresents the arguments and beliefs of those involved in what he calls 'the race relations industry' (Flew, 1986, p. 16). Second, he makes leaps of imagination, based on flawed and simplistic analogies, which he presents as logical 'fact'. The consequences of his arguments are familiar; they deny the existence of institutional racism and discrimination, blame the victim and thereby protect the status quo.

Flew begins by referring to recent definitions of equal opportunity which emphasize the importance of achievement.

> differences in outcome are ... confidently construed as by themselves sufficient to demonstrate corresponding differences in opportunity. Yet we have here a valid argument only when we are in a position to supply a further premise stating that, in whatever may be the relevant respects, the members of all the [social or racial] sets compared were equally able, equally eager and equally well qualified. And this we almost never are. (Flew, 1986, p. 24)[3]

The crucial issue concerns the definition of 'relevant respects'. Flew does not include financial circumstances, the level of school resourcing and the quality of teacher–pupil relationships as 'relevant'. He rejects the validity of all definitions of equal opportunity except the narrow original version which stresses formal equality of access: 'the equality which justice always demands is: not a substantial equality of outcome, either for individuals or for sets, but rather a formal equality of treatment for all relevantly like cases' (Flew, 1986, p. 16).

Flew goes on to attack another supposed fallacy of recent approaches to equal opportunity:

> It consists in inferring that, if the contestants in any competition are all treated fairly by the organisers, and thus have equal opportunities for success, then the success of any one such contestant must be equiprobable with the success of any other. To accept this argument we should have to allow that any competition in which it is most probable that

the best competitor will win must, for that reason alone, be put down as being unfairly conducted. (Flew, 1986, p. 25)

This passage perfectly demonstrates Flew's approach. It simultaneously dismisses his opponents and uses a striking commonsensical analogy which, in every way, misrepresents the recent approaches to equal opportunity. The passage begins by likening education to a competition (a common analogy). In this case, however, the analogy simply does not work – in an athletic competition we expect individual athletes to perform differently. Similarly, in the examination hall we expect individual pupils to perform differently. Yet Flew is talking about groups. Although he uses the singular 'contestant' and 'competitor', his analogy is an attempt to justify differences in the average performance of social groups. When he talks of 'the best competitor' Flew really means the best group or, to be more precise, the best 'race'. This leads us back to Flew's understanding of what constitutes a 'relevant' group difference, an issue on which he seems uncharacteristically reticent. His inexplicitness reflects the racist history of previous work which has tried to establish the genetically determined nature of intelligence.

'RACE', INTELLIGENCE AND HEREDITARIAN INVENTION:

There is no adequate evidence for the heritability of IQ within the white population. To attribute racial differences to genetic factors, granted the overwhelming cultural-environmental differences between races, is to compound folly with malice. That compounding characterized the mental testers of the First World War, and it has not vanished. (Kamin, 1974, p. 228)

In the late 1960s and early 1970s publications on both sides of the Atlantic (notably by A.R. Jensen, 1969, 1972 and H.J. Eysenck, 1971, 1973) led to renewed controversy over the relative importance of heredity and environment in the development of human intelligence (the so-called nature–nurture debate). Limitations of space prevent a detailed commentary on these debates, but suffice it to say that (a) no generally agreed definition of 'intelligence' has yet been framed, and (b) intelligence tests, therefore, merely measure an individual's ability to answer intelligence tests – they do not reveal differences in innate, natural and/or fixed levels of intellectual capability. For decades, prejudice, ignorance and bias have characterized many additions to a field of study which dresses itself in apparent 'scientific' respectability yet reveals an incredible disregard for the normal procedures of data collection and analysis (cf. Kamin, 1974, 1981; Lawrence, 1977).

A summary of Hans Eysenck's version of 'the facts' of 'racial differences' can be deduced by considering the subheadings which he uses in a discussion of 'racial and cultural factors' in relation to average intelligence quotient (IQ) test results. Eysenck's headings include 'Blacks: a 15-point lag'; 'Whites are more extreme'; 'Japanese and Chinese outstrip whites', and 'Jews do best of all' (Eysenck, 1981, pp. 74–7). Such views are echoed in Antony Flew's attempt to discredit those who judge equality of opportunity by reference to achievement. For example, he makes much of the fact that 'in the USA blacks are heavily overrepresented in professional basketball, while Jews have been about nine times overrepresented among America's Nobel Prizewinners' (Flew, 1986, p. 21).

As Flew's argument unfolds it becomes clear (although he never quite states it in so many words) that a belief in the genetic determination of intelligence ranks among the principal 'relevant respects' which he feels explain average differences in achievement between members of different 'racial sets'. Towards the end of his paper, for instance, Flew argues that since 'racial' surface differences are so obvious, surely there is good reason to suppose that there are other genetically determined factors which explain group differences in average achievement:

> given that no-one is so rash as to dispute the genetic determination of the racial and hence biological defining characteristics, we can have little reason for confidence that there is no significant difference in the distribution of the other genes within the relevant gene pools ... the possibility of differences between the gene pools of different races and different racial groups constitutes a further reason for rejecting inferences from inequalities of outcome to corresponding inequalities of opportunity. (Flew, 1986, p. 28)

Flew's attempt to 'clarify the concepts' qualifies as racist according to every definition of that much used word (see chapter 1 above). Flew believes in the existence of discrete human 'races' and he argues that the 'genetically determined' factors which distinguish 'races' may also explain average differences in their academic performance. Flew's analysis implies that some 'races' are better (faster, more motivated, more intelligent) than others. An accurate summary of his tactics is available in a paper written by a fellow contributor to the new right collection in which Flew's paper appeared; writing about the differences between education and 'indoctrination', Caroline Cox discusses the use of 'foregone conclusions' which 'can be identified by the following':

(1) Presentation of conclusions in such a way as to pre-empt serious consideration of alternative points of view.

(2) The use of loaded references and loaded questions.

(3) The association of ideas so that one complex issue is mentioned in the context of other issues to make it appear as if all come into the same category and can be subject to the same criticisms.

(4) The omission of relevant evidence which is needed to present a balanced, rounded appreciation of complex issues. (C. Cox, 1986, p. 75).

Flew's criticisms of the equal opportunity philosophy admirably demonstrate each of these tactics.

The 'radical' critique: equal opportunity as a facade; underachievement as a stereotype

Flew's critique of the equal opportunity philosophy is part of a more general attack on any approach which attempts to recognize and meet the needs of a culturally diverse pupil population. However, academics with a strong record of support for anti-racist initiatives have also challenged some of the evidence and background assumptions which underlie recent debates concerning the underachievement of certain ethnic groups. The 'radical' critique has identified some particularly important weaknesses in previous work.

In his paper 'Fact or Artefact? The "Educational Under-achievement" of Black Pupils' (1984), Barry Troyna critically appraises previous work in this area and explicitly challenges 'conventional wisdoms' concerning the relative performance of pupils from different ethnic groups. Unlike Antony Flew, however, Troyna's aim was not to protect the system from change, but quite the reverse; he argued that common notions of underachievement may act against curricular and pedagogical change by reinforcing stereotyped, racist images of relatively fixed and inferior intellectual potential among 'black' (Afro-Caribbean) students.

UNDERACHIEVEMENT AND INTER-GROUP COMPARISON: Troyna notes that comparisons between group achievements assume that research is 'comparing like with like' (Troyna, 1984, p. 158). Like Flew, Troyna argues that this assumption is spurious. However, whereas Flew suggests that 'racial' groups are themselves somehow different in their 'genetically determined' make-up, Troyna argues that the groups' experiences are so different as to invalidate direct comparison. In particular he highlights the importance of racism as a major barrier to Afro-Caribbean achievement.

> the relationship of black pupils to society generally, and education in particular, are so profoundly and qualitatively different from those of their white classmates (and, to a lesser degree, pupils of South Asian origin) that they militate against the use of inter-group comparison as a valid or reliable measurement of performance ... The results generated via this method therefore provide a particular and contentious conception of underachievement, one which ignores the pervasive influence of racism in the lives of black children. (Troyna, 1984, pp. 158–9)

Racism, Troyna argues, pervades the worlds of school and employment; Afro-Caribbean pupils are well aware of this additional barrier to post-school success and, therefore, may decide that school has little to offer. Troyna echoes Bagley's assertion that under these conditions a rejection of school may be the most sensible response:

> Black children may have low motivation in the educational and vocational systems (and therefore low test motivation) if it is clear to them that conventional education does not bring rewards, but rejection ... Only fools strive hard when there is little chance of reward. (Bagley, 1975, p. 44)

Troyna's critique of 'inter-group comparison', therefore, springs from his concern to recognize the importance of racism in our society and to combat stereotyped images of 'black' pupils as educational failures. However, his argument risks confirming another common racist stereotype, that 'black' young people fail in education because they are not sufficiently motivated. In fact, research suggests that Afro-Caribbean young people are at least as motivated as their white counterparts — frequently they show higher levels of motivation and effort in their attitudes to school and the amount of time spent on homework (Eggleston, Dunn and Anjali, 1986, pp. 74–9).

The relatively 'greater motivation' of Afro-Caribbean and Asian young people 'towards self-improvement and achievement' is also reflected in the greater proportions of students who pursue further study (full-time and part-time) after leaving school (Smith and Tomlinson, 1989, pp. 14–16). The continued effort of Afro-Caribbean and Asian students reflects the determination and resilience of young people whose parents and communities have suffered, and fought, insecurity, mass exploitation and gross inequalities over successive generations.[4]

Troyna's speculation concerning the effects of racism upon motivation is not, therefore, supported by recent research. Similarly, I have already mentioned work which shows that despite the proven influence of racism within the labour market (cf. Hubbuck and Carter, 1980; Brown, 1984; Ohri and Faruqi, 1988) examination results can still have a major effect upon the life-chances of Afro-Caribbean and Asian school-leavers, as possession of higher grade passes is associated with lower levels of unemployment for all ethnic groups (Clough and Drew, 1985). Furthermore, academic success destroys the common racist myths that Afro-Caribbean young people are (a) unintelligent, and (b) unqualified for the higher levels of the economy and education. Although Troyna's observations highlight the complexity of the situation, he does not make out a convincing argument for the rejection of achievement as one (not necessarily the only) indicator of educational opportunity.

Although his rejection of the concept of underachievement is somewhat unconvincing, as the following section demonstrates, his critique of the existing evidence of underachievement is much more telling.

AGAINST THE STEREOTYPE OF 'BLACK' FAILURE: During the early and mid 1980s a strong consensus developed concerning the relative underachievement of Afro-Caribbean pupils as a group. I have already presented a summary of some of the major survey findings in this area (see Table 5.1). The surveys conducted by the DES Statistics Branch were particularly influential because the data were gathered especially for the Committee of Inquiry into the Education of Children from Ethnic Minority Groups, and formed the basis for the Committee's assertion that, as a group, pupils of 'West Indian' ethnic origin were underachieving.

Troyna's purpose in questioning the empirical basis of such conventional wisdom was to challenge the commonly held stereotype of 'black' pupils as being destined to fail as a pathological or 'deficit' (Troyna, 1988) view of Afro-Caribbean pupils which absolves teachers of responsibility for 'black' pupils' achievements.

> The greatest danger lies in the possibility that ill-conceived and poorly formulated studies will perpetuate the notion of black educational underachievement as a *given* rather than as a problematic that requires sensitive and systematic interrogation. (Troyna, 1984, p. 164; original emphasis)

In order to counter this danger, Troyna identified several weaknesses which, in his view, undermined the validity of existing data on underachievement. In particular he emphasized:

i)   Failure to consider the possibility of 'race-of-tester' effects where 'a white tester may depress significantly the score of a black child on cognitive ability tests' (Troyna, 1984, p. 160).

ii) The uncritical use of group tests and teacher assessments, especially where the latter may present a distorted picture of 'ability' as perceived by teachers.

iii) The use of dated material without consideration of potential problems of change over time. As Troyna and others (Tomlinson, 1986; Smith and Tomlinson, 1989) have pointed out, most of the 1980s debate on underachievement was founded upon data generated during the 1960s and 1970s.

iv) The use of samples of varying sizes without due attention to sampling errors and the way these affect the conclusions and comparisons which can be legitimately drawn.

v) Failure to allow for 'other factors which may impinge on performance' (Troyna, 1984, p. 162). In particular, social class is well known to be strongly associated with educational achievement.

Although Troyna's critique ran contrary to popular belief, he succeeded in raising questions about previous studies which had frequently been overlooked or ignored. In retrospect, his paper can be seen to coincide with the beginnings of a period of more sophisticated and systematic research in which quantitative inquiries sought to explore the relationships between, and relative importance of a variety of factors, including social class, gender, ethnicity and the particular effects of individual schools.

The complexity of achievement

Despite a wide variety of criticisms, measures of academic achievement continue to play a crucial role in educational debate. The relative achievement of different social and ethnic groups is a vitally important question for anyone concerned to identify and act upon existing strengths and weaknesses in current educational provision. The lessons of the liberal and radical critiques are that such measures are at best partial and must be used carefully within the wider context of the many complex factors which may influence educational experience and achievement. In this section I chart some of these issues through recent attempts to investigate patterns of pupil achievement.

Achievement and the influence of social class, ethnic origin and pupil gender

The first major findings concerning educational achievement broken down by ethnic origin and social class were published by Maurice Craft and Alma Craft in 1983. Their findings seemed to indicate that 'West Indian' pupils were underachieving in relation to other ethnic groups, even when the data were controlled for social class. As I noted earlier, most analyses of underachievement have been criticized because they make no allowance for possible variations in the social class composition of the different ethnic groups (cf. Reeves and Chevannes, 1981;

Troyna, 1984, 1988). Given the over-representation of Afro-Caribbean workers in manual/working-class occupations (Brown, 1984), it has been argued that social class differences alone might explain variations in achievement between ethnic groups. Consequently, some viewed Craft and Craft's research as a major contribution to the field. On closer inspection, however, the study was far from conclusive.

Craft and Craft reported questionnaire and survey data on the background characteristics and educational achievements of fifth- and sixth-form pupils in a single Outer London borough in the summer and autumn of 1979 (a total of more than 2,000 students). Unfortunately, the published account presents data on social class and ethnic origin in terms of crude aggregate groups. Social class was framed in terms of a simple distinction between 'middle class' (non-manual) and 'working class' (manual) occupations. Similarly, information on ethnic origin was reduced to a fourfold classification of 'White' (including British, Irish, Australian, North American and West European); 'West Indian'; 'Asian' (including Indian, Sri Lankan, Pakistani, Bangladeshi, South East Asian and Kenyan Asian); and 'Other' (including those of 'mixed ethnic origin') (Craft and Craft, 1983, pp. 18–19).

Such aggregates are problematic, especially in the case of the heterogeneous 'Asian' group, which includes people of very different cultural and political backgrounds (cf. Taylor and Hegarty, 1985). This is a criticism which can be made of many studies in this field. Furthermore, the research made no mention of gender, adding to a long line of projects which have failed to recognize the importance of this variable.

Table 5.3 summarizes Craft and Craft's findings concerning fifth-form examination performance by ethnic origin and social class. On the basis of this data, Craft and Craft concluded that the examination performance of pupils of 'West Indian' ethnic origin 'lagged behind that of all the other groups, even when controlled for social class' (Craft and Craft, 1983, p. 14). Although 'middle class West Indian' pupils did proportionately better than 'working class West Indians', neither group did as well as pupils of similar social class backgrounds from different ethnic groups.

The Swann report reproduced the Crafts' findings and stated that the research 'showed clearly that, irrespective of social class, West Indian children are markedly under-represented

Table 5.3 Fifth-form examination performance by ethnic origin and social class in an Outer London borough (percentages)

Exam performance*	White		Asian		W. Ind.		Other		All		Totals
	MC	WC	MC	WC	MC	WC	MC	WC	MC	WC	
High	31	18	32	16	20	9	26	16	30	16	21
Medium	55	62	58	64	49	51	59	63	56	61	59
Low	14	20	10	21	31	41	16	21	14	23	20
N=	445	786	165	359	31	176	114	155	761	1,476	2,237

* Examination performance was calculated as follows: 'High' = 5 or more passes at GCE (grades C and above) *or* 3–4 GCE passes *plus* 5 CSE grades 2–5. 'Low' = 1–4 CSE grades 2–5 (and no GCE passes), *or* no GCE (grade C and above) and no CSE grade 5 or above. 'Medium' = 1–4 GCE passes only *or* some combination of GCE and CSE not covered in the high and low categories: cf. Craft and Craft, 1983, p. 19.
Source: Adapted from Craft and Craft, 1983, Table 2, p. 14.

amongst high achievers and markedly over-represented amongst low achievers' (Swann, 1985, p. 60). More cautiously, Barry Troyna drew attention to the relatively small number of Afro-Caribbean pupils in the total sample and concluded that the work; 'hardly resolves the issues; rather, it provides a basis for an exploration of the widely held, though not empirically tested, assumption that black pupils at all social class levels underachieve' (Troyna, 1984, p. 163).

I have already commented on the problems of aggregated (and crude) categories of social class, ethnic origin and examination performance which should warn against over-generalising on the basis of Craft and Craft's research. Furthermore, it should be noted that the raw numbers presented in the bottom row of Table 5.3 do not add up. Specifically, the total of 761 middle-class pupils in the 'All' column adds six pupils to the total of the numbers presented under each of the four ethnic group columns. Such errors detract from the status of the material.[5]

Despite its limitations, Craft and Craft's analysis marked an important (if imperfect) first step. It should be remembered, however, that their data are already more than a decade old. More recent material has shown the wisdom of Troyna's caution. In particular, an analysis of a nationally representative sample of school-leavers has highlighted the complexity of the area and advanced our understanding of the relationships between social class, ethnicity and gender.

The youth cohort study

Earlier in this chapter I referred to the results obtained from part of the Youth Cohort Study, or YCS (Drew and Gray, 1989). YCS data for 1985 partly confirmed the pattern of previous surveys in as much as proportionately fewer Afro-Caribbean pupils achieved five or more 'O' level passes at sixteen-plus. In fact, 'Just over one in five (21%) Whites and just under one in five (19%) Asians had achieved five or more "higher grade" passes compared with fewer than one in ten (7%) Afro-Caribbeans' (Drew and Gray, 1989, p. 8) The Youth Cohort Study has been designed to facilitate sophisticated interrogation of the data and Drew and Gray's work reveals a great deal in addition to the distributions of examination results by ethnic origin shown in Table 5.1.

The YCS follows successive cohorts of young people between the ages of sixteen and nineteen. Each cohort is questioned at three points via a postal questionnaire. The first 'sweep' is carried out six to nine months after the end of compulsory schooling and subsequently the samples are contacted again at two twelve-month intervals. YCS samples are large, up-to-date and nationally representative of those attending state-maintained schools. The latter fact is a major advance on previous research which has typically focused on pupils in relatively more disadvantaged inner-city areas, such as the Inner London Education Authority – ILEA (Kysel, 1988) – and LEAs with a high proportion of ethnic minority pupils (DES data reproduced in Rampton, 1981, and Swann, 1985). In the past this practice may have presented a somewhat depressed picture of overall achievement levels.

The YCS data are not, of course, perfect. Drew and Gray point out that despite the large total samples, when controlling for several factors at once some individual cell sizes become very small. Furthermore, they follow the common practice of combining Indian, Pakistani and Bangladeshi pupils in a single 'Asian' category. The YCS is, however, a vast improvement on most previous work and offers the opportunity to monitor developments through the analysis of several successive cohorts. In addition, it allows for comparison between pupils on the basis of ethnic origin, social class and gender.

Although YCS data for the 1985 cohort confirmed previously found differences in group performance at the highest levels of examination achievement (that is, concerning pupils who gained five or more 'O' level and equivalent passes), Drew and Gray argue that more attention should be given to the considerable variation in performance within ethnic groups and the significant overlap between groups. Table 5.4 and Figure 5.1 indicate the complexity of the situation.

Table 5.4 shows examination results broken down by ethnic origin in terms of three summary measures: the average number of 'O' level and equivalent passes, average number of passes at any grade, and the average 'exam score'. The figures in parenthesis concern the degree of spread within the group and indicate 'a considerable degree of overlap in the scores of the

Table 5.4 The fifth-year examination results of YCS respondents by ethnic origin

	Ethnic origin			
Measures of exam results	Afro-Caribbean	Asian	White	All*
Average number of GCE grade A-C/CSE grade 1 passes	1.09 **(1.92)	1.93 (2.73)	2.15 (2.83)	2.12 (2.82)
Average number of passes at any grade	5.07 (2.80)	5.67 (2.87)	5.70 (3.03)	5.69 (3.03)
Average exam score***	16.6 (12.3)	21.1 (15.4)	22.1 (16.0)	22.0 (15.9)
Number of cases	244	435	12,669	13,448

* This column includes all those on whom information was obtained and not just those who declared that their ethnic backgrounds were Afro-Caribbean, Asian or White.
** The figures in brackets show the standard deviations (or spread) for each average.
*** The exam score is based on a scoring system first developed by researchers at the ILEA (cf. Byford and Mortimore, 1985). See Table 5.2 above.
Source: Drew and Gray, 1989, Table 4.

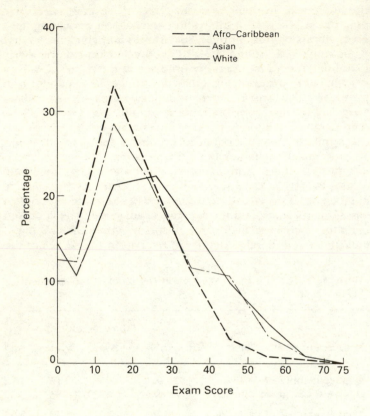

Figure 5.1 Distribution of exam scores by ethnic group

Source: Drew and Gray, 1989, Figure 2.

groups' (Drew and Gray, 1989, p. 8). Figure 5.1 graphically represents the overlap between pupils in each ethnic group. The data show that many Afro-Caribbean young people do well, although it would seem that high scores (over thirty-six points, or equivalent to six grade B's at 'O' level) are more rare than for 'Asian' and white young people.

YCS data on social background are originally coded according to the Registrar General's classification of socioeconomic status (in seventeen groups). Drew and Gray, however, present their analysis in terms of a simplified version aggregated into three broad categories: 'professional/managerial', 'intermediate' (including junior non-manual workers, personal service workers and some self-employed) and 'manual' (including all manual workers whether skilled, semi-skilled or unskilled).

Table 5.5 summarizes the findings when the 1985 YCS data are analysed by social class, ethnic group and gender. The children from professional/managerial backgrounds scored highest in all ethnic groups. In each group the average exam score for Afro-Caribbean young people was lower than their Asian and white peers of similar social backgrounds. This repeats the pattern reported by Craft and Craft (1983). In terms of gender there is a significant difference between White girls and boys, with female pupils outperforming the males in all social groups.

Drew and Gray emphasize that caution must be exercised when dealing with small subgroups. In Table 5.5, for example, there are only twelve and seventeen Afro-Caribbean and Asian pupils, respectively, from professional backgrounds. Nevertheless they highlight the 'relatively high performance of young people of Asian origin (and notably males) in the intermediate and manual socio-economic groups' (Drew and Gray, 1989, pp. 9–10).

Drew and Gray used the statistical technique of analysis of variance to judge the relative importance of social background, ethnic group and gender as influences upon exam scores. Each of the three variables was found to be statistically associated with exam scores. Individually, social class background was found to explain more of the variance than either ethnic group or gender. However, 'the larger part of the variance in exam scores remained unexplained by these three factors' (Drew and Gray, 1989, p. 10). This is a crucial finding. It suggests that the three main variables which commentators usually associate

Table 5.5 Average exam score broken down by ethnic origin, gender and socioeconomic group

Ethnic and socioeconomic group	* Average exam score		Number of cases
	Male	Female	
AFRO-CARIBBEAN			
Professional/Managerial	27.1	24.9	12
Intermediate	21.1	18.1	68
Manual	14.3	15.6	115
Other**	12.1	16.1	49
All	(16.4)	(16.8)	(244)
ASIAN			
Professional/Managerial	30.7	27.8	17
Intermediate	27.2	25.9	95
Manual	23.3	22.5	189
Other**	12.9	14.1	133
All	(21.2)	(20.9)	(435)
WHITE			
Professional/Managerial	30.4	32.3	2,118
Intermediate	23.7	25.0	3,903
Manual	17.6	20.0	5,218
Other**	13.0	13.4	1,430
All	(20.9)	(23.4)	(12,669)

* For the exam scores formula see notes to Table 5.2.
** This group includes all those who did not report sufficient information for their socioeconomic grouping to be established.
Source: Adapted from Drew and Gray, 1989, Table 5.

with achievement (social class, 'race' and gender) account for a minority of the variation in exam scores. This begs the question, 'What *does* account for the majority of variation?' Clearly, individual variations between pupils are very important and it will never be possible to point to any single factor which will explain all remaining differences. Recent work has, however, highlighted the important effects of individual schools: a consideration which has too often been ignored in quantitative analyses in the field of ethnicity and education.

Achievement, progress and school effects

There is a strong tradition of quantitative research which has focused upon differences in school effectiveness, usually measured in terms of examination achievements, although other 'outcomes', such as participation, attendance etc. may also be considered (cf. Ouston and Maughan, 1985). The central aim of such work is to identify 'successful' schools after controlling for different intake characteristics, such as social class composition.

It is crucial to understand that schools with the best examination results may not necessarily be the most successful. Variations in the levels of attainment on entry, and background factors such as social class, mean that pupils begin their secondary education from very different starting points. Consequently, although School A may achieve more total examination passes than School B, it may be that pupils in School B have made more *progress* during their secondary education and have achieved better results than would have been predicted (based on family circumstances and/or prior attainment) when they entered the school. Similarly, although pupils in School A appear to have done relatively well, they may not in fact have achieved the levels which would have been predicted when they entered the school.

Research on school effectiveness has grown in both the USA and the UK, and includes important studies of schools in England (Rutter *et al.*, 1979; Mortimore *et al.*, 1988), Scotland (Gray, McPherson and Raffe, 1983) and Wales (Reynolds, 1976). Unfortunately, many of these studies did not include ethnically diverse samples. Although 1970s' research in twelve London schools (Rutter, *et al.*, 1979) gathered data on ethnic origin, the main account of findings in this area was published separately at a later date (Maughan and Rutter, 1986). Recent research goes some way towards meeting the obvious need for investigations of the effectiveness of multi-ethnic schools.

The PSI/Lancaster study

A research project based at the Policy Studies Institute (PSI) and Department of Educational Research at Lancaster University followed the secondary school careers of pupils in urban multiracial comprehensives in four English education authorities; two in the South-East, one in the Midlands and one in the North of England.

131

The research was designed to 'measure differences between schools in the outcomes they achieve, in academic and other terms, after taking full account of differences in the attainment and background of children at the point of entry' (Smith and Tomlinson, 1989, p. 3). Furthermore, the researchers hoped to (a) identify the processes underlying school success, and (b) 'describe the educational experience of children belonging to racial minority groups'.

Originally twenty schools took part but by the end of the research the number had fallen to eighteen. The schools were selected so as to offer a range of characteristics, including;

> working-class areas and areas with a strong middle-class element;
>
> schools with high, medium and relatively low proportions of pupils belonging to minority groups in aggregate;
>
> schools containing both Asians and West Indians, and schools containing only Asians and only West Indians [among their ethnic minority intake];
>
> Moslems, Hindus and Sikhs, and Asians speaking various sub-continental languages. (Smith and Tomlinson, 1989, p. 32)

All sample schools had a 'significant' proportion of ethnic minority pupils, ranging from 12 to 89 per cent. In addition, since the project was primarily concerned with differences in school achievements, the researchers made efforts to include both schools which were 'thought to be successful, and others less so' (p. 32). The sample was specifically chosen, therefore, to facilitate a particular analysis and so, unlike the YCS (Drew and Gray, 1989), was not nationally representative of all pupils in state-maintained secondary schools.

The project monitored children who entered secondary school aged eleven in the autumn of 1981, and gathered information concerning their experiences and achievements until they left compulsory education aged sixteen in the summer of 1986. This was done via a series of attainment tests (administered during the pupils' first and second years); two pupil questionnaires (including one on option choices); a teacher questionnaire, and an analysis of school data on absences and final examination achievements at age sixteen. In addition, the pupils' parents were interviewed about their views of the school and their children's progress.

DIFFERENCES IN OVERALL ACHIEVEMENT: Surprisingly, pupils in the eighteen schools (not a nationally representative sample) achieved on a par with national averages: '10 per cent had five or more higher grade passes, while 32 per cent had one to four; the remaining 58 per cent had none' (Smith and Tomlinson, 1989, p. 242). There was a strong association between social class and examination achievement so that, 'on average, children from professional and managerial families obtained nearly eight times as many higher grade passes as those from families belonging to the "underclass" group (where neither parent had had a job in the five years before the survey was carried out)' (Smith and Tomlinson, 1989, p. 245).[6]

The researchers found differences in the examination successes of ethnic groups which were in the same direction as previous studies. The mean (average) number of higher grade passes was 1.40 for the UK/Eire group; 1.18 for the South Asian group; and 1.14 for the 'West Indian' group (Smith and Tomlinson, 1989, p. 253). Smith and Tomlinson describe these differences as 'small' (p. 245) yet, as David Drew has pointed out (personal communication) the difference between the UK/Eire and 'West Indian' averages is equivalent to more than 20 per cent of the 'West Indian' average.

Table 5.6 shows a breakdown of pupils who gained higher grade passes in particular subject groups across the eighteen schools. The table reveals something of the complexity of the situation where, as a group, 'West Indian' pupils achieved relatively more passes in English than both UK/Eire and South Asian pupils, yet did significantly worse in mathematics. South Asians did as well as, or better, than UK/Eire pupils in science, commerce and Asian languages.

These findings, therefore, indicated that although broad (and all too familiar) patterns of underachievement persisted across the eighteen sample schools, the picture was a complex one; no ethnic group was most successful in all subject areas. This is an important finding, but the report's authors (and subsequent media attention) stressed the rather different picture which emerged when statistical techniques were used to control for the influence of background characteristics (such as social class) and take account of differences in attainment levels when the pupils entered secondary school. Such measures concern rates of progress rather than absolute levels of achievement.

Table 5.6 Percentage of children obtaining an 'O' level (or equivalent) pass grade in each subject group by ethnic origin in eighteen urban comprehensive schools (percentages)

Ethnic origin						*Subject groups				
	English	Maths	Science	Practical 'male'	Practical 'female'	Humanities & soc. sciences	Commerce	Asian languages	European languages	Creative subjects
UK/Eire	23	18	14	6	5	22	2	less than 0.5	6	13
South Asian	18	15	15	4	4	20	2	5	3	8
West Indian	26	11	11	5	5	19	1	1	5	11
Mixed/other	23	18	10	8	4	10	3	1	6	15
Not known	14	11	11	0	0	18	18	0	0	4
Total	22	17	14	6	5	20	2	2	5	11

* Science = the traditionally higher-status sciences: physics, chemistry, biology, human biology, technology; electronics, computing. Practical 'male' = traditional 'male' practical subjects such as graphical communications, woodwork and engineering. Practical 'female' = traditionally 'female' practical subjects such as home economics, food and nutrition and child care. Humanities and social sciences include history, geography, social studies, religious education, English literature, economics etc. European languages = French, German, Spanish, Italian and Latin. Asian languages = Bengali, Punjabi, Urdu. Commerce = typing, office practice and commerce. Creative subjects include art, art & design, drama, music etc. See Smith and Tomlinson, 1989, pp. 207–8.
Source: Adapted from Smith and Tomlinson, 1989, Table 16.9, pp. 261–2.

DIFFERENCES IN PROGRESS: Smith and Tomlinson used the recently developed statistical technique of multi-level modelling to try to explain the pupils' exam results by reference to their sex, social class, ethnic group and attainment at the end of the second year taking into account differences between schools (Smith and Tomlinson, 1989, p. 265). Earlier in the pupils' secondary school careers, attainment tests had indicated that 'West Indian' and some South Asian children (especially those of Bangladeshi and Pakistani origin) had entered the schools with lower than average scores in reading and maths. However, by the time the pupils sat their external examinations as fifth-years they had narrowed the gap and achieved higher results than would have been predicted on the basis of their earlier attainment levels. Consequently, although (as a group) South Asian and 'West Indian' pupils achieved worse examination results than white pupils, they had made relatively greater progress during the last three years of compulsory education – that is, they achieved better results than would have been expected on the basis of earlier assessments.

Although Smith and Tomlinson took care to explain the complexities of their findings, some statements lent themselves to misinterpretation or misuse by others. They stated, for instance, that their work showed both South Asians and 'West Indians' doing 'distinctly *better* than pupils originating from the UK, when allowance is made for social class and attainment in reading at the end of the second year' (Smith and Tomlinson, 1989, p. 266; original emphasis). Ray Honeyford, ex-headteacher and new right author, stated that the report 'laid to rest . . . one of the great myths of modern Britain . . . West Indian and Asian children, the study found, are doing as well in our schools as white children – and in some cases better' (Honeyford, 1989). When young people enter the labour market it is their examination achievements that potential employers consider, not their rates of progress. In terms of absolute achievements in examination results, Honeyford's summary is simply wrong. This demonstrates the need for researchers to clearly distinguish between data on *progress* and examination *achievement*: a distinction which is becoming increasingly blurred as politicians and the media try to use the results of research on school effectiveness.

SCHOOL EFFECTS: By employing a statistical model which attempted to control for the effects of pupils' previous attainment and background characteristics, Smith and Tomlinson were able to demonstrate very significant differences in the performance of individual schools. There is insufficient space here to allow a detailed summary of their techniques and findings, but suffice it to say that schools were able to achieve very different results with children of similar backgrounds and earlier attainments. Smith and Tomlinson's data implied, for example, that a boy with an above average reading score would fail to get a CSE grade 3 in English at one school, but would achieve a pass at grade B in the GCE 'O' level examination at another school. Similarly dramatic differences emerged in mathematics. This pattern was repeated, to a lesser extent, for total achievements across the schools.

The researchers compared the relative importance of ethnic group and school effects, and concluded:

> the differences in exam results attributable to ethnic group are very much smaller than those attributable to the school level. In other words, what school a child goes to makes far more difference than which ethnic group he or she belongs to. (Smith and Tomlinson, 1989, p. 281)

Clearly this is a very important statement. To some extent it restates what many Afro-Caribbean parents and teachers have believed for decades (witness the development of the black voluntary school movement described by Chevannes and Reeves, 1987). However, the statement has also been taken up (and twisted) by elements of the media and new right who argue that the education system should be left alone to 'Forget about skin colour. Forget about race' (Honeyford, 1989). Indeed, Honeyford described the PSI/Lancaster report as 'a damning reversal of everything the race relations industry has pumped out about ethnic children's educational prospects in this country'. In the light of such responses it is necessary to put the school effects research into perspective.

The PSI/Lancaster research is important. It is, however, only a first step in a field which has few certainties and many confusions. Data on three cohorts of school-leavers in ILEA, for example, confirm the notion that some ethnic minority groups progress faster than white pupils in the ESWI group (Nuttall *et al.*, 1989). On the other hand, the ILEA data make no allowance for social class (which the authors state may depress the ESWI performance) and offer no information on the actual examina-

136

tion achievements of the pupils. In addition, Nuttall and his colleagues clashed with Smith and Tomlinson over the appropriateness of their sample (a single cohort) and the notion that school effectiveness can be measured as a single quantity. The ILEA team argues that schools are not equally effective for all subgroups of their pupil populations and concludes that the concept of 'overall effectiveness' (used by Smith and Tomlinson) 'is not useful' (Nuttall *et al.*, 1989, p. 776).

Clearly, research into school effects will attract great interest in the future. Existing work points to the complexity of achievement in schools and argues against the stereotyping of groups as in any way destined to fail. But current knowledge is rather limited and to date there is no school effects research based on a nationally representative sample, there is dispute concerning the usefulness of 'overall' measures, and there is a need to draw clear distinctions between data on progress and data on actual examination achievements. In addition, statistical studies of school effects raise questions, concerning the reasons for effectiveness, which they are not generally able to answer – a fact which has wider implications for future research in this field.

THE LIMITS OF QUANTITATIVE ANALYSES: Although the PSI/Lancaster study achieved its 'central objective' of measuring differences in school effects, in general the authors could only offer speculation concerning their remaining aims of explaining the reasons for the differences and describing the educational experiences of ethnic minority pupils. There were several reasons for this failure. One was that the response rate for the teacher questionnaire was so poor that the researchers had no usable data on management styles, organizational structures or even general teacher perspectives.

In addition, partly because of lack of funds, the study included no classroom observation and was only able to infer something of the pupils' experiences via the parental interviews, held during the lower-school years, and pupil questionnaire items, which included feelings about starting a new term and recent experience of praise and criticism from staff. Such data are limited and open to very many interpretations. The finding that both South Asian and 'West Indian' pupils felt more positively than their white peers about starting a new term, for example, is presented as meaning either that difficulties such as racial harassment 'are rare, or that children have learnt to live with them' (Smith and Tomlinson, 1989, p. 106). Some have chosen to believe the former explanation (cf. Honeyford, 1989), but on the basis of two years of ethnographic work in one of the study schools (coincidentally City Road was in the PSI/Lancaster sample) I have already presented data to indicate that the latter explanation is closer to the truth – especially in the case of Asian pupils, for whom racial harassment was an almost daily experience. Such problems highlight the complexity of life in multi-ethnic schools, a complexity which quantitative measures alone cannot adequately investigate.

Investigating inequalities of opportunity through qualitative research: the case of subject option choices

Most of the large-scale studies referred to in this chapter have given great weight to educational outcomes, especially examination achievements. Data on the processes which led to these outcomes are either absent or sketchy. Yet important differences in substantive opportunity may exist but not be revealed in the final pattern of outcomes. This is demonstrated by the case of subject option choices in City Road Comprehensive.

A body of literature already exists on differences in the academic nature of the subjects which pupils 'choose' according to their social class and/or gender (cf. Reid, Barnett and Rosenberg, 1974; Pratt, Bloomfield and Seale, 1984). Several researchers have used qualitative methods to examine the processes which underlay such patterns (see, for instance, Woods, 1976; Ball, 1981; Gillborn, 1990a). However, very few studies have considered the importance of ethnic origin at this crucial point in pupils' school careers. Data generated by the PSI/Lancaster study offer the first major indication of differences in this area (Tomlinson, 1987; Smith and Tomlinson, 1989). The work shows that ethnic minority pupils tend to appear in option subjects of lower academic status. Statistical modelling, however, indicated that this was a reflection of social class and attainment and 'it is not because ethnic group is itself being used as a criterion in the allocation to course levels' (Smith and Tomlinson, 1989, p. 216).

The option choice process was a major focus of my study of City Road Comprehensive. I followed three mixed ability form groups through the entire options process; I interviewed pupils both before and after decisions were taken; I spoke with teachers; read departmental reports, and watched as the pupils negotiated their choices in a series of meetings (both formal and informal) with teachers. During my observations an important trend emerged which would not have appeared in quantitative analyses.

In City Road, Afro-Caribbean pupils were more likely than others to experience apparently spontaneous inquiries from teachers who wanted to know which subjects they had chosen. Such inquiries frequently turned into a challenge, with the teacher 'recommending' a different option (usually of lower academic status). The following extract is taken from a spontaneous inquiry which resulted in the teacher advising the pupil (an Afro-Caribbean male) to change to a less academic, 'applied' option:

> There's a lot of science there.
> Physics — a lot of maths, which you don't get on with do you? You can tell me to [blows a 'raspberry'] ... but I'm wondering if you should do applied science (...)
> [After recapping on the mathematics involved in Physics] They might not explain it properly, just quickly mention it, then expect you to know it. And there's nothing worse than not knowing what's going off.
> If I were you I'd avoid physics like the plague.　　(field notes)

It appeared that Afro-Caribbean pupils experienced such spontaneous challenges more often than other pupils; this means that in fact they did not have the same opportunities as other pupils: Afro-Caribbean pupils had to fight harder to retain their high status choices. The fact that they were very successful in resisting such challenges meant that Afro-Caribbean pupils were not under-represented in high status subjects in City Road. In isolation, therefore, a measure of the academic level of pupils' options provides a very limited indication of the problems which they may have faced during the 'choice' process itself.

Conclusions: achievement, opportunity and inequality

> There is no 'proper' definition of equality of opportunity; the
> definition adopted remains an act of political choice. (Fowler
> and Melo, 1974, p. 94)

Although no single understanding of equality of opportunity
generates universal support, many have adopted an approach
which measures outcome in order to judge the relative
opportunities which were substantively available to different
groups of pupils. This is by no means a perfect definition; both
liberal and radical critics have identified weaknesses, especially
concerning the narrow, somewhat elitist, emphasis on academic achievement and the problems of evidence and
interpretation associated with much of the survey data in this
field. Furthermore, qualitative research has highlighted the
intricate, sometimes hidden, nature of school processes which
are rarely (if ever) fully captured through large-scale quantitative approaches.

Despite these problems, broad-based information on equality
of opportunity is vitally important, and recent advances in
quantitative methods have finally begun to reveal something of
the complex interaction between background factors (such as
social class, ethnicity and gender) and particular effects at the
individual school level.

Social class is known to be very strongly associated with
differences in academic achievement and recent research
suggests that such inequalities of outcome also persist within
different ethnic groups.

The achievement of different ethnic groups is a complex and
changing field. Many pupils (of all ethnic origins) do very well
in external examinations, but it is still the case that, as a group,
Afro-Caribbean pupils are not leaving school with qualifications
which match those of certain other groups at the highest levels.
Although their plight receives less attention, survey data also
point to the inequalities suffered by other ethnic minority
groups, such as children of Bangladeshi and Turkish parentage.

Studies of school effectiveness have confirmed what many
parents and students already knew, which is that a 'good' or
'bad' school can have a greater influence upon examination
results than membership of a particular ethnic group. This
work is important, but should not obscure the fact that group

inequalities of achievement still persist and must be critically addressed.

Although school effects research concerning multi-ethnic populations is still in its infancy, the work to date highlights the complexity of educational processes and confirms that schools and teachers have the power to influence the achievement of their pupils. In view of these findings it is perhaps time to reconsider the appropriateness of the term underachievement.

It has been argued that the concept of underachievement might become a stereotype which teachers, administrators and politicians use to absolve themselves of responsibility. Furthermore, the very term itself can be interpreted as in some way locating the problem within the group that is suffering. Thus educationists speak of the underachievement of Afro-Caribbean pupils rather than the underachievement of the educational system. In view of these points it has been argued that we need to move away from the concept of underachievement.

the nature of the education experience of black students, especially those of Afro-Caribbean origin, may be better understood in terms of 'educational disadvantage' or 'inequality' rather than in terms of 'underachievement'. In advancing this type of analysis, we are drawing attention to the structural and institutional realities within which the situation of the black student within the education system needs to be understood. (Wright, 1987, p. 126)

Whatever terms we use, it is still the case that many ethnic minority pupils suffer inequalities of opportunity. Schools and teachers are not powerless; they retain the ability to affect their pupils' progress and achievement drastically. A vital part of pupils' school experience is determined by curricular content and pedagogical styles. These form the subject of the next chapter, which focuses upon the debates concerning multicultural and anti-racist education.

Chapter 6

'Race', ethnicity and the curriculum

Towards anti-racist schooling

I used to write down all this stuff about kings and queens and all the European history because I wanted to get through. There was nothing about Asian or black history. It's as if we didn't exist. (Kussar, a sixth-form student of South Asian parentage, quoted by Mac an Ghaill, 1989, p. 282)

Denis Lawton (1975) has stated that the school curriculum 'is essentially a selection from the culture of a society' (p. 6). Yet it is questionable whether the United Kingdom has (or has ever had) a single culture. Sociologists were generally slow to recognize the importance of the curriculum as an area for critical study, but, following the publication of *Knowledge and Control* (Young, 1971), there has been increasing interest in the selection, use and consequences of different curriculum models (Burgess, 1986, pp. 202–4). Heated debates concerning the proper influence of ethnic minority cultures within the curriculum have involved claim and counter-claim by multiculturalists, anti-racists and, of course, the 'anti-anti-racists' of the political right (Klein, 1988a). The rapid introduction of the national curriculum during the late 1980s and early 1990s has made curriculum issues paramount in the minds of many teachers and marks a new phase in the continuing battle for a curriculum which is of relevance to *all* pupils in this country.

This chapter focuses upon the debates concerning the kind of curriculum which is appropriate for children growing up in a multi-ethnic society. As this has been a contested area for many years, these debates must be viewed within the wider political context of changing perspectives on the whole issue of 'race' relations in this country.

In considering the development of contrasting approaches to curriculum issues, various authors have used different terms to describe the same features. Chris Mullard (1982), for example, has analysed developments in terms of three 'power models', while James Lynch (1986) has described five 'phases'; the analyses use different labels and cite varying start- and end-dates for each model/phase of educational response, yet they describe the same progression of contrasting, but inter-connected, perspectives on issues of 'race' and education. This reflects the slow, evolutionary, often piecemeal character of different approaches to education in our multi-ethnic society. There have been no unequivocal points of revolutionary change in perspective; rather there has been continual discussion and argument involving teachers, academics, pressure groups, politicians and, most importantly, the ethnic minority communities themselves. The lines of attack and defence, indeed, the very language and issues at the heart of the struggle, have been continually contested and reconstructed. If we are to move ahead, an analysis of how we arrived at the present situation is crucially important. Any such analysis, however, must of necessity impose crude labels on the shifting and often haphazard developments. The following description builds upon previous work and, in order to avoid adding to the already confused vocabulary, I have tried to adopt the terms which have been most commonly taken up and used by those involved in the debates.

Assimilation

James Lynch (1986) has described the period between the early postwar years and the 1960s as a time of 'ignorance and neglect' (p. 42). By the late 1950s, however, there was growing resistance to immigration among the white population. Although immigration had been deliberately encouraged as a means of meeting Britain's need for labour, the experience of racism in the housing and employment markets was mirrored in violent attacks upon Afro-Caribbean and South Asian people. In the latter part of 1958 a series of attacks by white youths

143

culminated in 'riots', first in Nottingham, and then in Notting Hill, London.[1] Although many contemporary accounts clearly identified the 'immigrant' populations as victims rather than aggressors, parts of the popular press and politicians (on both sides of the House of Commons) sought to excuse the action of convicted whites (cf. Ramdin, 1987, pp. 208–10).

Following the 1958 riots, calls for an end to immigration reached new levels. The underlying assumption was that as more immigrants entered the country, so there would be more 'friction'. Consequently, the best way to handle 'the colour problem' was to limit the numbers of 'coloured' people: a rationale which the Conservative Party continues to invoke in debates on immigration today (cf. Cashmore, 1989). This reasoning was reflected in the 1962 Act to limit the immigration of peoples from the Commonwealth – the first of a series of acts and amendments to immigration rules which have systematically removed the rights of 'immigrants with dark skins. White Australians, Americans and Germans are never defined as a problem' (Dickinson, 1982, p. 75).

As this brief summary of events indicates, from the late 1950s and into the 1960s, the political mood changed from one of relative neglect to one which actively stressed the need to assimilate immigrants into British society. It was assumed that once they had mastered the English language, traditions and values, immigrants would be absorbed into white society without further conflict. The Department of Education and Science (DES), for example, began gathering statistical data on pupils who were themselves immigrants or whose parents had entered the country within the last ten years, clearly assuming that ten years was ample time to assimilate into the 'British' way of life.

During this period, therefore, immigrants from the Caribbean and the Indian subcontinent were defined as a problem which could be solved by helping them to fit into the existing (white) system. In the field of education, the assimilationist perspective led to a concern with teaching English as a second language (E2L) to South Asian pupils (see chapter 7) and fostering middle-class values. To take one example, Williams (1967) reported that teachers in Sparkbrook saw their role as 'putting over a certain set of values (Christian), a code of behaviour (middle-class), and a set of academic and job aspirations in which white-collar jobs have higher prestige than manual' (p. 237).

Hence the key aims of educational policy at this time were to safeguard the stability of the existing educational system and to protect the (often racist) sensitivities of white parents; nowhere was this more apparent than in the policy of dispersal.

In November 1963, Sir Edward Boyle (then Conservative Minister of Education) told the House of Commons that 'If possible, it is desirable on educational grounds that no one school should have more than about 30 per cent of immigrants' (*Hansard*, vol. 685, cols 439–40). Subsequently, the practice of dispersal, which some education authorities had already instigated, was officially sanctioned in DES Circular 7/65:

> It is inevitable that, as the proportion of immigrant children in a school or class increases, the problems will become more difficult to solve, and the chances of assimilation more remote ... Experience suggests ... up to a fifth of immigrant children in any group fit in with reasonable ease, but that, if the proportion goes over about one third either in the school as a whole or in any one class, serious strains arise. (DES Circular 7/65, quoted in Swann, 1985, pp. 193–4)

The circular concluded that 'every effort should be made to disperse the immigrant children round a greater number of schools.' Hence the notion of ethnic minority pupils as an educational problem was institutionalized. It lay at the very heart of the dispersal policy, a policy which explicitly gave priority to the opinions and prejudices of white parents.

> *It will be helpful if the parents of non-immigrant children can see that practical measures have been taken to deal with the problems in their schools, and that the progress of their own children is not being restricted by the undue preoccupation of the teaching staff with the linguistic and other difficulties of immigrant children.* (DES Circular 7/65, quoted in Swann, 1985, p. 194; original emphasis)

The dispersal policy was opposed by many groups. As Farrukh Dhondy has noted, by 'busing' ethnic minority children away from their own communities and into 'white' areas, dispersal policies increased pupils' vulnerability to racial harassment – including physical attacks, which contributed to at least one death (Dhondy, 1982, p. 36).

The assimilationist phase saw the emergence of a number of policy assumptions which continue to influence debate today. Although 'busing' has now been abandoned, the view that ethnic minority pupils represent a threat to educational standards and that a high concentration in a school will lower the performance of white pupils, has been clearly reflected in incidents such as the Honeyford affair (cf. Foster-Carter, 1987) and the successful campaign by white parents to remove their children from a predominantly Asian school in the Kirklees LEA (*Times Educational Supplement* 15 July 1988). Perhaps even more importantly, as Mullard (1982) has emphasized, assimilationist policies reflected a 'belief in the cultural and racial superiority of the "host" metropolitan society', a view which is still espoused, even by apparently 'learned' academics.[2]

Integration

A 1966 speech by Roy Jenkins, then Labour Home Secretary, is often taken as a turning point in the movement away from the assimilationist model and towards an apparently more liberal, integrationist phase. Jenkins advocated 'not a flattening process of assimilation but equal opportunity, accompanied by cultural diversity, in an atmosphere of mutual tolerance' (quoted in Mullard, 1982, p. 125). Jenkins' speech was important, not least because it represented official acknowledgement that substantive equality of opportunity did not already exist. Furthermore, Jenkins' public rejection of the 'flattening process' seemed to mark a significant move away from the previously sanctioned racist assumptions of white-British cultural superiority and the associated goal of the cultural 'absorption' of minorities. Diversity, so the policy-makers stated, was no longer to be ignored.

Educational responses to this phase in British 'race' relations were characterized by the appearance of various teaching materials and courses which sought to examine the differences between different ethnic groups and increase awareness of minorities' cultural traditions and historical backgrounds. Unfortunately, much of the material was poorly prepared and frequently reflected and reinforced crude stereotypes of ethnic minorities as, at best, exotic and strange, and, at worst, backward and primitive. James Lynch (1986) has referred to the latter half of the 1970s as the 'deficit phase' in the development of multicultural education, a time when the 'emphasis was on life styles rather than life chances' (p. 41).

Some significant progress was made during this period, not least with regard to the official end of dispersal policies and the establishment of limited legal protections in the Race Relations Act (1976). The Act also set up the Commission for Racial Equality (CRE), a much maligned body which has in fact achieved important victories in numerous cases of individual and institutional discrimination.[3] Despite these small gains, however, the assumptions and operation of the integrationist model were not so very different to those of the earlier assimilationist period. Despite the rhetoric of 'tolerance' and 'diversity', the basic aim of educational policies remained the protection of the existing system.

> By allowing limited diversity in respect of religious beliefs, customs, dress and even language, it is assumed within the framework of the [integrationist] model that blacks will be more likely to accept than to reject outright those [values and beliefs] which actually shape our society. (Mullard, 1982, p. 128)

Towards a multicultural curriculum

Policies based on the assumptions of assimilation/integration were, therefore, ill-conceived, partial and often racist. The basic values of such policies devalued ethnic minority people, reducing them to the status of a problem which would eventually go away as they became just another part of society. Such an approach was bound to fail.

The cultural variety, social cohesion and active resistance of ethnic minority groups ensured the failure of the 'flattening process' (cf. Sivanandan, 1982). Yet the education system faced increasingly difficult issues concerning 'race' and achievement. In 1971 Coard's pamphlet, *How the West Indian Child is Made Educationally Subnormal in the British School System*, was a landmark publication, identifying the active role which white racism played in the labelling of 'West Indian' pupils. Throughout the 1970s Afro-Caribbean parents' concern that their children were being failed by the system gained support from teachers who began to develop the theme of diversity (central to integrationist rhetoric) and broaden their perspectives to consider the whole curriculum and general pedagogical issues.

During the 1970s 'black studies' courses were designed and implemented in some schools. These were usually aimed at Afro-Caribbean children and sought to counter the problems of poor self-image (which at the time were offered as a reason for 'black educational failure') by imparting information on the history and culture of black people. Although these courses were often designed and implemented by ethnic minority teachers and seemed a radical development when they first appeared, they were criticized for their 'compensatory' assumptions which located the problem within the ethnic minority child. Such courses sought to treat the problem by focusing on the victims of the system, rather than targeting the system itself (cf. Stone, 1981). It was in recognition of this fact that momentum grew for change across the entire curriculum and for all pupils, not only those of ethnic minority background. This change in emphasis is often taken as a key factor in identifying a multicultural approach to education. One of the major problems in this field, however, is the lack of any single commonly accepted definition of just what multicultural education is or should be.

Problems of definition

Building upon the work of Phillips-Bell (1981), Sally Tomlinson (1983, p. 90) has noted the confusion generated by contrasting assumptions and approaches to education which have been lumped together under the 'umbrella-term' of multicultural education. Jenny Williams (1979) describes this definitional confusion as a major factor inhibiting the growth of the multicultural curriculum. In an attempt to 'aid debate among those working for change' (p. 127) she developed a typology of three contrasting perspectives. These were, firstly, the *technicist perspective*, based on a compensatory ideology which resulted in programmes of 'remedial' work and an emphasis on the need for basic E2L tuition; secondly, the *moral perspective*, reflecting a child-centred pedagogy, and stressing the use of discussion and self-analysis as a means of reducing prejudice and discrimination (cf. Stenhouse *et al.*, 1982); thirdly, the *socio/political ideology*, seeking the creation of 'a plural society of relatively separate but equal groups' and with a central focus on 'the problem of identity' (Williams, 1979, p. 30). Williams' typology graphically illustrates the range of values and approaches which can be confused under the general heading of multiculturalism. As she pointed out, 'None of the perspectives outlined ... is straightforward, unambiguous, without problems and without critics' (p. 131).

To some degree the ad hoc development of different, and sometimes conflicting approaches to multicultural education reflects the lack of clear centrally defined policy statements. Although the DES has stated its support for the principles of equal opportunity it has been reluctant to give a policy lead in the field of 'race' and education. Consequently it has fallen to the minority communities, individual teachers, schools and authorities (often concerned with special local pressures) to address multicultural issues within the curriculum. Despite the ad hoc nature of many initiatives, however, the Swann committee was able to highlight two important characteristics which they felt distinguished multicultural approaches from the previous 'compensatory' perspectives: 'firstly, meeting the particular educational needs of ethnic minority children and secondly, the broader issue of preparing *all* pupils for life in a multiracial society' (Swann, 1985, p. 199; original emphasis). At this point it is useful to examine some attempts to translate the themes of multiculturalism into curricular and pedagogical practice.

Multiculturalism in practice

Cohen and Manion (1983) have drawn upon the work of Robert Jeffcoate (1979) in describing a multicultural curriculum as 'one in which choice of content reflects the multicultural nature of British society and the world and draws significantly on the experiences of British racial minorities and cultures overseas' (Cohen and Manion, 1983, p. 181). There are a number of important differences between this approach and earlier integrationist courses on minority 'lifestyles'. Curriculum content, for example, should no longer deal in stereotypical images of exotic, far-away peoples using 'primitive' technologies; the experiences of minority communities in Britain should be explored, giving an accurate picture of similarities as well as differences. In particular, Jeffcoate has stressed the need to avoid applying Western value judgements blandly to other cultures which have 'their own validity' and should not be judged exclusively by British norms. When considering the lives and cultures of people in other parts of the world European norms can become redundant; technologically simple means of farming or transport, for instance, may be much better suited to local conditions than complex and highly fragile equipment which might at first appear to offer a 'superior' (Western) solution.

Advocates of multicultural approaches have emphasized the need for 'permeation' as a strategy of curricular reconstruction. Hence multicultural issues should permeate the entire curriculum and not be limited to a single audience (such as earlier 'black studies' courses), nor be treated as an extra to be bolted on to existing syllabuses. All teachers should be aware of multicultural issues and sensitive to possible bias, regardless of their various subject specialisms and the ethnic origin of their pupils.

> No subject should be excused the need for self-examination ... There is no such thing as a neutral subject. No matter how little a subject refers to culture and society it cannot be taught in a cultural or social vacuum. In chemistry, for example, black children receive an important subliminal message if the illustrations always show test tubes in white hands ... If we take a world view of scientific and other research it quickly becomes apparent that the original papers appearing in learned journals are produced by people of all races from universities in every country. (AMMA, 1987, pp. 47–8)

A great deal of work is available which helps to identify good practice and useful materials for teachers in all schools. Gillian Klein has played a particularly important role, first as author of major reviews of curriculum materials (Klein, 1982, 1985) and more recently as editor of the journal *Multicultural Teaching* (Trentham Books) which publishes reviews and short original articles by teachers and academics who are active in this field. However, current spending restrictions and the advent of local financial management (or as the DES prefers, local management of schools; cf. Coopers & Lybrand, 1988) are likely to mean that many teachers will be unable immediately to replace old and biased materials. Under such circumstances the Assistant Masters and Mistresses Association (AMMA, 1987, p. 49) have suggested that teachers draw the bias to pupils' attention and use the material as the basis for discussion. Such treatment is 'at best a stop-gap technique', yet teachers can make great progress simply by recognizing ethnic diversity in their use of illustrations and asides in lessons.

Many multicultural approaches are possible which develop subject-specific themes without demanding new materials. Dyson (1986) has shown how spatial awareness can be investigated in mathematics by using Rangoli patterns which characterize Hindu decorations for Diwali celebrations. Similarly, other writers have suggested multicultural approaches and materials for the whole range of subjects, from familiar fields such as the humanities (Collicott, 1986; Hodgkinson, 1987), music (G. Cox, 1986) and arts (Lashley, 1986), to the less obviously applicable, and often resistant, subject areas such as science (Ashrif, 1986; Watts, 1986) and mathematics (Swetz, 1985; Joseph, 1986).[4]

Multicultural education is, therefore, a varied and complex field. In some respects, the complexity of different views is a strength which highlights the scale and importance of the issues being addressed (Chivers, 1987, p. x). On the other hand, the lack of any single definition has resulted in ad hoc developments which have often lacked clear aims and objectives.

Despite these problems, multicultural approaches have marked a significant move away from the distorted and stereotyped images of the assimilation/integration years. In particular, the identification of the need for multicultural education for all pupils, of whatever age, gender and ethnicity, is a crucial move away from the assumption that it is ethnic minority pupils themselves who are 'the problem'. Predictably, however, multicultural education has not been without its critics; indeed, writers of both the left and right have found plenty to condemn.

Multiculturalism under attack

For the conservative critics, it [multicultural education] represents an attempt to politicize education in order to pander to minority demands, whereas for some radicals it is the familiar ideological device of perpetuating the reality of racist exploitation of ethnic minorities by pampering their cultural sensitivities (Parekh, quoted in Modgil *et al.*, 1986, p. 5).

The quotation above neatly summarizes part of the dilemma faced by those who have worked towards a multicultural curriculum. Partly because the term multicultural education has been used in reference to so many different approaches, its critics have emerged from the whole range of political and educational thought. On the political right, those bent on protecting the status quo have argued that any movement away from the teaching of 'British' (white) history and values can only harm pupils and the interests of the country as a whole. Members of the influential Hillgate Group (cf. Quicke, 1988) are among these critics, claiming that multicultural curricula are both intellectually vacuous and politically motivated:

> it seems to me that there can be no real argument for a 'multi-cultural' curriculum. To adopt such a curriculum is to fail to transmit either the common culture of Britain or the high culture that has grown from it. And no other culture is put in the place of those: the result is nothing more than a void, existing in the child's consciousness ... (Scruton, 1986, p. 134)

> The potential in these attacks [upon institutional racism] for the endless generation ·of disaffection, confrontation and social conflict is obvious, as is the eventual consequence – the destruction and revolutionary transformation of all the institutions of our democratic society. (Marks, 1986, p. 37)

On the other hand, some writers have attacked moves towards a multicultural curriculum as nothing more than a defensive strategy meant to protect the interests of the capitalist ruling class by dampening the potential for resistance by a 'black' underclass (cf. Dhondy, 1978).

> As interpreted and practised by many, multiracial education has appeared to become an instrument of control and stability rather than one of change, of the subordination rather than the freedom of blacks in schools and or society as a whole. (Mullard, 1982, p. 131)

Mullard's analysis of multicultural education as a means of social control has been echoed in comparative studies of other countries. On the basis of six comparative case studies,

Bullivant (1981) concluded that curriculum policies of cultural maintenance of minority groups could be 'managed' so that despite superficial change there was no shift in real life-chances and equality of opportunity. Similarly, Fazal Rizvi (1988) has offered an account of Australian educational policies which, while accepting that some advance has been made on earlier assimilationist practices, states that by encouraging minorities to 'celebrate their ethnicity' the shared political and economic interests of migrant groups have been obscured; 'multicultural education in Australia has thus become the instrument of control and stability, rather than change' (Rizvi, 1988, p. 348). Rizvi's conclusions mirror Christopher Bagley's verdict on the 'superficial multiculturalism of Canada, Britain and the Netherlands' which, he states, 'assists class exploitation by putting stress on what are in fact superficial differences between people. Multi-culturalism in its present form is little more than a masking ideology with which an artful and ruthless capitalism protects itself' (Bagley, 1986, pp. 56–7).

Unlike many of the critics from the political right, those of the left have not been content merely to shoot holes in existing multicultural practices. Chris Mullard, for example, has been particularly active in encouraging 'anti-racist' perspectives.[5]

Anti-racism

One of the criticisms frequently levelled against multicultural education is that it is 'soft' on racism: that the social, political and economic power relations which have resulted in the exploitation of minority groups are not properly addressed. Such criticisms have lain behind diverse moves towards establishing a more active and oppositional form of pedagogy and curriculum, one which is overtly anti-racist.

As with so much work in this field, there is no universally agreed model of what an anti-racist pedagogy and curriculum should in fact look like. The level of public and professional misunderstanding and prejudice concerning anti-racism was graphically illustrated in the circumstances surrounding the Macdonald panel's report into a Manchester school where an Asian pupil had been stabbed to death by a white peer (Macdonald *et al.*, 1989). Although the murder was racially motivated the news media somehow managed to twist the facts

153

so that they seemed to condemn the whole thrust of anti-racism (cf. Klein, 1988a; Lloyd, 1988). Manchester's education committee added to the confusion by refusing to publish most of the panel's report.

The Macdonald report was critical of the school's handling of certain issues, but the panel firmly supported the need to sensitively explore and develop anti-racist approaches (cf. Macdonald *et al.*, 1989, pp. 349–64); perhaps the clearest finding to emerge from the tragedy was that there was no magic formula which would bring about a change of attitudes at the chalk-face (Spencer, 1988a, b). There is no definitive anti-racist approach; rather, the term refers to a whole series of beliefs and practices concerning the proper role and nature of education in a multicultural society. It is, therefore, impossible to deal with every facet of the many different varieties of anti-racism which have been developed. In order to explore some of the central features of anti-racist approaches I will focus upon one example (Brandt, 1986) typifying some of the major themes which are characteristic of the general approach.[6]

The first key characteristic of Godfrey Brandt's approach is his rejection of previous multicultural strategies. Brandt offers a typology of different perspectives on the relationship between multiculturalism and anti-racism (Brandt, 1986, pp. 114–19). With very few references and no clear definition of what he understands by the term multiculturalism, Brandt argues that only an explicitly anti-racist perspective can begin to challenge the racist mechanisms of exploitation which are located within the very structure of our society. When anti-racists speak of institutional racism they often mean racially discriminatory beliefs and practices which are not only written into the workings of white institutions, but which reflect the deeper assumptions, goals and values of a white racist ruling class.

Brandt draws heavily on Mullard (1982) and Carby (1982) in arguing that any form of 'multicultural' education must itself be racist: 'multicultural education can be seen as the Trojan horse of institutional racism. Within it resides an attempt to renew the structure and processes of racism in education' (Brandt, 1986, p. 117). Brandt argues that whereas multi-culturalists have sought to respond to ethnic minorities' experiences, anti-racist teaching should accord them an active and central role: 'anti-racism must be dynamic and led by the experience and articulations of the Black community as the ongoing victims of rapidly changing ideology and practice of racism' (p. 119).

A second characteristic of anti-racist perspectives is an emphasis upon oppositional forms. As the very term anti-racism suggests, a central feature of such approaches is the pivotal role which they accord the struggle against racism. 'The aims of anti-racist education must be, by definition, oppositional' (Brandt, 1986, p. 125): this is embodied in the use of oppositional language. Brandt makes much of the dynamic, active character of anti-racism. He uses a table, for example, to juxtapose the language of multiculturalism and anti-racism; the former is summarized in terms of monoculturalism/ethnicism, culture, equality, prejudice, misunderstanding, ignorance. Its process is characterized as providing information and increasing 'awareness'. Anti-racism, on the other hand, uses terms such as conflict, oppression, exploitation, fragmentation (divide and rule), racism, power, structure, struggle. Its process is described as *'dismantle, deconstruct, reconstruct'* (p. 121; original emphasis). These differences in language are important because they highlight the political nature of anti-racist approaches, political because they critically address questions of power in society. As the detailed material from the City Road case study indicates (see above), opposition to racism and ethnocentrism must challenge the ways of operating within society in general, and schools in particular, which are simply taken for granted.

The oppositional language of anti-racism is both a strength and a weakness: although it points to the dynamic and active role which teachers must play in confronting racism, it also offers ammunition to those who criticize it as 'indoctrination' (cf. C. Cox, 1986) and, perhaps more importantly, can frighten off teachers who might otherwise make valuable contributions within their schools. In addition, the language of opposition and conflict can be misleading. One of the most important elements of Brandt's work concerns his data on classroom approaches to anti-racism, approaches which challenge racist assumptions yet bear no resemblance to right-wing portrayals of anti-racism as a revolutionary tactic employed by a hard core of political extremists (cf. Palmer, 1986).

Anti-racism in practice

In contrast to many previous statements of anti-racist intent, Brandt is notable for his attempt to address teachers' day-to-day concerns:

> Many teachers will say, 'I understand how I can make my teaching multicultural – I can add a wider range of cultural facts and a wider range of cultural examples to my teaching, but anti-racism tells me nothing but the fact that I ought to be against racism' (Brandt, 1986, p. 110).

Part of Brandt's answer to such a question is delivered through accounts of individual lessons in six multi-ethnic schools, two primary and four secondary. The lesson descriptions are valuable for a number of reasons, not least because they show the variety of school subjects and teaching strategies which can be used as a vehicle for challenging racism. The descriptions include formal didactic approaches, unstructured lessons, classroom discussion and the use of creative writing and art work to explore different perspectives on both historical and contemporary materials.

In addition, Brandt's observations highlight both the possibilities and the difficulties of addressing such issues within the classroom. Crucially, the reader is left with the realization that this kind of work is within everyone's grasp. Yet, at the same time, it will need careful handling and is unlikely to bring about change overnight. One of the lessons, for example, involved secondary pupils discussing common pictorial images of Christ and being led to realize (through discussions of 'climate, geographical location, etc.') that European representations of a white European Christ are likely to be inaccurate and in fact reflect social, not merely spiritual, issues (Brandt, 1986, pp. 161–5). Despite a lively and constructive discussion, however, the lesson could only be seen as a first step and had to be placed within the wider context of a subject area (religious education) which was dominated by the teachings of the Christian faith.

Brandt offers his lesson descriptions as examples of good anti-racist practice, yet the strategies which the teachers adopted (characterized by the creative and sensitive use of simple materials and people's own lived experiences) strongly echo the approaches described in earlier multicultural works of which Brandt is critical (cf. Twitchin and Demuth, 1981; Saunders, 1982). In terms of the curriculum, for instance, Brandt identifies 'three major activities' for the anti-racist:

- the overall critical reappraisal of the overt curriculum;
- the selection of materials which will further the aims of the curriculum framework;
- critical awareness of the importance of the 'hidden' curriculum (Brandt, 1986, p. 130).

The first two areas are familiar points of action within multicultural frameworks (see above). What gives Brandt's work its specifically anti-racist flavour is his use of oppositional language and determination to confront racism, even within the area of school 'ethos' which, he argues, must not be viewed as 'ethereal' but should be recognized as a crucial part of 'the social and cultural environment which is constructed out of the covert and/or overt policy, personal attitudes and ideological underpinnings' (p. 132). In other words, the implicit messages which are transmitted in the actions and statements of the school staff.

Brandt's work highlights key characteristics of the anti-racist perspective, most importantly in its criticism of multicultural-ism, the emphasis upon oppositional language and the over-riding goal of confronting racism. In terms of curricular and pedagogical strategies, however, there seems little to distin-guish good anti-racist practice from good multiculturalism. I have used Brandt as an example of the anti-racist argument, but his work is not unique. A recently published reader on *Anti-Racist Science Teaching* (Gill and Levidow, 1987) criticizes 'multiculturalism' while advancing anti-racist practice which echoes the best 'multicultural' approaches.

The importance of this conclusion cannot be overstated. Like most attempts to improve practice, multicultural work has not been a universal success. Undoubtedly, some teachers have presented an array of images which may have reinforced, rather than challenged, racism in their school and local community (cf. Stone, 1981) – such approaches have sometimes been dismissed as 'the 3Ss' (saris, samosas and steel bands). How-ever, the term multiculturalism has been used in relation to so many different forms of teaching that it is simply not possible to define all multiculturalism as falling short of challenging individual and institutional racism (cf. Green, 1982).

The literature on 'race' and education reveals fundamental differences between the political and philosophical positions of different authors. During the 1980s an 'us' and 'them' situation developed which seemed to pit writers who viewed racism as an individual/social psychological problem against writers who argued that racism should be analysed as a vital part of the functioning of a capitalist society. The two positions became virtually synonymous with multiculturalism and anti-racism, respectively (cf. Hatcher, 1987), yet such a characterization is highly simplistic and offers little support to teachers who are struggling to make sense of the issues within their classrooms. Too much of the debate on 'race' and education in the 1980s was characterized by bitter arguments between anti-racism and multiculturalism; one side accused the other of tokenism, and even racism (see above), only to be met by counter-claims of illiberalism (Jeffcoate, 1984, p. 150). As the then chair of the CRE noted in 1984 (*Times Educational Supplement*, 20 July), this dispute was a major 'diversion of effort'.

To date, one of the most significant attempts to move beyond the multicultural/anti-racist impasse is to be found within the recommendations of the Swann committee's report, *Education for All*.[7]

Education for all

From its original formation in 1979, Trevor Carter was a member of the Committee of Inquiry into the Education of Children from Ethnic Minority Groups. In his paper 'Working within the Power Structure in the Quest for Change' (1985), Carter gives a candid picture of life behind the scenes on the committee and makes several important points. Firstly, he reminds us that the committee was set up as a direct result of pressure from minority communities. Secondly, he reveals that the major dissident on the committee was its second chairperson, Lord Swann, author of a guide to the report which did not use the word racism once (this despite more than fifty pages of detailed discussion on the 'theory and practice' of racism within the main report).

The committee had a long and troubled history, including a restrictive reformulation of its terms of reference and the 'resignation' of its first chairperson, Anthony Rampton (cf. Troyna, 1986). These factors, plus several leaks to the press, considerably lessened the report's impact, yet, as Carter points out, the report itself contains important discussion of many areas and deserves to be more widely understood. This is especially true in relation to the report's central thrust, a policy termed 'education for all'.

The committee sought to identify the principles of an education which would meet the needs of *all* pupils. It stated that 'In the course of our deliberations we have increasingly been led to reflect on whether the term "multicultural education" is adequate or indeed appropriate. . .' (Swann, 1985, p. 317). In addition to widespread confusion over conflicting definitions, the committee noted that some LEAs and schools in 'all-white' areas had assumed that multicultural issues were irrelevant to their pupils' needs. In response the committee used the phrase 'education for all' to symbolize the universal need for change throughout the educational system.[8] The report identified two major strands to such an approach: the principles of a 'good education' and the need to challenge racism.

The committee emphasized that if education is to prepare pupils for life in the late twentieth century an appreciation of ethnic diversity must be an essential and central concern:

> An out of date and inaccurate text book is indefensible on educational grounds and a history syllabus which presents world history exclusively in terms of British interests, experiences and values could in no way be regarded as 'sound' history. Thus, we regard 'Education for All' as essentially synonymous with a good and relevant education for life in the modern world. (Swann, 1985, p. 318)

Hence the Swann committee reaffirmed the need to help pupils understand and value ethnic diversity and constantly to ensure that syllabuses and teaching materials do not carry ethnocentric messages of 'white' British superiority. This might be thought of as the multicultural element of 'education for all'.

The second principle of the committee's approach concerned the need to challenge racism. As Trevor Carter (1985) has emphasized, the committee gave serious and thoughtful consideration to racism, as both an individual and (in the case of institutional racism) a structural phenomenon: 'racism is an insidious evil ... We believe that for schools to allow racist attitudes to persist unchecked in fact constitutes a fundamental *mis*-education for their pupils' (Swann, 1985, p. 36; original emphasis). The committee went on to emphasize that it was not seeking 'separate' or 'tokenist' additives to existing curricula: its main concern was to address the very assumptions which underlay curricula and pedagogy in all classrooms. This element of 'education for all' drew upon anti-racist critiques by overtly targeting the very process of education as being in need of change. The committee described its primary aim as:

> bringing about a fundamental reorientation of the attitudes which condition the selection of curriculum materials and subject matter and which underlie the actual teaching and learning process and the practices and procedures which play such an important part in determining how the educational experience impinges on the lives of pupils. (Swann, 1985, p. 324)

Having outlined the broad principles of 'education for all', the committee went on to examine the implications for the curriculum and prefaced its comments by again stressing the need for all schools to evaluate their teaching; 'in our view the curriculum offered to all pupils, whether in multi-racial or "all-white" schools, must be permeated by a genuinely pluralist perspective' (p. 327). The committee did not restrict itself to broad statements of principle: it made relatively detailed comments concerning some subject areas and the need to address the messages implicit in schools' 'hidden' curricula. Political education, for example, has often been treated with great caution by teachers wary of accusations of bias and indoctrination. Yet the Swann committee emphasized that preparation to take an active and informed role in politics should be an essential part of pupils' schooling in a democratic society. Building upon evidence from Her Majesty's Inspectorate (HMI) the committee stated that political education should lead pupils to 'consider fundamental issues such as social justice and equality and this should in turn cause them to reflect on the origins and mechanism of racism and prejudice' (Swann, 1985, p. 336).

Sociologists have increasingly drawn attention to the importance of the hidden curriculum; 'those unstated norms, values, and beliefs embedded in and transmitted to students through the underlying rules that structure the routines and social relationships in school and classroom life' (Giroux, 1983, p. 47). As I have already noted, a concern with the hidden curriculum is characteristic of some anti-racist approaches (cf. Brandt, 1986). Once again, this was an area which the Swann committee addressed, using evidence on school 'ethos' and pastoral workings to highlight the ways in which racist values of assimilation/integration still find expression in school policy and teacher perspectives:

> Local (Asian) girl was excluded from school ... when her father requested she be allowed not to take part in the once weekly swimming classes (mixed sex) which runs for half an academic year! Despite letters from Islamic authorities to Head teacher and Education Department supporting father in his view, the Head teacher maintained his stance that swimming was 'a vital and integral part of the school's curricula', and that the girl 'was excluding herself by refusing school discipline' ... Comments to Assistant Community Relations Officer from Head during discussions included, 'It's the thin end of the wedge' – 'These people have got to be shown that they can't have everything to their convenience' (Quoted in Swann, 1985, p. 342)

In its statements concerning the need actively to confront racism in school and society the Swann committee seems to have attempted to take on board some of the anti-racist message. The committee's view of 'education for all' attempted to blend multicultural and anti-racist perspectives into the beginnings of a curricular and pedagogical strategy of relevance to all pupils. In order to help teachers critically evaluate their schools' curricula, the report detailed six criteria. The first four were taken from evidence submitted by the now-abolished Schools Council and reflect previous multicultural guidelines (cf. Jeffcoate, 1979); the fifth and sixth criteria were added by the committee to 'reflect the principles of "Education for All"'.

(i) The variety of social, cultural and ethnic groups and a perspective of the world should be evident in visuals, stories, conversation and information.

(ii) People from social, cultural and ethnic groups should be presented as individuals with every human attribute.

(iii) Cultures should be empathetically described in their own terms and not judged against some notion of 'ethno-centric' or 'Euro-centric' culture.

(iv) The curriculum should include accurate information on racial and cultural differences and similarities.

(v) All children should be encouraged to see the cultural diversity of our society in a positive light.

(vi) The issue of racism, at both institutional and individual level, should be considered openly and efforts made to counter it. (adapted from Swann, 1985, p. 329)

These guidelines represent a crude attempt to map out a basic checklist for schools and teachers to consider and act upon. The final criterion is perhaps the most important, as it reflects the basic message of anti-racism concerning the need to oppose (not merely disapprove of or ignore) racism within the school and society.

As Ahmed Gurnah (1987) has noted, the Swann report (like all other government inquiries before it) stands as part of the state's response to 'problems' which seem to threaten the stability of the system. In addition, however, such inquiries also 'seek to represent popular grievances. In that role they converge State interests and popular perceptions into a programme for moderate change' (Gurnah, 1987, p. 11). Given these somewhat contradictory forces it is little surprise that most inquiries are limited in their views and fail to satisfy the majority of readers. The Swann report exemplifies these problems, yet within its 800-plus pages there are some important sections. John Rex, for example, has argued that the report offers real opportunities for anti-racists who are prepared to look beyond the chairperson's 'guide' and engage the detail of 'education for all':

> In principle this is a very thoroughgoing agenda ... It emphasizes the notion of equality of opportunity; it does not base its concept of multiculturalism on a paternalistic and caricatured concept of minority cultures; and it targets racism both indirectly through a syllabus for all which treats minority culture with respect and directly through anti-racist teaching. It certainly gives me a charter for the kind of anti-

racist reform of the education system which I wish to bring about. (Rex, 1987, p. 15)

Despite the criticism which has been heaped upon the report from all parts of the political spectrum, therefore, the policy of 'education for all' may offer a limited, though important, first step towards officially sanctioned good anti-racist practice, the details of which (as usual) will have to be worked out on a day-to-day basis by classroom teachers. Unfortunately, statements within official inquiries are not guaranteed to see fruition in practice. Although Rex identifies a real opportunity for progress towards anti-racist teaching, there are powerful forces which may prevent its realization – not least central government. In order to understand the possible consequences of recent 'reforms' (including the national curriculum), it is useful to reflect on the fate of previous initiatives in this field.

Policy and practice

'Colour-blindness' and the failure to change

Bringing about change in curricular and pedagogical practice is no easy matter, especially in the field of 'race' and ethnic relations. Britain's first national survey of teachers' attitudes to multiracial education was carried out in the 1970s by a team of researchers based at the National Foundation for Educational Research (NFER). They found overwhelming support for the statement, 'Schools have a responsibility to promote good race relations amongst pupils.' Ninety-four per cent of the 510 teachers who replied agreed with this statement. In contrast, 'only eight per cent more teachers agreed than disagreed with the [statement] suggesting that lessons on race relations should be given in schools' (Brittan, 1976a, p. 106). The responses also evidenced a high degree of crude racial stereotyping (especially concerning an image of slow-learning and disruptive 'West Indian' pupils; Brittan, 1976b, p. 190).

The NFER survey was carried out in 1972, so it is perhaps not surprising that many teachers clung to crude assimilationist perspectives which blamed educational failure on home circumstances and emphasized the need for 'immigrant' pupils to change to meet the demands of the system. However, educational research has continued to demonstrate many teachers' preference for a 'colour-blind' approach, based on the assumption that to address 'racial' issues directly might only inflame the situation (Williams, 1979, p. 126).

it is clear that there is a substantial body of opinion within the teaching profession which firmly believes that to recognise differences between people of various ethnic origins is divisive and can in fact constitute a major obstacle to creating a harmonious multi-racial society. We ourselves regard 'colour-blindness' however as potentially just as negative as a straightforward rejection of people with a different skin colour since both types of attitude seek to deny the validity of an important aspect of a person's identity. (Swann, 1985, p. 27)

The data from City Road Comprehensive (see especially chapter 2 above) clearly demonstrate the problems of the 'colour-blind' approach where white teachers, in fact, proved to be anything but blind to behaviour which did not easily fit with their own experience and ethnocentric perspectives.

In 'all-white' schools very little work seems to focus on the multi-ethnic nature of society (cf. Gaine, 1987). Even where there are clear signs of racism among the pupils, many schools assume that there is no need for multicultural/anti-racist work in the absence of a significant ethnic minority population. Work undertaken for the Swann committee (Matthews, 1985) graphically illustrated the need which is so often ignored:

School B2 – a formal, strictly disciplined co-educational comprehensive school – had a largely all white pupil population apart from a few West Indian, Asian, Iranian and Chinese pupils ... A multicultural approach to the curriculum was not considered necessary. The Deputy Head, who had previously taught in a multi-racial school observed 'there is little apparent need here for a multicultural curriculum so very little is being done'...

A class of mixed ability fourth year pupils was asked to write on some aspects of immigration into Britain ... Here are examples of pupil writings:

– We take everybody in because we're mugs...

– The foreigners takes up our houses our jobs our food and

164

sometimes our women. alot of them come from the more poorer countries, maybe if they got out and we got jobs we might be able to send some food and other supplies over because everybody would be better of then...
- I think that pakistanis should not be aloud to own shops because so many whites are out of jobs... (adapted from Matthews, 1985, p. 252–3)

These comments echo the popular racism which is frequently reinforced through the media (cf. Troyna, 1981; Twitchin, 1988). In schools such as this, where a 'multicultural approach to the curriculum was not considered necessary' such views will continue completely unchallenged. A strong policy lead, from the DES and others, may offer one way of promoting more action in 'all-white' schools. Unfortunately, previous policy statements have done little or nothing to improve the reality of school life for many pupils.

Government policy: what are words worth?

Official statements have often revealed a great deal about policy-makers and their tendency to equate ethnic diversity with 'educational problems'. The dispersal policy of the late 1960s graphically illustrated the desire to assimilate quickly 'immigrant' pupils while protecting the interests of the system and the sensitivities of white voters.

It is true that some important progress has been made since the early days of the assimilation/integration period: 'Section 11' funding, originally set up as an assimilationist measure, was extended during the 1980s and additional resources were targeted at some multi-ethnic areas through educational support grants (Craft, 1989). In addition, the criteria for the accreditation of initial teacher training (ITT) courses required some awareness of ethnic diversity.

David Kirp (1979) has described British policy on 'race' and schooling as 'doing good by doing little'. However, changes have been slow to come and incomplete in their application. The Swann committee, for example, recommended that all intending teachers should gain some practical experience in multi-ethnic schools, yet no such requirement was mentioned in the government's consultations concerning new ITT criteria (DES, 1989b). In fact a survey of ITT provision, conducted by Her Majesty's Inspectorate (HMI), revealed great variation in practice; one Post-Graduate Certificate in Education (PGCE) course included just six hours on multicultural issues and even that time was spent linking cultural diversity with 'deprivation' and expectations of low achievement (HMI, 1989, p. 5).

One of the principal reasons for the slow and piecemeal nature of progress in this field is the lack of clear policy direction from the DES and central government. The Swann report was particularly critical of official attempts to subsume ethnic minority issues within wider debates on educational failure and economic and social disadvantage (cf. Swann, 1985, pp. 212–16). Yet this practice has continued, indeed, it was evident in the government's response to the Swann report itself: 'under-achievement is not confined to the ethnic minorities ... [Our] policies apply to all pupils irrespective of ethnic origin. As they bear fruit, ethnic minority pupils will share in the benefit' (Sir Keith Joseph, then Secretary of State for Education and Science, *Hansard*, vol. 75, col. 451).

Although Kirp (1979) described this 'racial inexplicitness' as doing good by 'stealth', many critics have taken a less generous position. Andrew Dorn, for example, has argued that in the absence of 'overt policies on multiracial education [which] result in explicit measures to combat racism and tackle inequality ... *doing little* will be *doing nothing*' (Dorn, 1980, p. 51; original emphasis). This view has been confirmed by the recent introduction of a major package of educational 'reforms', including the imposition of a national curriculum.

The national curriculum

Regardless of widespread public and professional criticism (see, for instance, Haviland, 1988; Lawton and Chitty, 1988), the Education Reform Act 1988 established schools' legal duty to introduce a statutory curriculum as directed by the Secretary of State for Education.[9] This curriculum (the so-called national curriculum) comprises specified foundation subjects (including three core subjects) which must be included in all pupils' curricula. The core subjects are English, mathematics and science (plus Welsh in Welsh-speaking schools). The other foundation subjects are technology (including design), history, geography, music, art, physical education and, for pupils between the ages of eleven and sixteen ('key stages' three and four), a modern foreign language.[10] The provisional timetable for the implementation of the national curriculum required a phased introduction so that the final foundation subjects are 'in place' by 1996/7 (DES, 1989a).

The DES stated that the purpose of the national curriculum was to 'develop a broad consensus about what children are taught, accepting of course that children differ in what they learn and in their rates of learning' (DES/WO, 1988b, p. 5). Working groups were set up with the aim of defining programmes of study and attainment targets for each foundation subject. Subsequently, pupils would be tested on their progress at the key ages of seven, eleven, fourteen and sixteen.

In the field of 'race' and education, initial responses to the national curriculum were generally negative. John Eggleston, however, identified what he believed to be a positive aspect in its prescriptive nature:

> The National Curriculum, despite all misgivings, does offer one major advantage ... Schools will not be able to differentiate between curriculum delivery on grounds of race, gender, language or any other discriminatory criteria. (Eggleston, 1988, p. 25)

Unfortunately, Eggleston's hopes may have been misplaced. During the passage of the Education Reform Bill 'Baroness Hooper for the government emphasised that programmes of study and attainment targets would allow for "considerable differentiation by ability in each subject"' (Lowe, 1988, p. 11). In view of the scope for 'considerable differentiation', Eggleston's verdict seems to assume that (a) teachers' personal assessments will play no part in selection procedures, and (b) the formal programmes of study and attainment targets are without ethnic bias. On both counts there is great cause for concern. Firstly, regarding the status of teachers' personal judgements of pupils' ability, the Task Group on Assessment and Testing (TGAT) has emphasized the crucial role which teachers will play in stating that: 'the Group recommends that assessments be made by combining teachers' own assessments with the results of externally provided tests' (DES/WO, 1988b, p. 11). Given the research evidence on teachers' negative labelling of some pupils, especially those of Afro-Caribbean ethnicity (see chapter 2), it seems highly unlikely that the assessment procedures will automatically improve the educational opportunities afforded to ethnic minority pupils. Subsequent DES statements have suggested that teachers' assessments will be less important than pupils' performance in the standard assessment tasks (SATs), but the standard assessment instruments are themselves a cause for concern.

The TGAT showed some sensitivity to the second concern, that of the possibility of gender and 'racial' bias. In addition to recognizing the difficulties which pupils might face where English was not their mother tongue, TGAT recommended that 'assessment tasks be reviewed regularly for evidence of bias' (DES/WO, 1988a, para 52). Unfortunately, even if such reviews do eventually prompt changes in the assessment instruments, they will come too late for those who first suffer the bias.

Without constant review (and action) the recurrent theme of differentiation (cf. DES/WO, 1988a, c) could usher in a new period of institutionalized racism. The TGAT report noted that as early as the age of seven, the test results might indicate a minority of pupils who need additional help, either to catch up with the majority or to 'maintain their speedier progress' (DES/WO, 1988a, para 103). Past experience with disciplinary conflicts and pupil selection (to different streams/bands and even referrals to separate ESN schools – see chapter 2 and Tomlinson, 1981) suggests that particular attention should be paid to identifying quickly any association between ethnicity and pupils' experience of such differentiation. Otherwise selective judgements which disadvantage ethnic minorities (especially Afro-Caribbean pupils) might become institutionalized and so stay with pupils throughout their school careers.[11]

Many writers have commented on the total absence of multicultural issues from the government's curricular blueprint: Gillian Klein described it as 'monocultural ... narrow, elitist and nationalistic' (Klein, 1988b, p. 3). The Commission for Racial Equality (CRE) emphasized its extreme disappointment 'that the consultation document makes no mention of the need for a curriculum that reflects the multicultural nature of British society.' The CRE went on:

> If the pluralist nature of our national culture is not reflected in the criteria for curriculum selection we cannot see how the proposed national curriculum will be able to achieve its stated objective 'to develop the potential of all pupils and equip them for citizenship'. (quoted in Haviland, 1988, p. 48)

More detail of the national curriculum has slowly emerged as separate elements are designed and put in place. There are, however, still large areas of uncertainty. In addition, the available information is sometimes inconsistent. In 1989, for example, a DES guide to the national curriculum listed 'multicultural issues' as a 'cross-curricular theme' (DES, 1989a, para 3.8). Later in the same year the National Curriculum Council (NCC) issued a circular concerning 'Whole Curriculum Planning' which introduced a three-way distinction between cross-curricular 'dimensions', 'skills' and 'themes' (NCC, 1989d). Multicultural issues were now redefined as a cross-curricular 'dimension':

Cross curricular dimensions

These are concerned with the intentional promotion of personal and social development ... Whilst secondary schools may offer courses of personal and social education, it is the responsibility of all teachers and is equally important in all phases of education.

Major cross-curricular dimensions ... include equal opportunities, and education for life in a multicultural society. They require the development of positive attitudes in all staff and pupils towards cultural diversity, gender equality and people with disabilities. (NCC, 1989d, para 9–11).

At first sight this description looks quite promising; for example, the requirement that all staff and pupils should develop 'positive attitudes' towards cultural diversity could potentially be used to help schools develop anti-racist initiatives across the entire curriculum. Unfortunately, there is very little mention of cultural diversity in the statutory requirements and non-statutory guidance which the DES and NCC have set out for the three core subjects (DES/WO, 1989a, b, c; NCC, 1989a, b, c). This is a crucial omission: as teachers struggle to meet the requirements of the national curriculum and the SATs, it is the subject specific details (such as attainment targets and programmes of study) which seem likely to command most attention.

Cross-curricular 'skills' (such as communication skills, problem-solving and study skills) and cross-curricular 'themes' (like economic and industrial understanding, environmental

169

education and health education) are built into several of the statutory attainment targets. For example, every science attainment target includes reference to communication skills (cf. NCC, 1989b, p. A3). In direct contrast, only one science attainment target (AT17) refers to 'a different culture'. Worse still, the only mention of 'an interesting multicultural element' in the non-statutory guidance for science teachers refers to role play concerning the best type of power station to build in 'a Third World country' (NCC, 1989b, p. F3). This seems likely to reinforce the worse kind of narrow multiculturalism, equating multicultural issues with notions of far-off 'Third World' ('underdeveloped') countries.

In fact, there is plenty of opportunity for committed teachers to use anti-racist strategies as they cover the national curriculum attainment targets. In science, for instance, material focusing on the differences between individuals could be used to explode the racist myths concerning links between pheno-typical differences and supposed differences in intellect (cf. Gill and Levidow, 1987). Such work would challenge common racist stereotypes and help cover several science attainment targets (such as those concerning experimentation, advances in knowledge of DNA and the social and ethical context of science). Yet such possibilities are not highlighted in the NCC's non-statutory guidance. This means that the historical pattern of multicultural and anti-racist provision in Britain, as a locally defined and largely unco-ordinated aspect of the curriculum, seems likely to continue.

Unlike the foundation subjects, cross-curricular issues are not subject to statutory control, so individual schools and authorities may decide that the issues central to 'education for all' are irrelevant to their needs. Once again it has fallen to individual teachers and education authorities to ensure that schools positively address the complex issues raised by the ethnic diversity of our society. Unfortunately, the legal status of the national curriculum ensures that the government's views and values are placed at the heart of the curriculum. Judging by the views of the reform's architect, the outlook is rather bleak:

> there is evidence of little more than a token nod towards the exhortation from Swann by the [then] incumbent of the office of Secretary of State for Education, whose public

utterances have asserted the importance of English (*pace* Wales) traditions, English history, English literature, English culture, and standard English: Baker, 1986, 1989. (Kimberley, 1989, p. 238)

The pattern of ethnocentrism continued when John MacGregor (Baker's successor) told the history working group 'to reconsider its recommendation that less than 50 per cent of the history curriculum in secondary schools should be devoted to British history' (*Times Educational Supplement*, 11 August 1989).

Conclusions

The voices of ethnic minority communities were finally acknowledged when the then Labour government established the Committee of Inquiry into the Education of Children from Ethnic Minority Groups. The committee recognized the failures of past policies and acknowledged the racist nature of the assimilationist and integrationist perspectives which had labelled minority groups as a problem while seeking to protect the status quo. The committee tried to build on the good practice of multicultural and anti-racist approaches and, despite bitter disputes within its ranks and widespread criticism from both sides of the political arena, produced a useful policy agenda ('education for all') which potentially offered a starting point for important curricular and pedagogical changes. Unfortunately, even that policy was almost totally absent from the current government's recent 'reform' of the educational system.

The status of multicultural issues as a cross-curricular dimension in the national curriculum may have a variety of consequences. In those local authorities and schools which have already begun seriously to consider their work in a multi-ethnic context, the models of good practice (considered above) may be taken up and developed further. In other schools and authorities, especially where there are few or no ethnic minority pupils, curricula may continue to reflect and reinforce the crude 'racial' stereotypes and ignorance of ethnic diversity which characterize too much of the educational experience in the UK. These problems are considered further in the next chapter, which concentrates on language issues – an area of the curriculum which has generated considerable debate in relation to the ethnic diversity of the pupil population.

Chapter 7

Language issues

English as a second language, bidialectism and the mother tongue debate

Even if it is accepted that the overriding task of the school is to ensure that children become literate in standard English, then for English bidialectical pupils the learning of literacy in English, and for bilingual pupils the learning of oracy and literacy in English, need to start from a recognition of the social and linguistic contribution that their existing linguistic skills might make to their overall educational development. (Linguistic Minorities Project, 1983, pp. 11–12)

The identification of language as an educational issue

Although remarkably few people seem aware of it, Britain has always been home to people of many different ethnic origins and cultural traditions (Jeffcoate, 1984; Tierney, 1982b). In the late 1950s and the 1960s, however, the emigration to Britain of peoples from Pakistan and the New Commonwealth was seen to raise a 'new' issue for the educational system and the diversity of pupils' language was identified as a problem to which the system had somehow to respond. Too often teachers and policy-makers have assumed that language differences are synonymous with language deficiency, a view which has led many to devalue and reject non-standard English languages and those who use them.[1]

Over recent years much has been written in this field, although some would argue that relatively little has actually changed. Pupils of both South Asian and Afro-Caribbean ethnic origin have been identified as facing linguistic 'problems', although the complexity and seriousness of the issues continue to be hotly contested.

Building on the work of Derrick (1968, 1973), Cohen and Manion (1983) have argued that the identification and treatment of Asian pupils' language needs is much easier than for their Afro-Caribbean peers.

> In the case of the former, the position is relatively clear-cut in that the concern is to develop *bi-lingualism*, the ability to achieve some command over English as well as retaining skills in the original native language, an aim that can be achieved through the policy of extraction during normal school lessons and the setting up of special centres for the purpose. What complicates the language issue for the West Indian pupils is that they already speak a variety of English, though not the standard form. The need for them is to develop skills in *bidialectism*, a challenge greater for both pupils and teachers than that presented by bilingualism. (Cohen and Manion, 1983, p. 205; emphasis added)

The distinction between the goals of bilingualism (for South Asian pupils) and bidialectism (for Afro-Caribbeans) is an important one, but Cohen and Manion seriously underestimate the size and complexity of the task facing pupils, parents and schools where English is not the child's first language (also known as the mother tongue). Separate language centres and 'extraction during normal lessons', for example, have been heavily criticized (see below).

In this chapter I consider some of the most important work in this area; in particular, I concentrate on issues in the teaching of English as a second language, the language needs of Afro-Caribbean pupils and the debate concerning mother tongue teaching. As the chapter will demonstrate, there is little that is simple or 'clear-cut'.

English as a second language

The teaching of English as a second language (sometimes referred to as ESL or E2L) was the first area of education seriously to attempt any response to the presence of ethnic minority children. During the 1960s the dominant assimilationist perspective led policy-makers and many educationists to seek ways of helping South Asian pupils learn English so as to become quickly integrated into the existing system of educational provision. As Sally Tomlinson (1983) has noted, a great deal of research was sponsored in this field and, among a varied range, some excellent materials were produced, perhaps most notably through the Schools Council's *Scope* programme (Schools Council 1969, 1971, 1976).

In many ways the teaching of English as a second language appeared to be a natural or automatic response, based on the assumption that Asian pupils must learn English in order to participate in the English educational system. Indeed, the quotation from Cohen and Manion above illustrates the often taken-for-granted 'logic' of providing special provision for E2L learners in separate classes or centres. As a short-term, transitional measure, separate E2L provision may be a necessary first step for some pupils for whom English is not their first language, but many educationists now agree that we should be moving towards integrated language learning across the curriculum.

Both academics and practitioners have argued that, despite its laudable goals, separate provision might have adverse effects upon the educational opportunities of pupils who are excluded from normal classroom life. Hestor and Wright (1977) stated that an integrated approach involving second language learners in the same classroom as native speakers could use the latter as a motivational device and aid the acquisition of English without excluding pupils from the routine of school life. The Bullock report, *A Language for Life*, was among the first government inquiries to address seriously the educational consequences of a multi-ethnic pupil population. The report recognized the linguistic needs of children 'from families of overseas origin' and argued that 'Common sense would suggest that the best arrangement is usually one where the immigrant children are not cut off from the social and educational life of a normal school' (Bullock, 1975, p. 289). Furthermore, the Committee of Inquiry stressed the need for 'linguistic help right across the curriculum', not merely in particular subject areas (Bullock, 1975, p. 291).

It is difficult to get a full picture of current E2L provision in this country. Little and Willey (1981) reported the findings of two national surveys, the first involving all local education authorities in England and Wales, the second a sample of secondary schools in areas where there are ethnic minority pupils, in varying concentrations. The surveys revealed that despite some authorities' now considerable experience of meeting language needs the bulk of resources were still concentrated on the teaching of basic skills; even in secondary schools little or no work was happening in the more advanced areas of language learning and use.

> There is wide agreement among those responsible for E2L teaching that current provision for the more advanced stages of language work and for teaching specialist subject languages – *which are seen as being of crucial importance to academic achievement* – is inadequate ... At present the E2L resources of many authorities are almost wholly taken up in meeting 'first phase' needs ... and many teachers working in secondary schools, theoretically with responsibilities for the ·more advanced aspects of E2L, often find themselves in practice having to cope with basic 'first phase' needs. (Little and Willey, 1981, p. 17; emphasis added).

The Swann committee generally endorsed Bullock's views on the importance of language across the curriculum. The committee listed a number of damning criticisms of separate E2L provision, including the limited and sometimes disjointed curricula which pupils experience; the negative effect on the learning of English which exclusive contact with other E2L pupils might cause, and the low status of E2L work and consequent lack of interest from mainstream teachers (Swann, 1985, pp. 391–2). In fact, the Swann report went further than Bullock by declaring that the logic behind separate E2L provision in language centres was 'an example of institutional racism which, whilst not originally discriminatory in *intent*, is discriminatory in *effect* in that it denies an individual child access to the full range of educational opportunities available' (Swann, 1985, p. 389; original emphasis). The committee recommended that all secondary schoolteachers should see E2L as part of their responsibility, possibly using specialist teachers as a resource in co-operative and team-teaching approaches (Swann, 1985, pp. 394–5).

In common with most of the committee's recommendations, these views seem largely to have been ignored. In fact, the lack of additional resources and the imposition of the national curriculum (see below) may have had the effect of reinforcing specialist subject boundaries so that little or no general progress has been made in this area since the Swann committee reported.

Afro-Caribbean pupils and bidialectism

In contrast to pupils of South Asian ethnic origin, it was some time before the linguistic needs of Afro-Caribbean pupils were recognized as in any way different to those of the majority 'white' pupil population. During the 1970s, however, there was increasing concern with the consequences of Afro-Caribbean 'dialect', and like so many issues in this field, the central questions have aroused considerable argument and continue to engage teachers in many multi-ethnic schools.

Creole: its forms and uses

The term Creole had been used in a variety of ways to denote differences in ethnicity and in the origin and development of language, music and culture (cf. Cashmore, 1988). Monica Taylor (1983) states that Creole simply means 'locally born' or 'things, habits, ideas, native to the West Indies'. In the field of linguistics the term has been used to describe a dialect form of standard English (there are also French-based Creoles) which is spoken by the majority of Caribbean islanders. This form of speech is sometimes referred to by its speakers as 'patois' or 'dialect' (cf. Edwards, 1979, p. 16).[2] In fact, there has been disagreement as to whether Creole should be thought of as a separate language rather than as a dialect of English – especially where the word 'dialect' might be taken as signifying inferior status in relation to the 'standard' form.

In terms of its systems of meaning, rules of grammar and capacity as a medium of communication, Creole has all the characteristics of a fully developed language (Labov, 1969, 1972; Edwards, 1979). Creole is not a slang, or a lazy or broken form of English; it is a language of consistent rules and meanings in which people can achieve differing degrees of competence (cf. Edwards, 1986, pp. 94–5). However, the question as to whether Creole should be regarded as a language or dialect is essentially a political (rather than linguistic) matter (Edwards, 1979, p. 20).[3] The issue is complicated by the differing (sometimes conflicting) concerns of particular interest groups; some of the strongest critics of moves to accord Creole greater status, for example, have been Afro-Caribbean parents. Government spokespeople and the DES have continually reaffirmed the dominant status to be accorded standard English in state-maintained schools. The national curriculum English working group stated that 'Although Standard English can be analysed as a dialect, this does not mean that it should be regarded as just one among many. Standard English is dialect of a special kind' (DES/WO, 1989a, para 4.11).

Creole has its roots in the 'pidgin' English developed by slaves whose original tribal languages were systematically eroded by the slave trade (cf. Genovese, 1972). It is a dynamic language which has developed over more than three centuries in complex ways which reflect many different influences. Viv Edwards has described the linguistic situation in the West Indies in terms of a continuum bounded by broad Creole and standard English where 'Each speaker will command a span of the continuum rather than simply occupying a point on it' (Edwards, 1979, p. 16). Each speaker's general position is likely to reflect specific characteristics related to social class and regional differences. In this way, 'Rural, working-class speakers will be nearer the Creole end of the continuum than urban, middle-class speakers' (Edwards, 1979, p. 16). In addition, the different colonial histories of the Caribbean islands are reflected in each island's particular Creole dialect; hence in Barbados there was a relatively high proportion of Europeans and so there the Creole is considerably closer to standard English than is the case in Jamaica, where there were much fewer Europeans (Taylor, 1983, p. 69; after Evans and Le Page, 1967).

In addition, the strength of dialect in individuals' speech has been noted to vary with the degree of formality of different occasions. Both Sutcliffe (1982) and Edwards (1986), for example, have recorded greater use of Creole/patois during informal gatherings of students rather than in formal inter-actions with teachers.

Just as Creole in the West Indies has developed and changed, so have the dialect forms used by Afro-Caribbeans in this country; Sally Tomlinson has noted that the Caribbean Creoles used in British inner-cities have continued to change and adapt, reflecting the importance of language 'as part of a cultural identity' (Tomlinson, 1983, p. 111).[4] This is a particularly important point in relation to teacher–pupil relationships, and one to which I shall return later in this chapter.

The extent of creole bidialectism

The first real attempt to chart the extent of dialect-speaking in British schools was undertaken by members of the University of London Institute of Education who reported that of 4,600 children in twenty-eight London secondary schools, 15 per cent (N=712) used an overseas dialect of English, predominantly some form of Jamaican-derived Creole (Rosen and Burgess, 1980, p. 57). As Monica Taylor has noted, the research was also of importance because it highlighted the sheer diversity of languages spoken by London school pupils (fifty-five languages and twenty-four dialects) and pointed to the fluid, changing nature of language. The situation was particularly complex because of the interaction of London and Jamaican language continua:

> The dialect typically spoken was found to be London/Jamaican not Jamaican Creole, but in any one speech there could be a tremendous diversity depending on the interaction of a West Indian element derived from any part of the Creole continuum and a London element from any part of the London continuum. (Taylor, 1983, pp. 71–2)

Recent work by Viv Edwards (1986, pp. 121–2) and Roger Hewitt (1986, pp. 126–49) has further highlighted the dynamic qualities of language use where Creole words, phrases and patterns of speech have been adopted (sometimes unconsciously) by white youths. The work of Edwards and Hewitt shows the very widespread use of Creole among youths in certain inner-city areas; to date, however, the most significant attempt to chart the extent of bidialectism/bilingualism in England remains the work of the Linguistic Minorities Project (LMP).

The Linguistic Minorities Project (LMP, 1983, 1985) carried out extensive surveys of pupils between the ages of five and sixteen in five LEAs. In two of the LEAs Creole speakers accounted for a significant proportion of the bilingual pupils surveyed: 9 per cent in Haringey and 7 per cent in Waltham Forest. The LMP survey instruments, however, were explicitly aimed at measuring bilingualism, and the true incidence of bidialectism may have been somewhat underestimated by the teachers who responded. There is, therefore, no accurate measure of the extent of Creole bidialectism among all English schoolchildren. The survey results reported by Rosen and Burgess (of twenty-eight London secondary schools) and the LMP (of bilingual primary and secondary pupils in five LEAs) offer only a brief snapshot of the situation in particular areas. On the other hand, their work clearly demonstrates the diversity of languages used by British school pupils and highlights something of the linguistic complexities of teaching in multi-ethnic areas.

Creole as a 'problem': interference and identity

During the 1970s, amid growing concern over 'the West Indian language issue', a great deal of attention focused on the concept of linguistic interference, arising from the anxiety that the grammatical structures, meanings and sounds of the different languages (Creole and standard English) might become confused, leading to a lack of understanding and poor performance in spoken and written English. Viv Edwards (1979, pp. 60–81) has described in some detail the different areas where interference may occur and quoted the following description of a West Indian girl's feelings during a schools broadcast on moths:

'The teacher thought I was thick, but I didn't know what a moth was. If she had said butterfly or something it would have been different.' Consequently, she only understood a word here and there in that lesson – 'the sound was pouring over my ears but I couldn't catch the sense of it'. (*Observer Magazine*, 16 December 1973, quoted by Edwards, 1979, p. 61)

The girl quoted above had recently arrived from St Kitts, a factor which clearly influenced her lack of understanding of a word she had simply not heard before. A more recent study by Ashton Gibson (1986) has also stressed the role of language as a barrier for young 'Westindians'. The testimony of some of Gibson's interviewees is particularly revealing; the following quotation is from a twenty-year-old Jamaican woman:

> I came to Britain at the age of eight ... At the first school I
> went to in Britain I was placed in the lowest stream of my
> age group. I was really above the rest of my class, but I just
> could not talk to my teacher. I wanted to let her know that I
> had read *Janet and John* books before, that I knew them
> backwards. I can remember trying to say this to her and
> being told: "Please speak English". This made the other
> children laugh at me, which was very embarrassing ... I
> always had the greatest difficulty understanding the teachers.
> When I asked them to repeat something I was told that I
> should pay more attention. I *had* been paying attention, but
> could not follow what was being said. (Gibson, 1986,
> pp. 37–8; original emphasis)

Although several researchers have pointed to the important
effects of interference (cf. Cheshire, 1982), the Rampton/Swann
Committee's interim report stated that 'we do not believe that
for the majority of West Indian children in our schools, who
were born and brought up in this country, linguistic factors
play a part in underachievement' (Rampton, 1981, p. 25). The
Committee's final report stood by its earlier findings and
restated their view that where language might be causing
problems for Afro-Caribbean pupils it could be remedied via
more sensitive approaches by teachers who recognize the value
of other languages and try to build on the linguistic skills which
all pupils bring to the school – the 'repertoire' approach
(Rampton, 1981, pp. 24–5; Swann, 1985, pp. 421–2).

The concept of interference is only one part of a complex
interaction of factors which might relate Afro-Caribbean
language to pupils' achievements. Both the Rampton and Swann
reports noted the damaging effects which teachers' criticisms
of their speech could have upon 'West Indian' pupils. The
quote above from Gibson's book reflects the importance of
teachers as agents who can embarrass and effectively exclude
pupils from the learning process. This reflects the importance
of language as a symbol of individual and ethnic identity:
'Creole remains a symbol of West Indian identity; it defines
their membership of a particular group with particular values
and is the vehicle of their culture. As such it is cherished and
respected' (Edwards, 1979, p. 49). Little wonder, therefore, that

depreciation and ridicule of the language can amount to the depreciation and ridicule of the person, family and culture. The following quotation – from Leonie, a young Afro-Caribbean woman studying at an English sixth-form college – gives some impression of the hurt and anger which can be caused:

> It's the fact that they made you reject yer own way of talking. That really got me. It was rejecting another part of you, being black you know, being part of you. Like the teacher at junior school got mad when I said, wha instead of pardon and all that and I found out that if you did not want to be laughed at, the best way to keep in the background was to try and speak the best English I could. So, I learnt to stop saying things like filim and all that business, coz when I was in junior school and the teacher asked, what did you do at the week-end? I stood up and said, well, I went to see a filim and the whole class started laughing. I felt so bad inside, you can't understand. I mean the teacher laughing as well. I mean they're laughing at me, they're laughing at my parents, they're laughing at everything associated with Patois, with everything black. (quoted in Mac an Ghaill, 1988, p. 29)

This quotation is also of importance because of Leonie's statement that she 'learnt' to change her language in school. This is a crucial point. I have already noted that language is a dynamic medium which fulfils a powerful affective role as well as performing a technical function in relation to the communication of meanings and thoughts. I noted in chapter 3 that Paul Dixon (the highest achieving Afro-Caribbean male in City Road) did not emphasize his ethnicity through displays in his dress or demeanour (including language), a factor which undoubtedly helped to avoid further clashes with teachers (see also Gabriel, 1986, p. 342). Studies have shown that language can be a powerful means of exclusion, sometimes leading to very serious teacher–pupil conflict. Mac an Ghaill (1988), for example, has described male 'anti-school' groups of Afro-Caribbean and Asian pupils which both used language as a weapon in their battles with staff; the effectiveness (and danger) of such strategies is clear from one of Cecile Wright's interviews with a white deputy headteacher:

> We've got a problem at the moment, which is very nasty ...

we are being faced with a barrage of Patois. It is so worrying because you see when that happens we as teachers have a choice. We either ignore it, but if it's done in public you feel threatened, or you feel that you are showing weakness if you just ignore it. You can either react equally aggressively and verbally back in Spanish, or French, which in fact is what is happening, but that is not helpful, or as one member of staff said to me today, 'I came very close to clobbering him today'. (Wright, 1985a, p. 13)

Clearly, when they are on the receiving end, teachers can also experience some of the powerful feelings of anger and rejection which linguistic exclusion can engender in pupils! It is important to emphasize once again, however, that use of Creole should not be assumed to signify any deliberate challenge or rejection. Language is a powerful expression of ethnicity; to interpret a pupil's pride in his or her ethnic identity as a challenge to (white) authority is exactly the kind of ethnocentric reasoning which lay behind so much teacher–pupil conflict in City Road (see chapter 2).

The bidialectism of many Afro-Caribbean pupils need not be a 'problem', yet the Swann Committee's hope that more teachers would be trained to recognize its effects (in terms of possible interference) and to respond to it positively as a resource (rather than as a sign of deficit or threat) has so far not been realized. Indeed, Mac an Ghaill (1988) has suggested that even where notions of valuing Creole became a central part of some 'liberal' teachers' ideology, the uneven application of the school's language policy (centered on low ability streams) acted to reinforce the staff's already negative view of all Afro-Caribbean students (Mac an Ghaill, 1988, p. 56) – an observation which highlights the complexity of multicultural/anti-racist issues and the need for critical reflection among all staff when considering such issues.

The mother tongue debate

The bilingualism of thousands of British children is a liability in their lives and not because there is something inherently wrong in the nature of bilingualism, but purely because of society's attitude to and treatment of bilinguals within our education system. (Arora, 1988, p. 21)

Since the mid 1970s there has been increasing concern with various issues centred upon the role of, and educational status which should be accorded to, a child's mother tongue – defined chronologically as the first language which a child speaks (Brook, 1980).

The extent and nature of bilingualism in England

Many British-born pupils join the educational system with some command of English in addition to a different mother tongue which they have learnt at home (others join with little or no English; see above). Some pupils, especially those of South Asian ethnic origin, go through the educational system with a good command of two or even three languages: the standard English of the school, the spoken language of the home and community, and sometimes an additional community language in which they are literate.

There is no totally reliable figure on the extent of bilingualism in this country, neither within the population as a whole nor in relation to all children of school age. The national curriculum English working group stated that 'On the basis of the limited evidence available some 5% of all schools in England are likely to have a significant population of children for whom English is not their mother tongue' (DES/WO, 1989a, para 10.3). Between 1982 and 1984 a survey of pupils in multi-ethnic comprehensives in four LEAs revealed that 'Just over a quarter of the study children (27 per cent) reported speaking one or more community languages in addition to English' (Smith and Tomlinson, 1989, p. 92). Because the project specifically targeted multi-ethnic schools this figure is not, of course, representative of most urban secondary school populations in Britain. Perhaps the most important finding to emerge from the survey was that 'The great majority of South Asian children (85 per cent) were bilingual to some degree' (Smith and Tomlinson, 1989, p. 92).

The interaction of a variety of different factors will influence the particular pattern of language use in any one area; region, religion, national identity and the formality or nature of particular occasions are all likely to be reflected in the languages which are spoken and written in the community – where the latter (the language of literacy) is not always the same as the former. The Linguistic Minorities Project, for example, has summarized some of the main distinctions concerning families with their roots in Punjab as follows:

> most families in England with origins in the Panjab, whether in India or Pakistan, and whether they are Muslim, Sikh or Hindu by religion, will use spoken forms of Panjabi which are likely to be mutually intelligible. However, it would be desirable to distinguish the groups for purposes of language education planning: the Muslim, Sikh and Hindu communities would normally expect tuition in their distinct languages of literacy, e.g. Panjabi in the Gurmukhi script for the Sikh communities, Panjabi in the Gurmukhi script or Hindi for the Hindu communities from the Indian part of Panjab and Urdu for the Muslim community from the Pakistani part of Panjab. (LMP, 1983, p. 41)

This quotation highlights a further complicating factor in the mother tongue debate, which is that although pupils from different South Asian backgrounds (attending the same school) may speak 'mutually intelligible' community languages, their parents might wish them to receive formal instruction in different languages of literacy.

When policy-makers speak about the problems of implementing state-maintained mother tongue provision they frequently draw attention to the diversity of community languages in this country and argue that it would simply be impossible to resource instruction in so many different languages. It is in this area that the work of the Linguistic Minorities Project (1983, 1985) is perhaps most important.

The Linguistic Minorities Project was a DES-sponsored research programme which was designed primarily to survey the extent of bilingualism in England, both in schools and among adults. The research team developed and used a variety of survey instruments. I shall concentrate on the Schools Language Survey (SLS) which was devised to measure the use of languages other than English by pupils in five LEAs. Of the LMP's surveys this one had the largest sample and was the only survey which consistently included Creole as one of the languages to be researched (LMP, 1983, p. 32).

The survey was administered by teachers who asked pupils individually: 'Do you yourself ever speak any language at home apart from English?' Where pupils indicated that they did, teachers were asked to pose the further questions: 'What is the name of that language?'; 'Can you read that language?', and 'Can you write that language?' The teachers were given guidance on the names of the most common languages and some indication of possible problems where pupils might offer a region's name rather than the name of the language itself (LMP, 1983, pp. 35–8). The survey's main findings are reproduced in Tables 7.1 and 7.2.

Table 7.1 details data gathered between November 1980 and November 1981, covering pupils between the ages of five and sixteen. Of the five LEAs surveyed, the largest proportion of 'bilingual pupils' (those speaking at least one language at home other than English) was 30.7 per cent (Haringey); the smallest was 7.4 per cent (the Peterborough division of Cambridgeshire). Table 7.2 shows these details broken down in terms of the main languages which were reported in the five LEAs.

The most important finding to emerge from the survey concerned the significance of the main South Asian languages, which suggests that linguistic diversity does not necessarily argue against positive moves to support the learning of certain ethnic minority languages. Table 7.2, for example, confirms the massive diversity of different languages which were spoken by the pupils at home; the smallest number was forty-two different

Table 7.1 Proportions of bilingual pupils in five LEAs

	Bradford	Coventry	Haringey	Peterbor'	Waltham Forest
Age range surveyed	6–16	6–16	5–15	5–16	6–16
(A) Total number of pupils surveyed	79,758	49,990	24,140	32,662	29,379
(B) Total number of 'bilingual' pupils	14,201	7,189	7,407	2,408	5,521
(B) as a % of (A)	17.8%	14.4%	30.7%	7.4%	18.8%

Note: 'Bilingual' pupils were those who indicated to their teacher that they spoke at least one language at home other than English (see LMP, 1983, p. 42). *Source:* Adapted from LMP, 1983, Table 2.1, p. 43.

languages (Peterborough), the largest was eighty-seven (Haringey). Such diversity is often used as a reason why mother tongue provision cannot be guaranteed and thus becomes a rationale for minimalist efforts. Yet the LMP data show that taking only the three most common minority languages in each district would account for more than half the bilingual pupils. Even in Haringey (where the greatest number of distinct

Table 7.2 Main languages reported in five LEAs

	Bradford	Coventry	Haringey	Peterbor'	Waltham Forest
(A) Total number of 'bilingual' pupils*	14,201	7,189	7,407	2,408	5,521
(B) Total number of identifiably distinct languages reported	64	50	87	42	65
The 6 most frequently spoken languages or language groupings as a % of (A) to the nearest whole number	Panjabi (53%)	Panjabi (59%)	Greek (34%)	Panjabi (24%)	Panjabi (31%)
	Urdu (19%)	Gujerati (16%)	Turkish (15%)	Italian (24%)	Urdu (21%)
	Gujerati (9%)	Urdu (7%)	**Creoles (9%)	Urdu (18%)	Gujerati (8%)
	Bengali (3%)	Hindi (3%)	Gujerati (6%)	Gujerati (12%)	Greek (8%)
	Pushtu (3%)	Italian (2%)	Italian (6%)	Chinese (4%)	Creoles (7%)
	Italian (3%)	Bengali (2%)	French-based Creoles (4%)	Polish (2%)	Turkish (4%)

* 'Bilingual' pupils were those who indicated to their teacher that they spoke at least one language at home other than English (see LMP, 1983, p. 42).
** 'Creoles' here means English-based and other non-French-based Creole languages.
Source: Adapted from LMP, 1983, Table 2.2, p. 44.

languages were reported) the three most common minority languages account for 58 per cent of all the bilingual pupils; in Coventry and Bradford the figure is more than 80 per cent.

On the basis of this information the project authors concluded:

> What this suggests from the point of view of potential educational support for minority languages is that the kind of objection which is based on the logistical problems arising from extremely large numbers of different languages in particular areas has only limited force. Some LEAs are already showing how a considerable impact can be made by beginning with support for the most widespread three or four languages in an area, before going on to tackle, probably on a more centralised basis, the languages with fewer and more scattered speakers. (LMP, 1983, p. 45)

As this quotation suggests, some schools and LEAs are taking action to support community languages in their areas; at a national level, however, there has been confusion and a great deal of disagreement over attempts to clarify the role of community languages in state-maintained schools. In the following sections I consider the debates concerning two aspects of the wider mother tongue issue; first, the appropriateness of community languages as a medium for educational instruction for part of the school day or week (sometimes referred to as bilingual education or mother tongue maintenance); second, the place of community languages in the modern language curriculum.

The role of state-maintained schools in supporting and developing mother tongue skills

The exceptional strength of feeling which surrounds the debates over mother tongue provision was acknowledged by the Swann committee (Swann, 1985, p. 397); these debates have been complicated by disagreements over the legal status of mother tongue provision following a European Council Directive concerning the education of children of migrant workers. The directive was part of a package of measures designed to improve freedom of movement for workers within member states of the European Community, it stated that:

in order to permit the integration of such children into the educational environment and the school system of the host State, they should be able to receive suitable tuition including teaching of the language of the host state.

... host Member States should also take, in conjunction with the Member States of origin, appropriate measures to promote the teaching of the mother tongue and of the culture of the country of origin of the above mentioned children, with a view principally to facilitating their possible reintegration into the Member State of origin. (European Council Directive 77/486/EEC, 1977)

Pressure groups have argued that the spirit of the EC Directive supports their case that state schools have a role to play in the teaching of South Asian mother tongues and culture. The DES, however, has consistently stated that the directive only requires EC member states to 'promote' mother tongue teaching and it does not accord a right to such provision. Furthermore, the DES has interpreted the directive in a way which excludes the vast majority of ethnic minority pupils in this country. DES Circular 5/81 stated that: 'the Directive and accompanying agreement do not address themselves to the position of children whose parents are UK nationals with family origins in other countries' (DES, 1981, quoted in Swann, 1985, p. 402). The Swann committee concluded that 'Mother tongue provision cannot be justified simply by the provisions of the EC Directive' and went on to argue that the case for any such provision should be made on the basis of its merits 'in view of the multi-lingual pupil population in many of our schools' (Swann, 1985, p. 402). Many have argued that the case for such provision is very strong indeed. It has been stated, for example, that mother tongue maintenance in state schools would benefit ethnic minority pupils both directly, through increased confidence and knowledge of their parents' culture, and indirectly, by raising the standing of the communities themselves. This returns us to the important links between language and (personal/group) identity which I have already noted in relation to the language needs of Afro-Caribbean pupils (above). As the LMP authors have argued, 'If children or their parents interpret the process of schooling as an attempt to undermine or challenge such a personal and significant part of their existence, this will affect their interest and involvement too' (LMP, 1983, p. 12).

One argument which has been put against mother tongue teaching is that it might interfere with pupils' acquisition of standard English. As Ranjit Arora has observed, such a policy means that no positive use is made of the child's existing language skills and fails to recognize that the 'learning of a second language can only be successfully attempted if there is a firm linguistic base in the child's first language' (Arora, 1988, p. 22). Twitchin and Demuth (1981) have pointed to the small-scale experiments in mother tongue teaching which have been carried out in Bradford (with infant pupils) and Bedford (with primary pupils). In addition to greater confidence and skill in their mother tongue, the pupils who had received mother tongue instruction showed better understanding and use of standard English than their ethnic minority peers who had not received mother tongue tuition. 'One interpretation of these results is that linguistic and conceptual growth in the mother-tongue naturally fosters second language learning' (Twitchin and Demuth, 1981, p. 135).

Unfortunately, the Swann Committee remained unconvinced of the benefits of using community languages as the medium of instruction for part of the pupils' experience of mainstream education:

> the key to equality of opportunity, to academic success and, more broadly, to participation on equal terms as a full member of society, is good command of *English* and the emphasis must therefore we feel be on the learning of English. We find the research evidence that the learning of English can be assisted by bilingual education or mother tongue maintenance, unconvincing, since in many instances the most that can be claimed from particular projects is that the child's learning of English is not impaired and *may* in some respects be enhanced. (Swann, 1985, p. 407; original emphasis)

The Swann report recommended that ethnic minority communities should continue to shoulder the responsibility for the maintenance of community languages. Although schools and LEAs were encouraged to give what support they could, for instance, by allowing access to their buildings, Swann advised that priority should be given to the teaching of English. Despite the Swann report's rejection of mother tongue maintenance, however, some LEAs and schools are devoting considerable time and energy to supporting and valuing the community languages which are represented in their pupil populations.

The Elton report, *Discipline in Schools*, recognized the importance of good home–school links and stressed the need to make communications available in community languages as well as in English (Elton, 1989, pp. 128–9). Some schools have already adopted this practice as part of their strategy to encourage the greater involvement of ethnic minority parents; in addition, some have realized the important role which bilingual pupils can play in facilitating greater understanding between school and home. The following quotation is from a deputy headteacher of twenty-one years' teaching experience, sixteen of them in his current school (an inner-city comprehensive where more than 90 per cent of the pupils were of South Asian ethnic origin):

English is not the first language for many of our parents. One of the things we try and do is work via the children to try and give their parents more confidence. A couple of 'for instances'; always on reception we have children who are the first people to greet visitors to the school. The make-up of the school suggests that one of the people, if not *both* the people on reception, will be able to speak community languages – Punjabi or Urdu or Bengali. That immediately means that if mum comes up – who may have very little English – mum can talk to someone in her own language, in the language where she knows she will be understood and she will get some assistance. On parents' evenings, all our paperwork we send out is sent out in community languages and again we have young people who will assist the adults as soon as they come in. (quoted in Gillborn, Nixon and Rudduck, 1989, pp. 273–4)

In the school described above, the staff sought to demonstrate their recognition of the positive value of the local community languages through a variety of strategies. In addition to a modest library of books written in different languages, the school's entrance and corridors were signposted using each of the languages represented in the pupil population. I visited the school as part of a research project for the Elton committee and interviewed several staff, of both sexes, differing subject specialisms and lengths of experience (cf. Gillborn, Nixon and Rudduck, 1989; Gillborn, 1990b). The staff were particularly enthusiastic about the contribution made by ethnic minority teachers and those with some understanding of multicultural/ anti-racist initiatives. The following quotation highlights the simple but important steps which were being taken to emphasize the school's acceptance of community languages:

> We have had a multicultural development teacher, she has been working with us for two years. She has done a lot of work on language. Well, for instance, I have been painting the windows in the [assembly] hall (...) now Helen walked in and said to one of the pupils, 'Could you write that in Urdu?' Now I hadn't thought of saying that to him. So he did and wrote on the window ... So it's those sort of things.

Despite the positive moves which some schools and LEAs are making in this area, nationally the picture is rather depressing. Ranjana Ash, writing in anticipation of the Swann report, highlighted the extremely small numbers of bilingual pupils who were receiving formal instruction in their mother tongues. Data which the UK submitted to the European Community in 1984 indicated that of the '375,000 to 500,000 pupils aged between 5 and 16 whose first language is not English (excluding Welsh and Gaelic speakers)' only 8,300 received any kind of mother tongue instruction 'within the integrated educational system' (that is, between 1.6 and 2.2 per cent). A further 34,700 were receiving some form of mother tongue instruction in classes run by community (voluntary) organiza- tions or embassies (Ash, 1985, p. 22). According to these data, therefore, in 1984 at best only 12 per cent of those five- to sixteen-year olds whose first language was not English were receiving any kind of instruction in their mother tongue. Given the Swann report's rejection of mother tongue maintenance in state schools, there seems little reason to· suppose that the situation has improved since the data were collected.

Community languages and the modern language curriculum

One of the most effective ways of learning a language is

through social interaction in everyday life ... This process of language acquisition is a natural and mainly unconscious process. So, as more monolingual English youngsters have friends who regularly use two or more languages in their daily lives there is a greater chance that they may come to see the naturalness of these social skills. (LMP, 1983, p. 12)

The first report of the Linguistic Minorities Project (LMP, 1983) viewed the presence of bilingual pupils in England as a potential resource for all pupils, including the monolingual majority. The LMP authors argued that pupils should be encouraged to consider South Asian languages in the same terms as other modern languages. If community languages were taught in secondary schools as, say, French, Italian and German are at present, the presence of bilingual and multilingual pupils in the school and community could not only help improve the language skills of all pupils, but also generate greater understanding and respect between the different communities which make up the pupil population.

The everyday reality of multilingual England now is a means to help monolingual English speakers either to learn to communicate in other languages, or at least change negative or indifferent attitudes towards language learning in general and towards minority language speakers in particular. (LMP, 1983, p. 13)

In a policy statement the Commission for Racial Equality has emphasized the importance of ethnic minority languages not as 'foreign languages' but as the 'languages of the various communities in the UK' which should be made available for all children and adults to learn 'and not by virtue of their ethnic background only' (CRE, 1982, p. 11). In addition, several teachers' unions have issued statements in support of community languages; Sally Tomlinson, for example, has quoted from a document published by the National Union of Teachers (NUT) – England's largest teaching union – which stated that 'the Union would wish to see the same status accorded to ethnic minority languages as to other modern European languages' (NUT, 1982, quoted in Tomlinson, 1983, p. 113). Similarly, in a widely praised booklet on multicultural and anti-racist education, the Assistant Masters and Mistresses Association (AMMA) stated that 'all pupils should have the option of studying their mother tongue to examination level' (AMMA, 1987, p. 41).

As in so many areas of multicultural provision, some individual schools and local authorities have taken important steps towards making tuition in community languages available to students up to examination level at sixteen-plus. However, the pattern of provision is very patchy and even where tuition is available, the classes are frequently timetabled on the periphery of the main curriculum as an additional subject to be attended during lunch-breaks or even when the bulk of pupils are in other lessons. For example, a case has been documented where mother tongue work was offered in the same timetable slot as physics and mathematics (Twitchin and Demuth, 1981, p. 138).

Similarly, in City Road Comprehensive tuition in Urdu and Punjabi was offered through the use of LEA peripatetic staff; the lessons were timetabled at the same time as more 'mainstream' subjects and consequently only a handful of pupils (exclusively of South Asian ethnic origin) opted for them. Even limited provision of this kind is very much appreciated and valued by the pupils who attend, but in City Road the lack of resourcing and the peripheral timetabling allocations meant that staff viewed community languages as 'Asian-only' subjects; it was assumed that white and Afro-Caribbean pupils would not be interested. In City Road there was no attempt to highlight the potential benefits for all pupils which might derive from learning a community language – the option was simply not considered, even for those who indicated a desire to work in fields (such as education, health and social work) where such skills might prove particularly valuable.

The Swann Committee of Inquiry added its voice to those calling for greater provision of community languages as part of the modern language curriculum. Despite its rejection of community languages as a medium for instruction (bilingual education and mother tongue maintenance) the committee strongly attacked the 'artificial distinction' which secondary schools often draw between 'modern or foreign languages and ethnic minority community languages'. The committee recommended that ethnic minority community languages should form 'an integral part of the curriculum in secondary schools' (Swann, 1985, p. 409). Swann endorsed the sentiments of the earlier Bullock committee but went further by recommending that highly placed staff in every school (the headteacher at primary level; a deputy head at secondary level) should take on responsibility for co-ordinating language work throughout the school and across the curriculum (Swann, 1985, p. 418). The Swann committee recognized that it would require a significant change in attitudes before all pupils recognized ethnic minority community languages as a legitimate and worthwhile option, but it was convinced of the need for such a change (cf. Swann, 1985, p. 419).

More recently, the PSI/Lancaster study of multi-ethnic comprehensives has added its voice to calls for the teaching of non-European languages. Pupils' responses to questionnaire items on language use indicated that they 'tended to prefer high status languages ... even when they speak some other language better'. The authors concluded that 'One of the most important steps that schools can take towards a multi-cultural education policy is to develop the teaching of Asian languages and literatures within the framework of the National Curriculum' (Smith and Tomlinson, 1989, p. 107).

Ethnic minority community languages and the national curriculum

'Community languages merit equal status to any language.' (Arora, 1984, p. 9)

There was some praise when, in 1987, the government announced proposals to make the learning of a foreign language compulsory for all pupils between the ages of fourteen and sixteen.[5] Although many educationists criticized the national curriculum proposals as simplistic and likely to create a curricular straitjacket (cf. Haviland, 1988), in the modern languages field the proposals were generally welcomed. This was perhaps not surprising given the poor history of second language learning in Britain and, in particular, the tendency for greater numbers of boys to opt out of foreign language courses at the age of fourteen-plus (cf. Powell, 1984; Pratt, Bloomfield and Seale, 1984).

The demands of the national curriculum have prompted increasing concern with national and local provision for foreign language education, including DES moves to increase the supply of language teachers. Superficially, the national curriculum seemed to offer a golden opportunity for government,

LEAs and schools to increase provision for the teaching of ethnic minority community languages, as recommended (before the national curriculum was mooted) by the Swann committee. However, the ethnocentric tone of the reforms was defined in the very first statements of the government's intent; writing about the consultation document, issued in July 1987 (DES/ WO, 1987), Ranjit Arora stated:

> The total absence ... of any reference to community languages, to bilingualism or to the linguistic, racial and cultural diversity of British society is clearly illustrative of its narrow and ethnocentric ideology. (Arora, 1988, p. 22)

Although this omission was duplicated in the Education Reform Act 1988 itself, the government had stressed that there would be some flexibility in the ways in which schools might choose to fulfil the requirements of the national curriculum. Consequently, although the reforms did nothing to improve the situation of ethnic minority languages within the secondary curriculum it appeared that scope remained for schools and LEAs to promote their own policies within this area. Even this hope was threatened by subsequent government statements.

In early 1989 Kenneth Baker, then Secretary of State for Education, introduced a distinction between two groups of languages; the first included the languages of the European Community (such as Danish, Dutch, French, German, Italian and Spanish); the second included non-EC languages (such as Arabic, Bengali, Gujerati, Hindi, Punjabi, Russian and Urdu). All state-maintained secondary schools would be required to offer pupils the opportunity to study at least one language from the first group. Pupils 'may pick a language from the second list ... provided they have been given the option of an EC language'. If carried through into practice such a distinction would mean that by law at least one European language must be on offer to all pupils. Although schools would retain the right also to offer community languages from the second group, the government emphasized that schools would 'have to bear in mind that they should provide enough staff to teach all pupils an EC language' (*Times Educational Supplement*, 10 March 1989).

As Tara Mukherjee (1989) has noted, this distinction effectively defines the Indic languages of many British citizens as second-rate; priority is given to the languages of our

196

European economic 'partners' rather than the established ethnic minority communities which are a vital part of this country's social, economic and cultural make-up.

Regardless of whether Baker's two-part schedule is finally reflected in the prescriptions for modern language teaching under the national curriculum, it certainly seems unlikely that the 'reforms' will do anything to help ensure that (non-EC) community languages attain their rightful place within the mainstream language curriculum of English secondary schools.

Conclusions

Language education is a particularly complex area. In this chapter I have focused on the issues surrounding three principal language concerns: the teaching of English as a second language, the language use of Afro-Caribbean pupils and the debates concerning mother tongue education. A great deal has been written in this area, yet too little has changed within the classroom. E2L provision remains at a basic level, the use of Creole can lead pupils into damaging conflicts with white teachers, and most mother tongue education remains confined to voluntary provision and the periphery of state schools' curricula.

Despite statements by government and DES representatives, who claim to acknowledge and accept the valuable contribution of ethnic minorities, the situation in the field of language education appears particularly bleak. Although research projects repeatedly highlight the diversity and potential reward for all pupils which is offered by community languages; although government reports have emphasized the need for mainstream work on community languages across the curriculum; and despite the apparent opportunities opened up by the increased role of languages in the national curriculum, there seems little realistic hope of significant improvement on a nationwide scale in the foreseeable future.

Chapter 8

'Race' matters

Conclusion

> when a taxidriver said to me recently that 'There wouldn't
> be any racism if people didn't go on about it', he was only
> expressing a widespread view – though not one that I could
> let pass. I replied that racism is like cancer, and that people
> were suffering from it even when no one talked about it.
> More, really, because the shroud of silence inhibited the
> development of treatments. The first step in any cure has to
> be diagnosis – recognition of the condition. (Klein, 1988b,
> p. 3)

As Anselm Strauss (1987, p. 6) has reminded us, 'social
phenomena are complex phenomena'. There is no simple 'cure'
for racism. Indeed, at one level Gillian Klein's analogy between
racism and cancer understates the size of the problem: cancer
involves the *mis*functioning of biological organisms, while
racism is frequently part of the 'normal' routine life of
institutions. In schools, racism is to be found not only in crude
jokes about chocolate factories (Wright, 1986, p. 131), but also
in the basic assumptions which underlie curriculum structures
and content, pedagogical styles and disciplinary codes.

The field of 'race', ethnicity and education is extremely
contentious. As I noted in chapter 1, even the very terminology
of the debates shift and change so that there are few constants
or certainties; labels, analyses and arguments which were once
viewed as progressive, or even radical, can soon be described
as piecemeal or racist. Given the range of issues, and the

198

essentially political nature of many of the problems, it is hardly surprising that many teachers and policy-makers prefer to adopt a 'colour-blind' approach to education – they try to avoid 'racial problems' by simply treating everyone alike.

To some, the 'colour-blind' approach has much to recommend it: it appeals to 'commonsense' notions of justice, requires no change in pedagogy, structures or funding, and carries the weight of the new right who advise teachers to 'Forget about skin colour. Forget about race' (Honeyford, 1989).

One of the themes of this book has been the need to reject 'colour-blind' approaches, not because they clash with any favoured political perspective but rather because evidence gathered in schools and classrooms demonstrates that (whatever we may believe) human beings are far from blind when it comes to questions of ethnicity.

In order to understand the dynamics of the school processes which lie behind the statisticians' arguments about 'underachievement', 'progress' and 'attainment' we must move beyond the school gates and into the classroom. Hence the first part of this book focused on school processes through an examination of previous qualitative research and a detailed analysis of data gathered in a single inner-city comprehensive school. The black community has been critical of both official inquiries and much academic research which has tended to ignore issues at the school level (Troyna, 1986). By examining life in multi-ethnic schools something of the complexity and importance of the issues can be revealed.

Inside multi-ethnic schools

Teachers and pupils

Discipline is a major concern for most schools (cf. Elton, 1989) and has become a particularly important issue in relation to the culturally diverse nature of the pupil population. In chapter 2 I presented a variety of data from City Road Comprehensive which confirmed the findings of previous studies (such as Green, 1985; Wright, 1986; Mac an Ghaill, 1988) that, more than any other ethnic group, Afro-Caribbean pupils tend to experience conflictual relationships with white teachers. Perhaps even more important than the amount of criticism was the nature of the criticism and control to which Afro-Caribbean pupils were subject. Interview data and classroom observation indicated that where pupils of different ethnic groups were involved in identical behaviour, it was the Afro-Caribbeans who were most likely to be criticized. Furthermore, teachers sometimes acted against pupils' sense (and display) of their ethnicity so that certain forms of dress, speech and even ways of walking could lead to teacher–pupil conflict.

Thus conflict between white teachers and Afro-Caribbean pupils was frequently generated by the teachers' ethnocentric interpretation of actions and demeanour which were not a familiar part of their white cultural background and experience. It was not that Afro-Caribbeans simply broke school rules more than other pupils; an examination of the school's detention records revealed that proportionately more Afro-Caribbeans' 'offences' were described in terms of interpretative criteria, where teachers stressed the pupils' 'manner' or presumed intent rather than simply describing a rule which had been broken. This reflected the myth of an Afro-Caribbean challenge which was an important (though largely unspoken) part of staff culture in City Road. The teachers believed that Afro-Caribbean pupils were a likely source of trouble and consequently reacted to any supposed sign of arrogance or challenge which they perceived in the pupils' behaviour. A further consequence of this myth was that if an Afro-Caribbean pupil or parent complained of injustice, staff responded by assuming that the claim was at best mistaken, and at worst a smokescreen meant to draw attention away from a genuine offence.

In effect, therefore, although City Road teachers genuinely believed that 'treating everyone the same' was the best way to handle ethnic diversity (and almost all would strenuously reject crude 'popular' racism), the teachers' actions were racist in their consequences. In City Road Comprehensive Afro-Caribbean pupils were in a situation where their very ethnicity meant that they were likely to experience conflict with white teachers no matter how conscientiously they approached their work. Pupils of South Asian ethnic origin, on the other hand, experienced school quite differently.

Like their Afro-Caribbean peers, the ethnicity of South Asian pupils played a major part in their experience of school. Almost all Asian males within the age-group, for example, were united by a friendship network which reflected their shared perspectives and experiences in the local community, at the mosque and within the school. Racial harassment (mainly verbal, but sometimes physical) at the hands of white pupils was a particularly strong factor which united the Asian males. In terms of their relationships with white teachers, however, Asian pupils' ethnicity was not the influence it was for Afro-Caribbean pupils. This is not to say that white teachers did not hold stereotyped and sometimes negative views of Asian cultures and communities (for instance, concerning the role of women). In general, however, the teachers assumed that Asian pupils were likely to be quiet, well-behaved and backed up by a highly motivated and supportive family. The contrast in staff perspectives concerning Afro-Caribbean and Asian people was reflected in the pupils' experience of and adaptation to schooling.

Living with racism

Given a position in which they were likely to conflict with teachers, and knew that official lines of response were of little use, Afro-Caribbean pupils' adaptations to their situation were especially important. The size of the task facing academically ambitious Afro-Caribbean pupils was very great; 'ability' and hard work were not enough they also had to manage interactions with teachers so as to avoid seeming to confirm the myth of an Afro-Caribbean challenge to authority.

Case studies of Afro-Caribbean pupils' responses to this situation, presented in chapter 3, illustrated something of the range of possible reactions. During their third year both Wayne Johnson and Paul Dixon, for example, were described as intelligent, yet underachieving due to their poor 'attitude'. In fact both pupils accepted the importance of gaining educational qualifications and neither set out deliberately to cause trouble, yet Wayne became caught up in a spiral of increasing control and resistance which eventually led to his permanent exclusion from City Road. Although Paul managed his interactions so as to minimize conflict with teachers, his strategy involved a great deal of personal sacrifice and was negotiated in isolation, without the subcultural support of peers in a similar position. Both pupils' responses included elements of resistance and accommodation, and there was some evidence that their adaptations were mirrored among Afro-Caribbean girls. Most importantly, the experiences of Afro-Caribbean pupils in City Road confirmed the complex and negotiated character of pupil adaptations, and highlighted the crucial role which ethnicity played in relation to their educational opportunities.

In contrast to their Afro-Caribbean peers, South Asian pupils tended to experience teacher–pupil relations which crucially reflected teachers' views of their 'ability' rather than their ethnicity. Hence in chapter 4 the cases of Arif Aslam and Rafiq Ali displayed some of the characteristics of differentiation and polarization which were also apparent in the careers of white pupils of both sexes.

The City Road data, therefore, demonstrate the importance of ethnicity within multi-ethnic schools. Despite the teachers' attempts to treat everyone the same, their belief in the myth of an Afro-Caribbean challenge combined with their ethnocentric interpretation of pupils' actions and style of demeanour to place Afro-Caribbean pupils in a disadvantaged position. Although the teachers were generally 'liberal' in their intent, their actions were frequently racist in their consequences.

Ethnicity also influenced the way in which South Asian males experienced school, especially concerning their friendship choices and experience of racial harassment. In terms of their relationships with teachers, however, the Asian pupils did not always suffer because of the stereotypes which the teachers held. Thus Afro-Caribbean and South Asian pupils experienced City Road in very different ways. The basic lesson to emerge from these data is, therefore, that 'race' matters. To deny that the presence of ethnic minority communities within society has any consequences for the educational system is to compound error with ignorance. The fact that ethnicity does influence pupils' experiences of school has massive consequences for the educational system in this country. In the second part of this book, therefore, attention was turned to wider issues of debate and controversy within the field. Emphasis was placed on the specific areas of opportunity, achievement, curricula and language issues.

Issues for education in a multi-ethnic society

Achievement and 'underachievement'

During the 1980s, notions of efficiency and economy claimed centre stage as the 'batch processing' model came to dominate official discourse on educational issues. The concept of equality of educational opportunity, however, remained at the heart of much research and debate within the field. Although there is no universally accepted definition of this concept, many researchers judge the opportunities which were substantively available to different groups by comparing their average achievements at the end of compulsory education. Liberal, radical and new right critics have each attacked some element of this approach, but it remains a vital (though crude) guide to pupils' experiences and achievements.

Surveys of educational achievements at sixteen-plus have consistently shown differences in the average performance of different ethnic groups. In particular, proportionately fewer children of Afro-Caribbean origin have achieved the 'high hurdle' of five or more higher grade passes. This pattern appears to hold true even when surveys make allowance for the influence of social class, which is known to be strongly associated with educational achievement. As I noted in chapter 5, however, many pupils of all ethnic groups do very well; talk of 'underachievement' should not, therefore, be assumed to imply that pupils of any group are destined to fail. Indeed, recent studies have highlighted the complex and changing nature of academic success.

The achievements of a nationally representative sample of sixteen-year-olds (Drew and Gray, 1989), for example, have shown smaller differences than in previous studies which may have presented a depressed picture by concentrating on pupils in inner-city areas. Furthermore, much research has been analysed in terms of crude aggregate groups which may hide important differences between sexes, social classes and ethnic groups. South Asian pupils, for instance, are frequently lumped together into a single group, yet data from inner London have shown very great variations within that group (Kysel, 1988). In addition, recently developed statistical techniques have been used to explore the different effects which individual schools may have upon their pupils' progress. Although this work is still in its early stages it highlights the power of schools and teachers to influence the achievements of their pupils (whatever their gender, social class or ethnic group background).

Curricular issues

'Reforms' of the educational system, introduced in the late 1980s and early 1990s, place curricular issues at the forefront of teachers' minds and herald a new phase in the continuing struggle for a curriculum which is of relevance to all pupils. In the past, curricular responses to ethnic diversity have frequently reflected political pressures and philosophies at least as much as educational ones. During the late 1950s and into the 1960s, educational policies were premissed on the belief that 'immigrant' communities presented a problem which would be solved once they had been assimilated into the 'British' (white, middle-class) system of norms and values. The assumption that 'immigrants' represented a threat to white culture and interests was dramatically embodied in the officially sanctioned policy of dispersal. Although this policy was abandoned during the integrationist phase of the late 1960s and the 1970s, the underlying assumptions of white cultural superiority remained intact.

The efforts of ethnic minority communities, teachers, pressure groups, schools and individual local authorities were fundamental to the development of curricular approaches which sought to build upon the strengths of ethnic diversity, recognize the needs of minority communities and educate all children for life in a multi-ethnic society. These values were first articulated through so-called multicultural approaches which moved away from the stereotyped assumptions and materials which characterized earlier assimilationist/integrationist approaches. During the 1980s anti-racist critics attacked multiculturalism for failing to address the structural inequalities which lay behind the operation of racism in society. As I argued in chapter 6, however, despite differences in rhetoric, in some cases the application of multicultural and anti-racist approaches in classroom situations seem remarkably similar. In both cases, good practice involves opposition to racism through the sensitive use of materials and approaches which challenge Eurocentric assumptions and build upon the lived experiences of different groups.

To some degree, the Swann committee's policy guideline, 'education for all', offers an opportunity for schools to adopt multicultural/anti-racist initiatives within a mainstream (officially sanctioned) curricular approach, although (as usual) the details must be worked out on a day-to-day basis by classroom teachers. Unfortunately the history of curricular change in this country offers little room for optimism, especially in schools with few ethnic minority pupils, which usually assume (mistakenly) that 'race' issues are of no relevance. This situation has been compounded by the reluctance of the DES to take a clear policy lead. Indeed, the worst fears of many educationists were confirmed when plans for a national curriculum made no mention of ethnic diversity and subsequent statements (by successive Secretaries of State) confirmed the emphasis upon 'English' traditions, culture and history (cf. Arora, 1988; Klein, 1988b).

Languages for a multi-ethnic society

Many of the key issues which this book has addressed come together when attention is turned to language use and education, the first part of the curriculum in which conscious attempts were made to respond to the presence of ethnic minority pupils. In chapter 7 I examined the debates concerning the teaching of English as a second language, the language needs of Afro-Caribbean pupils and the controversies surrounding mother tongue teaching. As in so many areas of concern, the issues are complex. For example, many people assume that language issues relate solely to pupils of South Asian ethnic origin. Yet evidence suggests that Afro-Caribbean pupils' use of Creole – an important symbol of ethnicity and shared identity – often leads to conflict with white teachers who view such linguistic forms as slang or even as a challenge to their authority (see also chapters 2 and 3).

There is very great linguistic diversity among the pupil population of this country: the Linguistic Minorities Project (LMP, 1983, 1985) counted more than eighty distinct languages in one LEA alone. Such data are often used by policymakers to excuse their inaction by claiming that there are simply too many different languages for any practical support to be offered. Yet the LMP data also showed that merely by supporting the three most common community languages more than half of the bilingual pupils in their sample would have been helped. Unfortunately the DES has rejected calls for tuition in community languages, arguing that it might interfere with the learning of English. A small minority of pupils currently have the opportunity to study community languages as part of the modern languages curriculum and it has been argued that all pupils would benefit from greater awareness of the South Asian community languages which are already used by thousands of people in this country. Predictably, however, the provisions of the national curriculum have done nothing to extend this opportunity. Indeed, explicit emphasis was placed on European languages.

It is clear, therefore, that in many areas of school life there is an urgent need for conscious action to recognize and attack the inequalities of opportunity which currently act against the interests of ethnic minority pupils. Such changes would benefit all pupils, yet the chances of significant improvement in the near future appear slight.

'Race', ethnicity and education in the 1990s

I began this chapter by quoting Gillian Klein's remarks concerning the need constantly to recognize and confront racism. For educational researchers and practitioners the advent of the national curriculum, and related reforms of the state education system, present an important agenda for future action.

A nationalist curriculum?

The Education Reform Act 1988 made only cursory reference to cultural diversity but may have massive implications for the inequalities of opportunity suffered by many ethnic minority groups. Although the DES has stated that schools and teachers are free to decide how to deliver the national curriculum, in practice the programmes of study and statutory attainment targets will exercise a great deal of control over the content of the core and other foundation subjects which make up the vast majority of pupils' timetables. Successive Secretaries of State for Education have made it clear that the national curriculum is to be a nationalist curriculum, stressing 'English' language, history and 'culture'.

In tandem with schools' duties to enrol as many pupils as they are physically able to accommodate, the public nature of secondary schools' performance in the national system of testing will ensure that, as a matter of survival, emphasis will be given to the content of the programmes of study. Hence teachers may have only limited opportunities to evaluate critically aspects of 'English' history or use non-Eurocentric materials which clash with centrally defined subject content. Similarly, despite the increased number of students who will study modern languages, the national curriculum has done nothing to improve the status of non-European languages, whose second-rate status in the eyes of policy-makers was confirmed in Kenneth Baker's emphasis upon European languages (see chapter 7).

The politics of testing

As I noted in chapter 5, the history of testing has been marked by bitter controversy over the question of bias against certain ethnic groups (cf. Kamin, 1974, 1981) and it seems likely that this field will provoke a great deal more controversy in the future. Past experience, for example, concerning social class differentiation during selection at eleven-plus (Halsey, Heath and Ridge, 1980), warns that the tests might be the first step towards institutionalized racism on a massive scale. Recent school effects research has highlighted the variations in pupils' progress between different schools and ethnic groups, yet, if the TGAT proposals lead to increased selection throughout the education system (via increased streaming or banding) differences between pupils as young as seven years old might lead to labelling which will disproportionately affect certain ethnic minority groups (Kimberley, 1989).

TGAT's recommendation that 'assessment tasks be reviewed for evidence of bias' is not enough. Suppose that national results show that, as a group, Afro-Caribbean pupils do not achieve on a par with other pupils in the standard assessment tasks. Given the racist uses of testing and differentiation in the past, it seems highly unlikely that the tests would automatically be questioned as biased. It is more likely that the tests would remain unchanged while a renewed debate raged concerning supposed links between 'race' and 'intelligence' – two concepts for which there are not even agreed definitions. The warning signs are already appearing. Recently there have been attempts to rehabilitate the reputation of Sir Cyril Burt, a pioneer of intelligence tests in Britain who falsified key parts of his data (cf. Hearnshaw, 1990). Parents, minority communities, teachers and academics must work together to ensure that racist theories of white superiority do not re-emerge in the guise of science once the standard assessments of the national curriculum are applied.

The continuing need for research

Clearly, educational researchers have a great deal of work to do, examining how the reforms are put into practice and highlighting features which work against equality of opportunity for all pupils. In particular, there is a need for more research which blends aspects of qualitative and quantitative methodologies. As this book has demonstrated, quantitative measures have a crucial role to play (for instance, in mapping widespread patterns of experience and achievement). However, more sensitive qualitative approaches are also necessary if we are to understand the complex processes at work within schools. Clearly, the right mix of qualitative and quantitative research strategies cannot be assumed in advance; such approaches must be designed to reflect the particular demands of the research problem. David Drew and John Gray (1990), for example, have already identified an area where both qualitative and quantitative approaches are needed. They argue that newly developed statistical models, used in school effects research, could be applied to identify schools which are especially effective for pupils from different ethnic groups. Subsequent ethnographic studies of these schools might reveal the processes which lay behind their success.

Despite the potential contribution of educational research, however, the history of curricular and pedagogical initiatives in this field indicates that the most valuable work has often begun at the local level as a result of the struggles and imagination of particular communities, pressure groups and teachers.

Changes at the school level

Despite the rather bleak picture of life under the national curriculum which I have painted above, the status of multicultural issues as a cross-curricular dimension may yet offer an opportunity for the development of anti-racist approaches. Whether this potential is realized will depend upon the efforts of teachers and ethnic minority communities, since there seems little hope of positive action from policy-makers in the foreseeable future.

Similarly, the increased role of parent representatives on schools' governing bodies could serve to empower black communities whose views are not always reflected in school administration at present. Unfortunately, the same mechanisms might also act to limit teachers' abilities to counter racist views among the white communities whom they serve.

A measure of the educational system's progress towards a more egalitarian situation is the representation of ethnic minority people among the teaching force. The present situation is symptomatic of the general lack of progress on issues of 'race' and ethnicity within education:

> The overall picture which emerges from our research is that ethnic minority teachers are few in number, that they are disproportionately on the lowest salary scales, and that they are concentrated in subjects where there is a shortage of teachers or where the special needs of ethnic minority pupils are involved. They do not enjoy the same career progression as white teachers, even when their starting scales and length of service are similar, nor do their headteachers encourage them in the same way as they do white teachers to apply for vacancies within their school. (Ranger, 1988, p. 65)

Greater representation of all ethnic groups among the teaching force would provide tangible evidence (to both staff and pupils) of the ability of ethnic minority people, while simultaneously helping to facilitate a better understanding between schools and the communities which they serve (cf. Gillborn, Nixon and Rudduck, 1989, pp. 274–7). At the same time, it is important to recognize that Afro-Caribbean and Asian teachers are not born experts on multicultural and anti-racist issues and should not be subject to the forces which currently place many of them in narrow 'specialist' areas of the curriculum where chances for promotion may be restricted.

The recent introduction of massive reforms of the state education system may increase the inequalities of opportunity which already exist. Questions of 'race', ethnicity and education are, however, extremely complex. Although present policy-makers seem intent on a 'colour-blind' approach, which acts against the interests of many ethnic minority groups, action by those who have historically fought for equality of educational opportunities (including ethnic minority communities, teachers and pressure groups) may yet improve the quality of schooling for all pupils.

Notes

Chapter 1

1. 'White headteacher of a predominantly Asian school in Bradford, Ray Honeyford published articles in which he attacked multi-racial education, characterised Pakistan as a country unable to cope with democracy and argued that West Indian family structure and values were a root cause of "black educational failure". Local parents led a campaign to have him removed from his post. He was ultimately offered (and took) early retirement and £161,000 compensation.' Quoted from Paul Gordon, 1988, p. 98.
2. In order to protect confidentiality all names connected with 'City Road' have been changed.
3. One of the strengths of ethnographic work in general, and grounded theory in particular, is the emphasis upon categories and themes which emerge within the research setting. Unlike many previous studies, for example, I never explicitly asked teachers or pupils for their views about 'race' or gender issues. Whenever 'race' or gender was mentioned by an interviewee I would follow up the comment as I would any other, but I was never the first person to raise the issues as potentially relevant. In this way I avoided 'prompting' interviewees and did not encourage teachers or pupils simply to rehearse or generate stereotypes for my benefit. See Troyna and Carrington, 1989, pp. 213–17 for a critique of some previous approaches in this area.
4. When the age-group were fourth-years I began to explore issues which required greater involvement with fewer pupils. Consequently, I decided to concentrate on pupils in two (of my original three) case study forms. The forms included male and female pupils of each ethnic group within the school population.

I was able to build strong relationships of mutual trust with many pupils, who then introduced me to members of wider friendship networks beyond the limits of the case study forms. Full details of the fieldwork are available in my first account of the research: Gillborn, 1987.

Chapter 2

1. The Flanders system for classroom interaction analysis is fully documented in Flanders, 1970. The system requires an observer to note the character of the action in a classroom at frequent regular intervals. The observer chooses the most appropriate description from a list of ten categories:
    (i) Teacher accepts student's feelings;
    (ii) Teacher praises or encourages;
    (iii) Teacher accepts or uses the student's ideas;
    (iv) Teacher asks question(s);
    (v) Teacher lectures;
    (vi) Teacher gives directions;
    (vii) Teacher criticizes or justifies authority;
    (viii) Student talks in response to teacher;
    (ix) Student initiates talk;
    (x) Silence or confusion
    Adapted from Wragg and Kerry, 1978, p. 18.
2. It should be noted that Wright does not always use the same pseudonyms for the schools which she visited. In the short articles which first appeared as a result of her study (1985a, 1985b), she called the schools 'Upton' and 'Landley'. In the longer published versions of the research (1984, 1986), however, the schools are referred to simply as School A and School B respectively.
3. Many ethnographers have found that pupils seem most at ease addressing them as they would any other adult in the school, see for example, Hammersley, 1984 and Ball, 1985. Similarly, in quotations from City Road Comprehensive, where a pupil refers to me as 'sir' this should not be taken as signifying any confusion on his/her part; throughout the research I made it clear that I had no authority in the school, that I was not a teacher and that everything which I heard would be handled in confidence. The pupils fully understood this: 'sir' was simply a convenient shorthand.
4. See chapter 4.
5. Unfortunately the school records did not include reliable data on the multiple receipt of report cards. I was therefore unable to calculate the frequency with which some pupils received

additional cards during their careers in City Road.

6. The very small number of South Asian and mixed race females who were detained means that any further analysis by gender and ethnic origin would be meaningless.

Chapter 3

Much of the City Road data presented in this chapter has previously appeared in the *British Journal of Sociology of Education* (see Gillborn, 1988).

1. There was some indication that when answering the sentence completion items pupils tended to choose mainly from within their own gender; see Gillborn, 1987, pp. 376–80 for details of the design, administration and analysis of the sentence completion questionnaire.

2. By 'pass' grades at the age of sixteen-plus I mean those grades normally considered to be a pass by the main users of educational certification (employers and institutions of further and higher education):

   Pre-1988: Grades A, B and C in the General Certificate of Education (GCE, 'O', or ordinary, level) and/or grade 1 in the Certificate of Secondary Education (CSE).

   Post-1988: Grades A, B and C in the General Certificate of Secondary Education (GCSE).

   For research findings and a general summary of work in this area see Goacher, 1984, and Mortimore and Mortimore, 1984.

3. A recently completed study of second-generation Sikh girls in Nottingham focuses upon the influences of ethnicity and gender, and includes an interesting discussion of 'deviance' within a culturally pluralist context: Drury, 1989.

4. Both Wayne Johnson and Paul Dixon were members of the form groups which I followed throughout my research in City Road. From their third year onwards I was in constant contact with their form, observing and talking with the pupils on a frequent and regular basis. In contrast, none of the girls who were centrally involved in the parallel adaptations were members of my case study forms. This meant that I had to rely upon the female Afro-Caribbean pupils who were in my forms to act as sponsors, introducing me to key actors and vouching for my trustworthiness (as Wayne had done with Barry and Roger). Sponsors were particularly important in relation to the female clique because they were likely to be doubly suspicious of me, not merely as an outsider, but also because of my gender and ethnic identity as a white male. Unfortunately the two Afro-Caribbean girls who began to act as my sponsors suffered

prolonged absence from school during their fourth and fifth years. Consequently, although I got to know something of the group's experiences and concerns, I was unable to gain full access to the group.

Burgess, 1984, pp. 194–7 and Hammersley and Atkinson, 1983, pp. 56–63, offer summaries of the value and dilemmas involved in the use of sponsors in field research.

5. Mac an Ghaill, 1989, pp. 283–4, offers further examples of 'conflict limitation' strategies, as reported by Asian and Afro-Caribbean students at a sixth form college.

Chapter 4

1. The three girls were Muslims who to some degree mirrored the friendship patterns of their male peers. Because of their number and the fact they were mostly spread across tutorial forms which I did not study, however, I mainly concentrated on the male Asians in the age-group.

2. Within City Road the names used by the Asian pupils were very much anglicized versions which fitted the expectations of the school (and wider society) but lost the essence of their true names. In most cases, for example, the school was using a given name as if it were a family name. This is typical of the way that white institutions have misinterpreted and misused the names of South Asian people. For the sake of authenticity I have chosen to use pseudonyms which reflect the form of the names which were used within City Road. However, this should not be interpreted as sanctioning what is an offensive and (in the case of hospital records and the like) sometimes dangerous example of white ethnocentrism.

3. For details of duties during fast, see Caesar E. Farah's study of Islam in Farah, 1987, especially pages 143–5.

4. As Máirtín Mac an Ghaill has observed (personal communication) Aggleton (1987) has also noted the lack of shared consciousness among members of exploited groups, in this case, divided by ethnicity and gender.

5. Audrey Lambart's study of a girls' grammar school was also part of the Manchester research project; cf. Lambart, 1976.

6. It would be inappropriate to compare the three terms of the third year with the four upper-school terms for which I have data. The upper-school figures therefore relate to the spring and summer terms of the pupils' fourth year and the autumn term of their fifth year. I have omitted the first term of the fourth year since any polarization related to upper-school experiences or processes should have become more marked as the pupils moved

towards the end of their school careers. The calculations exclude Afro-Caribbean pupils, whose experience of control and criticism I have already shown to be significantly different to those of their peers of other ethnic origins.

7. Industrial action by the main teacher unions complicated the situation somewhat but the school continued to encourage all parents to come in and discuss their children's options.

Chapter 5

1. In some instances the data presented in the table have been reworked by Drew and Gray so as 'to obtain more nearly comparable estimates of performance'. See Drew and Gray, 1989, p. 11.
2. Palmer's collection uses the term anti-racist in a very loose way, meaning almost any perspective which seems sensitive to ethnic diversity. See chapter 6 for a discussion of genuinely anti-racist approaches.
3. Flew's use of the word 'set' is inconsistent and misleading. In a footnote he states that he uses it 'in order to avoid the *social* implications of "class" ... the sole essential feature of a set is that its members have at least one common characteristic, any kind of characteristic' – Flew, 1986, p. 30; emphasis added. It appears, therefore, that in Flew's view, sets are biologically determined rather than socially constructed. In his text Flew writes of 'distinctions between the whole race and one or more of its subsets'; see p. 28. Characteristically, however, the reader is offered no guidance on how to identify races, sets and subsets.
4. Chapter 3 includes a case study of such determination. Further examples appear in the work of Fuller, 1980, and Mac an Ghaill, 1988, pp. 11–36. For a description of 'race relations' developments and conflicts in Britain since 1945 see Cashmore, 1989.
5. It is perhaps revealing that the Swann report reproduced the table intact and without comment. Such occurrences seem to indicate that quantitative material is sometimes accepted at face value, without even checking the internal consistency of the data.
6. In total, 26 per cent of the pupils in the PSI/Lancaster sample belonged to a family without a parent at work; see Smith and Tomlinson, 1989, p. 42.

Chapter 6

1. 'Riot' is a difficult term to use with confidence. Both contemporary and historical accounts of the Nottingham conflicts, for

example, refer to 'riots'. Compare this with the official language of the 1980s which spoke of 'disturbances' – see for instance, the Scarman report, 1982. For a good introduction to this issue see Barry Troyna's section on the riots of 1981 in Cashmore's *Dictionary of Race and Ethnic Relations*, 1988.

2. For an example of this see Roger Scruton's essay, *The Myth of Cultural Relativism*, 1986.

3. Details of the Commission's work are published in its annual report. Some examples of cases where the CRE has successfully brought legal action against racist individuals and institutions are cited in Ben-Tovim *et al.*, *The Local Politics of Race*, 1986.

4. Alma Craft and Gillian Klein, 1986, have produced an excellent guide to materials and approaches for teachers in primary and secondary schools, which includes invaluable subject specific advice for the latter.

5. In 1985 Mullard was a central figure in the decision to change the title (and emphasis) of NAME – an important pressure group – from the National Association for Multiracial Education to National Anti-racist Movement in Education (see *Times Educational Supplement*, 1 May 1987).

6. A principal reason for focusing on Brandt's work is his explicit attempt to deal with the day-to-day realities of teaching in a multi-ethnic society. He is one of the few writers to move beyond theory and into practice. Another writer to engage in the real life of classroom teaching is Madan Sarup, in his book *The Politics of Multiracial Education*, 1986.

7. For the sake of clarity I have structured this chapter chronologically. As I noted at the beginning, however, the arguments have not developed in neat, distinct phases. Hence, although Brandt's book was published after the Swann report, I comment on his approach before examining the policy of 'education for all'. This is because the latter grew partly out of a response to anti-racist critiques (of which Brandt's is typical). In addition, although Brandt makes reference to the Swann report, his criticisms are not central to the development of his analysis.

8. In fact the term 'education for all' was already being used by many educationists; see, for example, Jon Nixon's book, *A Teacher's Guide to Multicultural Education*, 1985, which was written before the publication of the Swann report.

9. For a historical perspective on the origins of the national curriculum see Aldrich, 1988.

10. See the following chapter for a discussion of the national curriculum's consequences in relation to ethnic minority community languages.

11. A 'digest for schools' (summarizing the TGAT's main report) repeated the view that assessments at age seven might identify a

minority of pupils who need 'special provision'. The digest stated that 'There is no supposition that children in Levels 1 or 3 must be educated *outside* classes for their own age group'; see DES/WO, 1988b, p. 10 (emphasis added). Hence separate provision *within* the age-group remains a distinct possibility. Furthermore, while there was 'no supposition' of differentiation across age-groups, such a move has not been ruled out.

Chapter 7

1. Shepherd, 1987, has described teacher–pupil relationships in a school of predominantly South Asian intake. He identified language as one of the main factors which led teachers to form negative views of the pupils. Language has consistently emerged as an important issue in teacher–pupil interaction; for a general introduction to some of the major issues in language and schooling see Stubbs, 1983.
2. I agree with Viv Edwards, 1986, p. 10, that it would be preferable to adopt the community term for this linguistic style (that is, patois). However, because of the nature of this chapter I quote extensively from several works which refer to 'Creole'. For the sake of consistency I have therefore decided to use the term Creole.
3. I follow the practice of the Linguistic Minorities Project who, while recognizing the proper linguistic status of Creole as a language, referred to its speakers in terms of bi*dialectism*. This is a useful device for maintaining important distinctions in discussions of South Asian and Afro-Caribbean language needs and uses. However, my use of the term should not be taken as a denial of the true status of Creole/patois as a language rather than a dialect.
4. Poetry offers a dramatic example of language use where the 'tensions' between different linguistic styles and the lived experience of conflict and exploitation are given a powerful voice. 'You can see it in the writing. You can hear it in the words' – it is a 'language of pain': from Andrew Salkey's introduction to *'Dread Beat and Blood'* by Linton Kwesi Johnson, 1975.
5. The Education Reform Act 1988 makes provision for pupils who have been the subject of a statement of special educational needs to be exempt from some of the requirements of the national curriculum – as deemed appropriate by the school, LEA and parents – cf. Lowe, 1988, pp. 22–3.

Guide to further reading

'Race' and ethnic relations is a highly complex and dynamic field. This guide to reading is meant to highlight a small number of sources which offer distinctive perspectives and ideas about the problems encountered within society in general, and classrooms in particular.

Ashok Bhat, Roy Carr-Hill and Sushel Ohri (eds) (1988) *Britain's Black Population* (Aldershot: Gower) was written by members of the Radical Statistics Race Group and provides a critical introduction to some of the central issues concerning 'race' in Britain. E. Ellis Cashmore (ed.) (1988) *Dictionary of Race and Ethnic Relations* (London: Routledge) includes sensitive discussion of key activists and concepts by prominent writers. Each entry also includes suggestions for further reading. Barry Troyna (ed.) (1987) *Racial Inequality in Education* (London: Tavistock) brings together important original papers which address a range of issues concerning education in Britain.

Analyses of 'race' and inequality in education cannot be sustained in a social or historical vacuum. Centre for Contemporary Cultural Studies (1982) *The Empire Strikes Back* (London: Hutchinson) is a radical critique of previous 'race relations' policy and research, highlighting the complex interplay between 'race' and class structures. Amrit Wilson (1978) *Finding a Voice: Asian Women in Britain* (London: Virago), A. Sivanandan (1982) *A Different Hunger* (London: Pluto) and Beverley Bryan, Stella Dadzie and Suzanne Scafe (1985) *The Heart of the Race* (London: Virago) describe the struggle against racism within historical, social and personal contexts. E. Ellis Cashmore (1989) *United Kingdom?* (London: Unwin Hyman) summarizes the major political developments since 1945 and helps to identify similarities and differences between class, 'racial' and gender inequalities in Britain.

A distinctive feature of this book has been the concern to investigate the realities of life in multi-ethnic classrooms. Cecile Wright's chapter, 'School Processes – An Ethnographic Study', in J. Eggleston, D. Dunn and M. Anjali (1986) *Education For Some* (Stoke-on-Trent: Trentham) and Máirtín Mac an Ghaill (1988) *Young, Gifted and Black* (Milton Keynes: Open University Press) report detailed ethnographic research in multi-ethnic settings. Mac an Ghaill's work is particularly noteworthy for his attention to teachers' perspectives and his attempt to address 'race', class and gender issues within a single study.

Anne Wilson (1987) *Mixed Race Children* (London: Allen & Unwin) remains the only detailed study of the position of children who do not easily fall within the dominant socially constructed categories of 'race'. Similarly, there are very few studies of multicultural and anti-racist work in 'all white' schools: Chris Gaine (1987) *No Problem Here* (London: Hutchinson) and Sally Tomlinson (1990) *Multicultural Education in White Schools* (London: Batsford) are the main sources. Both books address some of the real-life problems faced by teachers at the classroom level. Elizabeth Grugeon and Peter Woods (1990) *Educating All* (London: Routledge) may prove especially interesting to primary teachers – the book reports case studies of multicultural and anti-racist work in selected schools.

In a field which changes so rapidly (and especially in view of the national curriculum) books on 'race' and education can date very quickly. Journals offer an up-to-date source of interesting and challenging papers on relevant initiatives, perspectives and research findings. *New Community* is published four times a year for the Commission for Racial Equality and includes articles on a range of topics related to racism, 'race' and ethnic relations. *Race & Class* is published quarterly by the Institute of Race Relations (London) and offers a radical analysis of contemporary issues both in the UK and internationally. *Multicultural Teaching* (Stoke-on-Trent: Trentham) is an excellent applied journal which publishes short articles of direct relevance to classroom teachers. All three journals include regular book reviews.

References

Aggleton, P. (1987), *Rebels Without a Cause: Middle Class Youth and the Transition from School to Work* (London: Falmer).

Aldrich, R. (1988), 'The National Curriculum: an historical perspective', in D. Lawton and C. Chitty (eds), op. cit., pp. 21–33.

Anyon, J. (1983), 'Intersections of gender and class: accommodation and resistance by working-class and affluent females to contradictory sex-role ideologies', in S. Walker and L. Barton (eds), *Gender, Class and Education* (Lewes: Falmer), pp. 19–37.

Arnot, M. (ed.) (1985), *Race & Gender: Equal Opportunities Policies in Education* (Oxford: Pergamon).

Arora, R. K. (1984), 'Teaching of community languages – sources and training', *Multicultural Teaching*, vol. 3, no. 1, autumn, pp. 9–12.

Arora, R. K. (1988), 'A monolingual gerbil in a multilingual school', *Multicultural Teaching*, vol. 6, no. 2, spring, pp. 19–22.

Arora, R. K. and Duncan, C. G. (eds) (1986), *Multicultural Education: Towards Good Practice* (London: Routledge).

Ash, R. (1985), 'Towards a bilingual education: anticipating Swann', *Multicultural Teaching*, vol. 3, no. 2, spring, pp. 22–4.

Ashrif, S. (1986), 'Eurocentrism and myopia in science teaching', *Multicultural Teaching*, vol. 5, no. 1, autumn, pp. 28–30.

Assistant Masters and Mistresses Association (1987), *Multi-Cultural and Anti-Racist Education Today* (London: AMMA).

Bagley, C. (1975), 'On the intellectual equality of races', in G. K. Verma and C. Bagley (eds), *Race and Education Across Cultures* (London: Heinemann), pp. 30–47.

Bagley, C. (1986), 'Multiculturalism, class and ideology: a European-Canadian comparison', in S. Modgil *et al.*, (eds), op. cit., pp. 49–59.

Baker, K. (1986), *Speech to Students at Pangbourne College, Berkshire* (London: DES Press Release).

Baker, K. (1989), *Terms of Reference for National Curriculum History Working Group* (London: DES Press Release).

Ball, S. J. (1973), 'The study of friendship groups in a multi-racial comprehensive school: research and methodology', MA Dissertation, University of Sussex.

Ball, S. J. (1981), *Beachside Comprehensive: A Case Study of*

Secondary Schooling (Cambridge: Cambridge University Press).

Ball, S. J. (1985), 'Participant observation with pupils', in R. G. Burgess (ed.), *Strategies of Educational Research* (Lewes: Falmer), pp. 23–53.

Ballard, R. and Ballard, C. (1977), 'The Sikhs: the developments of South Asian settlements in Britain', in J. L. Watson (ed.), op. cit., pp. 21–56.

Banton, M. (1977), 'The adjective 'black': a discussion note', *New Community*, vol. 5, no. 4, pp. 480–2.

Banton, M. (1983), *Racial and Ethnic Competition* (Cambridge: Cambridge University Press).

Banton, M. (1988a), 'Race', in E. E. Cashmore (ed.), op. cit., pp. 235–7.

Banton, M. (1988b), 'Institutional racism', in E. E. Cashmore (ed.), op. cit., p. 146.

Becker, H. S. (1951), 'Role and career problems of the Chicago public school teacher', Doctoral thesis, University of Chicago.

Becker, H.S. (1952), 'Social-class variations in the teacher–pupil relationship', reprinted in H. S. Becker (1970), op. cit., pp. 137–50.

Becker, H. S. (1963), *Outsiders: Studies in the Sociology of Deviance* 1973 edn, (New York: Free Press).

Becker, H. S. (1970), *Sociological Work: Method and Substance* 1977 edn, (New Brunswick, N.J.: Transaction Books).

Becker, H. S and Geer, B. (1960), 'Latent culture: a note on the theory of latent social roles', reprinted in B. R. Cosin *et al.*, (eds) (1971), op. cit., pp. 52–6.

Becker, H. S., Geer, B., Hughes, E. C. and Strauss, A. L. (1961), *Boys in White: Student Culture in Medical School* (Chicago: Chicago University Press).

Bell, L. (1988), 'Local financial management in schools: efficiency, economy and administration', *School Organisation*, vol. 8, no. 2, pp. 121–9.

Bennett, A. (1988), *Talking Heads* (London: BBC Books).

Ben-Tovim, G., Gabriel, J., Law, I. and Stredder, K. (1986), *The Local Politics of Race* (London: Macmillan).

Bhachu, P. (1985), *Twice Migrants: East African Sikh Settlers in Britain* (London: Tavistock).

Bird, C. (1980), 'Deviant labelling in school: the pupils' perspective', in P. Woods (ed.) (1980b), op. cit., pp. 94–107.

Blackledge, D. and Hunt, B. (1985), *Sociological Interpretations of Education* (London: Croom Helm).

Brandt, G. L. (1986), *The Realization of Anti-racist Teaching* (Lewes: Falmer).

Brittan, E. M. (1976a), 'Multiracial Education: 2. Teacher opinion on aspects of school life. Part One: changes in curriculum and school organization', *Educational Research*, vol. 18, no. 2, pp. 96–107.

Brittan, E. M. (1976b), 'Multiracial Education: 2. Teacher opinion on aspects of school life. Part Two: pupils and teachers', *Educational*

Research, vol. 18, no. 3, pp. 182–91.

Brook, M. R. M. (1980), 'The mother-tongue issue in Britain: cultural diversity or control?', *British Journal of Sociology of Education*, vol. 1, no. 3, pp. 237–56.

Brown, C. (1984), *Black and White Britain: The Third PSI Survey* (Aldershot: Gower).

Brown, P. (1987), *Schooling Ordinary Kids: Inequality, Unemployment, and the New Vocationalism* (London: Tavistock).

Bullivant, B. M. (1981), *The Pluralist Dilemma in Education: Six Case Studies* (Sydney: Allen and Unwin).

Bullock, A. (1975), *A Language for Life* (London: HMSO).

Bulmer, M. (1986), 'Race and ethnicity', in R. G. Burgess (ed.), *Key Variables in Social Investigation* (London: Routledge), pp. 54–75.

Burgess, R. G. (1984), *In the Field: An Introduction to Field Research* (London: George Allen and Unwin).

Burgess, R. G. (1985), 'Introduction', in R. G. Burgess (ed.), *Strategies of Educational Research: Qualitative Methods* (Lewes: Falmer) pp. 1–22.

Burgess, R. G. (1986), *Sociology, Education and Schools: An Introduction to the Sociology of Education* (London: Batsford).

Byford, D. and Mortimore, P. (1985), *School Examination Results in the ILEA 1984*, RS977/85, (London: Inner London Education Authority).

Carby, H. V. (1982), 'White woman listen! Black feminism and the boundaries of sisterhood', in Centre for Contemporary Cultural Studies, op. cit., pp. 212–35.

Carmichael, S. and Hamilton, C. V. (1967), *Black Power: The Politics of Liberation in America* (London: Penguin).

Carrington, B. (1983), 'Sport as a side-track: an analysis of West Indian involvement in extra-curricula sport', in L. Barton and S. Walker (eds), *Race, Class and Education* (London: Croom Helm), pp. 40–65.

Carter, T. (1985), 'Working within the power structure in the quest for change: serving on the Swann committee', *Multicultural Teaching*, vol. 3, no. 3, summer, pp. 4–5.

Cashmore, E. E. (ed.) (1988), *Dictionary of Race and Ethnic Relations* 2nd edn (London: Routledge).

Cashmore, E. E. (1989), *United Kingdom? Class, Race and Gender since the War* (London: Unwin Hyman).

Centre for Contemporary Cultural Studies (1982), *The Empire Strikes Back: Race and Racism in 70s Britain* (London: Hutchinson).

Cheshire, J. (1982), 'Dialect features and linguistic conflict in schools', *Educational Review*, vol. 34, no. 1, pp. 53–67.

Chevannes, M. and Reeves, F. (1987), 'The black voluntary school movement: definition, context, and prospects', in B. Troyna (ed.), op. cit., pp. 147–69.

Chivers, T. S. (ed.) (1987), *Race and Culture In Education: Issues Arising from the Swann Committee Report* (Windsor: NFER-Nelson).

Clough, E. and Drew, D. with Wojciechowski, T. (1985), *Futures in Black and White: Two Studies of the Experiences of Young People in Sheffield and Bradford* (Sheffield: Pavic Publications & Sheffield City Polytechnic).

Coard, B. (1971), *How the West Indian Child is Made Educationally Subnormal in the British School System* (London: New Beacon Books).

Cohen, A. K. (1955), *Delinquent Boys: The Culture of the Gang* (London: Collier-Macmillan).

Cohen, L. and Manion, L. (1983), *Multicultural Classrooms* (London: Croom Helm).

Cohen, P. and Bains, H. S. (1988), *Multi-racist Britain* (London: Macmillan).

Cohen, P. S. (1968), *Modern Social Theory* (London: Heinemann).

Cohn, T. (1987), 'Sticks and stones may break my bones but names will never hurt me', *Multicultural Teaching*, vol. 5, no. 3. summer, pp. 8–11.

Collicott, S. (1986), 'Approaches to multicultural curriculum – humanities', in R. K. Arora and C. G. Duncan (eds), op. cit., pp. 74–83.

Commission for Racial Equality (1982), *Ethnic Minority Community Languages: A Statement* (London: Commission for Racial Equality).

Commission for Racial Equality (1985), *Swann: A Response from the Commission for Racial Equality* (London: Commission for Racial Equality).

Commission for Racial Equality (1987), *Racial Attacks: A Survey in Eight Areas of Britain* (London: Commission for Racial Equality).

Commission for Racial Equality (1988), *Learning in Terror: A Survey of Racial Harassment in Schools and Colleges* (London: Commission for Racial Equality).

Coopers & Lybrand (1988), *Local Management of Schools* (London: HMSO).

Cosin, B. R., Dale, I. R., Esland, G. M., Mackinnon, D. and Swift, D. F. (eds) (1971), *School and Society: A Sociological Reader* 2nd edn, (London and Henley: Routledge and Kegan Paul in association with The Open University Press).

Cox, C. (1986), 'From "Auschwitz – yesterday's racism" to GCHQ', in F. Palmer (ed.), op. cit., pp. 74–81.

Cox, G. (1986), 'Music in the multicultural curriculum: an evaluation of the first year of an in-service project', *Multicultural Teaching*, vol. 4, no. 2, spring, pp. 19–21.

Craft, A. and Klein, G. (1986), *Agenda for Multicultural Teaching* (London: Longman for School Curriculum Development Committee).

References

Craft, M. (1989), 'Race: mixed prospects', *Education*, vol. 73, no. 13, pp. 306–7.

Craft, M. and Craft, A. (1983), 'The participation of ethnic minority pupils in further and higher education', *Educational Research*, vol. 25, no. 1, pp. 10–19.

Cross, M. (1989), 'Soapbox' in *Network: Newsletter of the British Sociological Association* no. 43, January, p. 20.

Demaine, J. (1989), 'Race, categorisation and educational achievement', *British Journal of Sociology of Education*, vol. 10, no. 2, pp. 195–214.

Department of Education and Science (1989a), *National Curriculum: From Policy to Practice* (London: HMSO).

Department of Education and Science (1989b), *Future Arrangements for the Accreditation of Courses of Initial Teacher Training: A Consultation Document* (London: DES).

Department of Education and Science and the Welsh Office (1987), *The National Curriculum 5–16: A Consultation Document* (London: HMSO).

Department of Education and Science and the Welsh Office (1988a), *National Curriculum: Task Group on Assessment and Testing: A Report* (London: HMSO).

Department of Education and Science and the Welsh Office (1988b), *National Curriculum: Task Group on Assessment and Testing: A Digest for Schools* (London: HMSO).

Department of Education and Science and the Welsh Office (1988c), *National Curriculum: Task Group on Assessment and Testing: Three Supplementary Reports* (London: HMSO).

Department of Education and Science and the Welsh Office (1989a), *English for ages 5 to 16: Proposals of the Secretary of State for Education and Science and the Secretary of State for Wales* (London: HMSO).

Department of Education and Science and the Welsh Office (1989b), *Science in the National Curriculum* (London: HMSO).

Department of Education and Science and the Welsh Office (1989c), *Mathematics in the National Curriculum* (London: HMSO).

Derrick, J. (1968), 'The work of the Schools Council Project in English for immigrant children', *Times Educational Supplement*, 25 October.

Derrick, J. (1973), 'The language needs of immigrant children', *London Educational Review*, 24 September, pp. 25–30.

Dhondy, F. (1974), 'The Black explosion in British schools', *Race Today*, February, pp. 44–7.

Dhondy, F. (1978), 'Teaching young Blacks', *Race Today*, May/June, pp. 80–85; reprinted in F. Dhondy, B. Beese and L. Hassan (eds) (1982), op. cit., pp. 8–20.

Dhondy, F. (1982), 'Who's Afraid of Ghetto Schools?', in F. Dhondy, B. Beese and L. Hassan (eds), op. cit., pp. 36–42.

223

Dhondy, F., Beese, B. and Hassan, L. (eds) (1982), *The Black Explosion in British Schools* (London: Race Today Publications).

Dickinson, P. (1982), 'Facts and figures: some myths', in J. Tierney (ed.), op. cit., pp. 58–85.

Dorn, A. (1980), 'Review of "Doing Good by Doing Little" by David L. Kirp', *Multiracial Education*, vol. 9, no. 1, autumn, pp. 49–51.

Dorn, A. (1985), 'Education and the Race Relations Act', in M. Arnot (ed.), op. cit., pp. 11–23.

Drew, D. and Gray, J. (1989), 'The fifth-year examination achievements of Black young people in England and Wales', *unpublished paper*, (Sheffield: University of Sheffield Educational Research Centre).

Drew, D. and Gray, J. (1990), 'The black–white gap in exam achievement: a statistical critique of a decade's research', paper presented at the British Sociological Association annual conference, *Social Divisions and Social Change*, University of Surrey, 2–5 April.

Driver, G. (1977), 'Cultural competence, social power and school achievement: West Indian secondary school pupils in the West Midlands', *New Community*, vol. 5, no. 4, spring–summer, pp. 353–9.

Driver, G. (1979), 'Classroom stress and school achievement: West Indian adolescents and their teachers', in V. Saifullah Kahn (ed.), op. cit., pp. 131–44.

Driver, G. (1980a), 'How West Indians do better at school (especially the girls)', *New Society*, 17 January, pp. 111–14.

Driver, G. (1980b), *Beyond Underachievement: Case Studies of English, West Indian and Asian School-leavers at Sixteen Plus* (London: Commission for Racial Equality).

Driver, G. (1984), Letter to the editor, *Times Educational Supplement*, 10 February, p. 19.

Drury, B. (1989), 'Ethnicity amongst second generation Sikh girls: A case study in Nottingham', PhD thesis, University of Nottingham.

Dyson, D. (1986), 'Multicultural approach to mathematics', in R. K. Arora and C. G. Duncan (eds), op. cit., pp. 117–34.

Edwards, V. (1979), *The West Indian Language Issue in British Schools: Challenges and Responses* (London: Routledge and Kegan Paul).

Edwards, V. (1986), *Language in a Black Community* (London: Multilingual Matters).

Eggleston, S. J. (1988), 'The new Education Bill and assessment – some implications for black children', *Multicultural Teaching*, vol. 6, no. 2, spring, pp. 24–5, 30.

Eggleston, S. J., Dunn, D. K. and Anjali, M. (1984), *The Educational and Vocational Experiences of 15–18 year old Young People of Ethnic Minority Groups*, report submitted to the Department of Education and Science (Keele: University of Keele).

Eggleston, S. J., Dunn, D. K. and Anjali, M. (1986), *Education For Some: The Educational & Vocational Experiences of 15–18 year old*

References

Members of Minority Ethnic Groups (Stoke-on-Trent: Trentham).

Elmore, R. F. (1987), 'Reform and the culture of authority in schools', *Educational Administration Quarterly*, vol. 23, no. 4, pp. 60–78.

Elton, R. (1989), *Discipline in Schools: Report of the Committee of Enquiry* (London, HMSO).

Etzioni, A. (1961), *A Comparative Analysis of Complex Organizations: On Power, Involvement, and Their Correlates* (New York: Free Press).

European Communities (1977), 'Council Directive of 25 July 1977 on the education of the children of migrant workers' (77/486/EEC), reprinted in M. Swann (1985) op. cit., pp. 441–2.

Evans, P. C. C. and Le Page, R. B. (1967), *The Education of West Indian Immigrant Children* (London: National Committee for Commonwealth Immigrants).

Evetts, J. (1970), 'Equality of educational opportunity: the recent history of a concept', *British Journal of Sociology*, vol. 21, no. 4, pp. 425–30.

Evetts, J. (1973), *The Sociology of Educational Ideas* (London: Routledge and Kegan Paul).

Eysenck, H. J. (1971), *Race, Intelligence and Education* (London: Temple Smith).

Eysenck, H. J. (1973), *The Inequality of Man* (London: Temple Smith).

Eysenck, H. J. (1981), in H. J. Eysenck versus L. Kamin, *Intelligence: The Battle for the Mind* (London: Pan).

Farah, C. E. (1987), *Islam* 4th edn (London: Barron's).

Flanders, N. A. (1970), *Analyzing Teacher Behaviour* (London: Addison-Wesley).

Flew, A. (1984), *Education, Race and Revolution* (London: Centre for Policy Studies).

Flew, A. (1986), 'Clarifying the concepts', in F. Palmer (ed.), op. cit., pp. 15–31.

Fordham, S. (1988a), 'Racelessness as a factor in black students' school success: pragmatic strategy or pyrrhic victory?', *Harvard Educational Review*, vol. 58, no. 1, pp. 54–83.

Fordham, S. (1988b), 'Racelessness, collectivity, and individuality in the black community: reply to Hawkins', *Harvard Educational Review*, vol. 58, no. 3, pp. 420–5.

Foster-Carter, O. (1987), 'The Honeyford affair: political and policy implications', in B. Troyna (ed.), op. cit., pp. 44–58.

Fowler, G. and Melo, A. (1974), *Political Concepts in Education*, unit 9 of course E221 (Milton Keynes: Open University).

Fuller, M. (1980), 'Black girls in a London comprehensive school', reprinted in M. Hammersley and P. Woods (eds) (1984), op. cit., pp. 77–88.

Furlong, V. J. (1976), 'Interaction sets in the classroom: towards a study of pupil knowledge', reprinted in M. Hammersley and P. Woods (eds) (1984), op. cit., pp. 145–60.

Gabriel, J. (1986), 'Education and racism: some recent contributions', *British Journal of Sociology of Education*, vol. 7, no. 3, pp. 341–7.

Gaine, C. (1984), 'What do we call people?', *Multicultural Teaching*, vol. 3, no. 1, autumn, pp. 4–6.

Gaine, C. (1987), *No problem here: a practical approach to education and race in white schools* (London: Hutchinson).

Genovese, E. D. (1972), *Roll, Jordan, Roll: The World the Slaves Made* (New York: Pantheon).

Gherardi, S. and Turner, B. (1987), *Real Men Don't Collect Soft Data* Quaderno 13 (Trento: Dipartimento di Politica Sociale, Universita di Trento).

Gibson, A with Barrow, J. (1986), *The Unequal Struggle: The Findings of a Westindian Research Investigation into the Underachievement of Westindian Children in British Schools* (London: Centre for Caribbean Studies).

Giddens, A. (1984), *The Constitution of Society* 1986 edn, (Cambridge: Polity Press).

Giddens, A. (1989), *Sociology* (Cambridge: Polity Press).

Gill, D. and Levidow, L. (eds) (1987), *Anti-racist Science Teaching* (London: Free Association Books).

Gillborn, D. (1987), 'The negotiation of educational opportunity: the final, years of compulsory schooling in a multi-ethnic inner-city comprehensive', PhD thesis, University of Nottingham.

Gillborn, D. (1988), 'Ethnicity and educational opportunity: case studies of West Indian male–white teacher relationships', *British Journal of Sociology of Education*, vol. 9, no. 4, pp. 371–85.

Gillborn, D. (1989), 'Talking heads: reflections on secondary headship at a time of rapid educational change', *School Organisation*, vol. 9, no. 1, pp. 65–83.

Gillborn, D. (1990a), 'Sexism and curricular 'choice'', *Cambridge Journal of Education*, summer, vol. 20, no. 2, pp. 161–74.

Gillborn, D. (1990b), 'Management and teachers – discipline and support', in N. Jones (ed.), *Special Educational Needs Review: Volume 3* (Lewes: Falmer).

Gillborn, D., Nixon, J. and Rudduck, J. (1989), 'Teachers' experiences and perceptions of discipline in ten inner-city comprehensive schools', in R. Elton, op. cit., pp. 251–77.

Giroux, H. A. (1983), *Theory and Resistance in Education: A Pedagogy for the Opposition* (London: Heinemann).

Glaser, B. G. and Strauss, A. L. (1967), *The Discovery of Grounded Theory: Strategies for Qualitative Research* (Chicago: Aldine Press).

Goacher, B. (1984), *Selection Post-16: the Role of Examination Results* Schools Council Examinations Bulletin 45 (London: Methuen).

Goffman, E. (1952), 'On cooling the mark out', *Psychiatry*, vol. 15, pp. 451–63.

Goffman, E. (1959), *The Presentation of Self in Everyday Life*

(Harmondsworth: Penguin).

Gordon, P. (1988), 'The new right, race and education – or how the Black Papers became a White Paper', *Race & Class*, vol. 29, no. 3. pp. 95–103.

Gray, J., McPherson, A. F. and Raffe, D. (1983), *Reconstructions of Secondary Education: Theory, Myth and Practice since the War* (London: Routledge and Kegan Paul).

Griffin, C. (1985), *Typical Girls?: Young Women from School to the Job Market* (London: Routledge and Kegan Paul).

Green, A. (1982) 'In defence of anti-racist teaching: a reply to recent critiques of multicultural education', *Multiracial Education*, vol. 10, no. 2, pp. 19–35.

Green, P. A. (1983a), 'Teachers' influence on the self-concept of pupils of different ethnic origins', PhD thesis, University of Durham.

Green, P. A. (1983b), 'Male and female created He them', *Multicultural Teaching*, vol. 2, no. 1, autumn, pp. 4–7.

Green, P. A. (1985), 'Multi-ethnic teaching and the pupils' self-concepts', in M. Swann, op. cit., pp. 46–56.

Gurnah, A. (1987), 'Gatekeepers and caretakers: Swann, Scarman, and the social policy of containment', in B. Troyna (ed.), op. cit., pp. 11–28.

Halsey, A. H., Heath, A. F. and Ridge, J. M. (1980), *Origins and Destinations: Family, Class, and Education in Modern Britain* (Oxford: Clarendon Press).

Hammersley, M. (1984), 'The researcher exposed: a natural history', in R. G. Burgess (ed.), *The Research Process in Educational Settings: Ten Case Studies* (Lewes: Falmer).

Hammersley, M. (1985), 'From ethnography to theory: a programme and paradigm in the sociology of education', *Sociology*, vol. 19, no. 2, pp. 244–59.

Hammersley, M. and Atkinson, P. (1983), *Ethnography: Principles in Practice* (London: Tavistock).

Hammersley, M. and Turner, G. (1980), 'Conformist pupils?' in P. Woods (ed.) (1980b), op. cit., pp. 29–49.

Hammersley, M. and Woods, P. (eds) (1976), *The Process of Schooling* (London: Routledge and Kegan Paul).

Hammersley, M. and Woods, P. (eds) (1984), *Life in School: The Sociology of Pupil Culture* (Milton Keynes: Open University Press).

Hargreaves, D. H. (1967), *Social Relations in a Secondary School* (London: Routledge and Kegan Paul).

Hargreaves, D. H. (1976), 'Reactions to labelling', in M. Hammersley and P. Woods (eds), op. cit., pp. 201–7.

Hargreaves, D. H., Hester, S. and Mellor, F. (1975), *Deviance in Classrooms* (London: Routledge and Kegan Paul).

Hatcher, R. (1987), '"Race" and education: two perspectives for change', in B. Troyna (ed.), op. cit., pp. 184–200.

Haviland, J. (1988), *Take Care, Mr Baker!*(London: Fourth Estate).

Hearnshaw, L. S. (1990), 'The Burt affair – a rejoinder', in *The Psychologist*, vol. 3, no. 2, pp. 61–4.

Her Majesty's Inspectors (1989), *Responses to Ethnic Diversity in Teacher Training* (London: DES).

Hestor, H. and Wright, J. (1977), 'Language in the multi-ethnic classroom', *Forum*, vol. 20, no. 1.

Hewitt, R. (1986), *White Talk Black Talk: Inter-racial Friendship and Communication amongst Adolescents* (Cambridge: Cambridge University Press).

Hodgkinson, K. (1987), 'Eurocentric world views – the hidden curriculum of Humanities maps and atlases', *Multicultural Teaching*, vol. 5, no. 2, spring, pp. 27–31.

Home Office (1981), *Racial Attacks* (London: HMSO).

Honeyford, R. (1989), 'At last ... the truth about black pupils', *Daily Mail* 29 June, p. 6.

Hubbuck, J. and Carter, S. (1980), *Half a Chance? A Report on Job Discrimination against Young Blacks in Nottingham* (London: Commission for Racial Equality).

Hughes, E. C., Becker, H. S. and Geer, B. (1958), 'Student culture and academic effort', reprinted in B. R. Cosin *et al.* (eds)(1971), op. cit., pp. 47–51.

Issues in Race and Education no. 50 (1987), 'Section 11: who needs special funding?' (London: Issues in Race & Education).

Jeffcoate, R. (1979), 'A multi-cultural curriculum: beyond the orthodoxy', *Trends in Education*, vol. 4, no. 4, pp. 8–12.

Jeffcoate, R. (1984), *Ethnic Minorities and Education* (London: Harper & Row).

Jelinek, M. M. and Brittan, E. M. (1975), 'Multiracial education: 1. Inter-racial friendship patterns', *Educational Research*, vol. 18, no. 1, pp. 40–53.

Jensen, A. R. (1969) 'How much can we boost IQ and scholastic achievement?', *Harvard Educational Review*, vol. 39, no. 1, pp. 1–123.

Jensen, A. R. (1972), *Genetics and Education* (London: Methuen).

Johnson, L. K. (1975), *Dread Beat and Blood* (London: Bogle-L'Ouverture).

Joseph, G. (1986), 'A non-Eurocentric approach to school mathematics', *Multicultural Teaching*, vol. 4, no. 2, spring, pp. 13–14.

Kamin, L. J. (1974), *The Science and Politics of I.Q.* (Harmondsworth: Penguin).

Kamin, L. (1981), in H. J. Eysenck versus L. Kamin, *Intelligence: The*

Battle for the Mind (London: Pan).

Kawwa, T. (1968), 'Three sociometric studies of ethnic relations in London schools', *Race*, vol. 10, no. 2, pp. 173–80.

Keddie, N. (ed.) (1973), *Tinker, Tailor ... The Myth of Cultural Deprivation* (Harmondsworth: Penguin Education).

Kimberley, K. (1989), 'National assessment and testing: the TGAT Report', in *British Journal of Sociology of Education*, vol. 10, no. 2, pp. 233–9.

Kirp, D. L. (1979), *Doing Good by Doing Little: Race and Schooling in Britain* (London: University of California Press).

Klein, G. (1982), *Resources for Multi-cultural Education: An Introduction* 2nd edn 1984, (London: Longmans Resource Unit for the Schools Council).

Klein, G. (1985), *Reading into Racism* (London: Routledge).

Klein, G. (1988a), 'Rise of the anti-anti-racist', *Times Educational Supplement*, 24 June, p. 4.

Klein, G. (1988b), 'Editorial: the nature of the beast. . .', *Multicultural Teaching*, vol. 6, no. 2, spring, p. 3.

Kysel, F. (1988) 'Ethnic background and examination results', *Educational Research*, vol. 30, no. 2, pp. 83–9.

Labov, W. (1969), 'The logic of nonstandard English', reprinted in N. Keddie (ed.) (1973), op. cit., pp. 21–66.

Labov, W. (1972), *Language in the Inner City* (Pennsylvania: University of Pennsylvania Press).

Lacey, C. (1970), *Hightown Grammar: the School as a Social System* (Manchester: Manchester University Press).

Lacey, C. (1988), 'Preface', in M. Mac an Ghaill, op. cit., pp. vi–vii.

Lambart, A. M. (1976), 'The Sisterhood', in M. Hammersley and P. Woods (eds), op. cit., pp. 152–9.

Lashley, H. (1986), 'Arts education as an element of multicultural education', in R. K. Arora and C. G. Duncan (eds), op. cit., pp. 84–100.

Lawrence, D. (1977) 'The continuing debate on heredity and environment', *Patterns of Prejudice*, vol. 2, no. 3, pp. 5–9.

Lawton, D. (1975), *Class, Culture and Curriculum* (London: Routledge and Kegan Paul).

Lawton, D. and Chitty, C. (eds) (1988), *The National Curriculum* Bedford Way Paper no. 33 (London: University of London Institute of Education).

Linguistic Minorities Project (1983), *Linguistic Minorities in England* (London: University of London Institute of Education).

Linguistic Minorities Project (1985), *The Other Languages of England* (London: Routledge and Kegan Paul).

Little, A. and Willey, R. (1981), *Multi-ethnic Education: The Way Forward* Schools Council Pamphlet 18 (London: Schools Council).

Lloyd, J. (1988), 'RAT race dilemmas', *Times Educational Supplement*, 3 June, p. 4.

Lowe, C. (1988), *Education Reform Act 1988: Implications for School Management* (London: Secondary Heads Association).

Lynch, J. (1986), *Multicultural Education: Principles and Practice* (London: Routledge and Kegan Paul).

Mabey, C. (1986), 'Black pupils' achievement', *Educational Research*, vol. 28, no. 3, pp. 163–73.

Mac an Ghaill, M. (1988), *Young, Gifted and Black: Student-Teacher Relations in the Schooling of Black Youth* (Milton Keynes: Open University Press).

Mac an Ghaill, M. (1989), 'Coming-of-age in 1980s England: reconceptualising black students' schooling experience', *British Journal of Sociology of Education*, vol. 10, no. 3, pp. 273–86.

Macdonald, I. Bhavnani, R. Khan, L. and John, G. (1989), *Murder in the Playground: The Burnage Report* (London: Longsight Press).

McRobbie, A. (1978), 'Working class girls and the culture of femininity', in Women's Study Group (ed.), *Women Take Issue* (London: Hutchinson) pp. 96–108.

Malone, M. (1983), *Racial Discrimination: Your Right to Equal Opportunity* (Bolton: Ross Anderson).

Marks, J. (1986), '"Anti-Racism" – revolution not education', in F. Palmer (ed.), op. cit., pp. 32–42.

Mason, D. (1986), 'Introduction. Controversies and continuities in race and ethnic relations theory', in J. Rex and D. Mason (eds.), op. cit., pp. 1–19.

Matthews, A. (1985), 'A report of visits to schools with few or no ethnic minority pupils', Annex C to chapter 5 of M. Swann, op. cit., pp. 244–76.

Maughan, B. and Rutter, M. (1986), 'Black pupils' progress in secondary schools: II. Examination achievements', *British Journal of Developmental Psychology*, vol. 4, no. 1, pp. 19–29.

Meyenn, R. J. (1980), 'School girls' peer groups', in P. Woods (ed.) (1980b), op. cit., pp. 108–42.

Middleton, B. J. (1983), 'Factors affecting the performance of West Indian boys in a secondary school', MA thesis, University of York.

Modgil, S., Verma, G. K., Mallick, K. and Modgil, C. (eds) (1986), *Multicultural Education: The Interminable Debate* (Lewes: Falmer).

Moreno, J. L. (1953), *Who Shall Survive? Foundations of Sociometry, Group Psychotherapy and Sociodrama*, revised and enlarged edition (New York: Beacon House).

Mortimore, J. and Mortimore, P. (1984), *Secondary School Examinations* Bedford Way Paper 18, (London: University of London).

Mortimore, P., Sammons, P., Stoll, L., Lewis, D. and Ecob, R. (1988), *School Matters: the Junior Years* (Wells, Somerset: Open Books).

Mukherjee, T. (1984), 'I'm not blaming you – an anti-racist analysis', *Multicultural Teaching*, vol. 2, no. 3, summer, pp. 5–8.

Mukherjee, T. (1989), 'Speaking in mother tongues', *Guardian*, 14 March.

Mullard, C. (1982), 'Multiracial education in Britain: from assimilation to cultural pluralism', in J. Tierney (ed.), op. cit., pp. 120–33.

National Curriculum Council (1989a), *English Key Stage 1: Non-statutory Guidance* (York: NCC).

National Curriculum Council (1989b), *Science: Non-statutory Guidance* (York: NCC).

National Curriculum Council (1989c), *Mathematics: non-statutory Guidance* (York: NCC).

National Curriculum Council (1989d), *The National Curriculum and Whole Curriculum Planning: Preliminary Guidance Circular no. 6* (York: NCC).

National Union of Teachers (NUT) (1982), *Mother-Tongue Teaching* (London: NUT).

Newsam, P. (1984), 'One Flew over the cuckoo's nest', *Times Educational Supplement*, 23 March, p. 2.

Nixon, J. (1985), *A Teacher's Guide to Multicultural Education* (Oxford: Blackwell).

Nuttall, D. L., Goldstein, H., Prosser, R. and Rasbash, J. (1989), 'Differential school effectiveness', *International Journal of Educational Research*, vol. 13, pp. 769–76.

Ohri, S. and Faruqi, S. (1988), 'Racism, employment and unemployment', in A. Bhat, R. Carr-Hill and S. Ohri (eds), *Britain's Black Population: A New Perspective* (Aldershot: Gower), pp. 61–100.

Oldman, D. (1987), 'Plain speaking and pseudo-science: the "New Right" attack on antiracism', in B. Troyna (ed.), op. cit., pp. 29–43.

Ouston, J. and Maughan, B. (1985), 'Issues in the assessment of school outcomes', in D. Reynolds (ed.), *Studying School Effectiveness* (Lewes: Falmer), pp. 29–44.

Palmer, F. (ed.) (1986), *Anti-Racism – An Assault on Education and Value* (London: Sherwood Press).

Phillips-Bell, M. (1981), 'Multi-cultural education: what is it?', *Multiracial Education*, vol. 10, no. 1, pp. 21–6.

Powell, B. (1984), 'Where have all the young men gone?', *Times Educational Supplement*, 2 March, pp. 43–4.

Pratt, J., Bloomfield, J., and Seale, C. (1984), *Option Choice: A Question of Equal Opportunity* (Windsor: NFER-Nelson).

Quicke, J. (1988), 'The "New Right" and education', *British Journal of Educational Studies*, vol. 26, no. 1, pp. 5–20.

Ramdin, R. (1987) *The Making of the Black Working Class in Britain* (Aldershot: Wildwood House).

Rampton, A. (1981), *West Indian children in our Schools* Cmnd 8273 (London: HMSO).

Ranger, C. (1988), *Ethnic Minority School Teachers* (London: Commission for Racial Equality).

Reeves, F. and Chevannes, M. (1981), 'The underachievement of Rampton' *Multiracial Education*, vol. 10, no. 1, pp. 35–42.

Reid, M. I., Barnett, B. R., and Rosenberg, H. A. (1974), *A Matter of Choice: a Study of Guidance and Subject Options* (Windsor: NFER).

Rex, J. (1987), 'Multiculturalism, anti-racism and equality of opportunity in the Swann Report', in T. S. Chivers (ed.), op. cit., pp. 1–16.

Rex, J. and Mason, D. (eds) (1986), *Theories of Race and Ethnic Relations* (Cambridge: Cambridge University Press).

Reynolds, D. (1976), 'The delinquent school' in M. Hammersley and P. Woods (eds), op. cit., pp. 217–29.

Rizvi, F. (1988), 'Multiculturalism in Australia: the construction and promotion of an ideology', *Journal of Education Policy*, vol. 3, no. 4, pp. 335–50.

Rosen, H. and Burgess, T. (1980), *Languages and Dialects of London School Children: An Investigation* (London: Ward Lock Educational).

Rowley, K. G. (1968), 'Social relations between British and immigrant children', *Educational Research*, vol. 10, no. 2, pp. 145–8.

Rutter, M., Maughan, B. Mortimore, P. and Ouston, J. with Smith, A. (1979), *Fifteen Thousand Hours: Secondary Schools and their Effects on Children* (Shepton Mallet: Open Books).

Saifullah Khan, V. (1977), 'The Pakistanis: Mirpuri villagers at home and in Bradford', in J. L. Watson (ed.), op. cit., pp. 57–89.

Saifullah Khan, V. (ed.) (1979), *Minority Families in Britain: Support and Stress* (London: Macmillan).

Sarup, M. (1986), *The Politics of Multiracial Education* (London: Routledge).

Saunders, M. (1982), *Multicultural Teaching: A Guide for the Classroom* (London: McGraw-Hill).

Scarman, Lord (1982), *The Brixton Disorders: 10–12 April 1981* (Harmondsworth: Penguin).

Schools Council (1969), *Scope, Stage One: An Introductory English Course for Immigrant Children* (London: Longman).

Schools Council (1971), *Scope, Handbook 2: Pronunciation* (London: Longman).

Schools Council (1976), *Scope, Handbook 3: English for Immigrant Children in the Infant School* (London: Longman).

Schutz, A. (1964), 'The stranger: an essay in social psychology', reprinted in B. R. Cosin *et al.* (eds) (1971), op. cit., pp. 27–33.

Scruton, R. (1986), 'The myth of cultural relativism', in F. Palmer (ed.), op. cit., pp. 127–35.

Sharp, R. and Green, A. (1975), *Education and Social Control* (London: Routledge and Kegan Paul).

Sharpe, S. (1976), *'Just Like a Girl': How Girls Learn to be Women* (Harmondsworth: Penguin).

Shepherd, D. (1987), 'The accomplishment of divergence', *British Journal of Sociology of Education*, vol. 8, no. 3, pp. 263–76.

Sivanandan, A. (1982), 'From resistance to rebellion', in A. Sivanandan, *A Different Hunger: Writings on Black Resistance* (London: Pluto Press) pp. 3–54.

Smith, D. J. and Tomlinson, S. (1989), *The School Effect: A Study of Multi-Racial Comprehensives* (London: Policy Studies Institute).

Solomos, J. (1988), 'Institutionalised racism: policies of marginalisation in education and training', in P. Cohen and H. S. Bains (eds), op. cit., pp. 156–94.

Spencer, D. (1988a), 'Trial and error approach to anti-racist education', *Times Educational Supplement*, 6 May, p. 8.

Spencer, D. (1988b), 'The truths that colour-blindness hides', *Times Educational Supplement*, 13 May, p. A16.

Stenhouse, L., Verma, G. K., Wild, R. D. and Nixon, J. (1982), *Teaching About Race Relations: Problems and Effects* (London: Routledge and Kegan Paul).

Stone, M. (1981), *The Education of the Black Child in Britain: The Myth of Multiracial Education* (London: Fontana).

Strauss, A. L. (1987), *Qualitative Analysis for Social Scientists* (Cambridge: Cambridge University Press).

Stubbs, M. (1983), *Language, Schools and Classrooms* 2nd edn (London: Methuen).

Sutcliffe, D. (1982), *Black British English* (Oxford: Blackwell).

Swann, M. (1985), *'Education For All'* Final Report of the Committee of Inquiry into the Education of Children from Ethnic Minority Groups, Cmnd 9453 (London: HMSO).

Swetz, F. J. (1985), 'Some traditional Malay systems of measurement', *Multicultural Teaching*, vol. 3, no. 3, summer, pp. 32–5.

Syer, M. (1982), 'Racism, ways of thinking and school', in J. Tierney (ed.), op. cit., pp. 86–107.

Taylor, M. J. (1983), *Caught Between: A Review of Research into the Education of Pupils of West Indian Origin* revised edn, (Windsor: NFER-Nelson).

Taylor, M. J. with Hegarty, S. (1985), *The Best of Both Worlds...? A Review of Research into the Education of Pupils of South Asian Origin* (Windsor: NFER-Nelson).

Tierney, J. (ed.) (1982a), *Race, Migration and Schooling* (London: Holt, Rinehart and Winston).

Tierney, J. (1982b), 'Race, colonialism and migration', in J. Tierney (ed.) op. cit., pp. 1–43.

Tomlinson, S. (1981), *Educational Subnormality: A Study in Decision-Making* (London: Routledge and Kegan Paul).

Tomlinson, S. (1983), *Ethnic Minorities in British Schools: A Review of the Literature, 1960–1982* (London: Heinemann Educational with the Policy Studies Institute).

Tomlinson, S. (1986), 'Ethnicity and educational achievement', in S. Modgil *et al.*, (eds), op. cit., pp. 181–93.

Tomlinson, S. (1987), 'Curriculum option choices in multi-ethnic schools', in B. Troyna (ed.), op. cit., pp. 92–108.

Troyna, B. (1981), *Public Awareness and the Media: A Study of Reporting on Race* (London: Commission for Racial Equality).

Troyna, B. (1984), 'Fact or artefact? The "educational underachievement" of black pupils', *British Journal of Sociology of Education*, vol. 5, no. 2, pp. 153–66.

Troyna, B. (1986), '"Swann's Song": the origins, ideology and implications of "Education for All"', *Journal of Education Policy*, vol. 1, no. 2, pp. 171–81, reprinted in T. S. Chivers (ed.) (1987), op. cit., pp. 26–43.

Troyna, B. (ed.) (1987), *Racial Inequality in Education* (London: Tavistock).

Troyna, B. (1988), 'Paradigm regained: a critique of "cultural deficit" perspectives in contemporary educational research', *Comparative Education*, vol. 24, no. 3, pp. 273–83.

Troyna, B. and Carrington, B. (1989), '"Whose side are we on?" Ethical dilemmas in research on "race" and education', in R. G. Burgess (ed.), *The Ethics of Educational Research* (Lewes: Falmer), pp. 205–23.

Twitchin, J. (ed.) (1988), *The Black and White Media Book: Handbook for the Study of Racism and Television* (Stoke-on-Trent: Trentham).

Twitchin, J. and Demuth, C. (1981), *Multi-Cultural Education: Views from the Classroom* (London: BBC).

van den Berghe, P.L. (1988), 'Race', in E. E. Cashmore (ed.), op. cit., pp. 237–9.

Wallman, S. (ed.) (1979), *Ethnicity at Work* (London: Macmillan).

Watson, J. L. (ed.) (1977), *Between Two Cultures: Migrants and Minorities in Britain* (Oxford: Blackwell).

Watts, S. (1986), 'Science education for a multicultural society', in R. K. Arora and C. G. Duncan (eds), op. cit., pp. 135–46.

Weber, M. (1904), 'The Ideal Type', excerpts from 'Objectivity', reprinted in K. Thompson and J. Tunstall (eds) (1971), *Sociological Perspectives: Selected Readings* (Harmondsworth: Penguin) pp. 63–7.

References

Weis, L. (1985), *Between Two Worlds: Black Students in an Urban Community College* (London: Routledge and Kegan Paul).

Wellman, D. T. (1977), *Portraits of White Racism* (Cambridge: Cambridge University Press).

Williams, J. (1967), 'The younger generation', in J. Rex and R. Moore (eds), *Race, Community and Conflict* (Oxford: Oxford University Press for the Institute of Race Relations) pp. 230–57.

Williams, J. (1979), 'Perspectives on the multicultural curriculum', *The Social Science Teacher*, vol. 8. no. 4, pp. 126–33.

Willis, P. E. (1977), *Learning to Labour: How Working Class Kids Get Working Class Jobs* (Farnborough: Gower).

Wilson, A. (1981), 'Mixed race children: an exploratory study of racial categorisation and identity', *New Community*, vol. 9, no. 1., pp. 36–43.

Wilson, A. (1987), *Mixed Race Children: A Study of Identity* (London: Allen & Unwin).

Woods, P. (1976), 'The myth of subject choice', *British Journal of Sociology*, vol. 27, no. 2, pp. 130–49.

Woods, P. (1977), 'How teachers decide pupils' subject choices', *Cambridge Journal of Education*, pp. 21–32.

Woods, P. (1979), *The Divided School* (London: Routledge and Kegan Paul).

Woods, P. (1980a), 'The development of pupil strategies', in P. Woods (ed.) (1980b), op. cit., pp. 11–28.

Woods, P. (ed.) (1980b), *Pupil Strategies: Explorations in the Sociology of the School* (London: Croom Helm).

Woods, P. (1983), *Sociology and the School: An Interactionist Viewpoint* (London: Routledge and Kegan Paul).

Wragg, E. C. and Kerry, T. L. (1978), *Classroom Interaction Research* (Oxford: TRC-Rediguides).

Wright, C. (1984), 'School processes – an ethnographic study', in S. J. Eggleston, D. K. Dunn and M. Anjali, op. cit., pp. 201–78.

Wright, C. (1985a), 'Learning environment or battleground?', *Multicultural Teaching*, vol. 4, no. 1, autumn, pp. 11–16.

Wright, C. (1985b), 'Who succeeds at school – and who decides?', *Multicultural Teaching*, vol. 4, no. 1, autumn, pp. 17–22.

Wright, C. (1986), 'School processes – an ethnographic study', in S.J. Eggleston, D. Dunn and M. Anjali, op. cit., pp. 127–79.

Wright, C. (1987), 'Black students – white teachers', in B. Troyna (ed.), op. cit., pp. 109–26.

Young, M. F. D. (ed.) (1971), *Knowledge and Control: New Directions for the Sociology of Education* (London: Collier-Macmillan).

Subject Index

Note: italicized numbers refer to figures

accommodation as pupil strategy
  60–3, 64, 66, 68, 70–1, 201
African Asian students' achievements
  Table 5.2
African students Table 5.2, 114
Afro-Caribbean
  as group label 5, 6
  students 8, 10, 14, 19–44, Table
    2.1, Table 2.2, 45–71, 72, 73, 74,
    78, 79, 87, 89, 90, 99–101, Table
    5.1, 110, Table 5.2, 112–14,
    119–22, Table 5.3, Table 5.4, *5.1*,
    124–9, Table 5.5, 132, 133, Table
    5.6, 135, 137, 139–41, 147–8,
    163, 167, 168, 174, 177–83,
    199–203, 205, 207, 212, 213–14,
    216
alienation 98
all-white schools 159, 160, 164–5,
  171, 204–5
anti-racism 115, 119, 153–8, 160,
  161, 162–3, 164, 169, 170, 171,
  192, 204, 208, 209, 214, 215
anti-school pupils, 56, 64, 65, 66, 70,
  81–2, 84, 85, 86, 95, 97, 99, 182
  see also alienation
Arabic 196
Arab students' achievements Table
  5.2
Asian
  as group label 5, 6
  students 6, 9, 10, 14, 20, 21, 26, 30,
    Table 2.1, 40, Table 2.2, 47, 53,
    54, 62, 67, 72–80, 85–101, Table
    5.1, 110, 114, 120, 121, 124,
    Table 5.3, 126, Table 5.4, *5.1*,
    129, Table 5.5, 132, 133, Table

5.6, 135, 137, 142, 144, 161,
  174, 175, 183–97, 200–3, 205,
  212, 213–14, 216
assemblies 25, 49, 83, 90, 95
assimilation 143–6, 147, 151, 153,
  161, 163, 165, 171, 175, 204
Assistant Masters and Mistresses
  Association (AMMA) 8, 150–1,
  193–4
attainment targets 105 *see also*
  national curriculum
attendance 25, 33, 83–4, 90, 93, 96,
  131, 132 *see also* truancy
attitude, teachers' perceptions of
  pupils' 25, 39, 40–1, 48, 58–9,
  60, 87, 93, 200–1
Australia 153

banding 21, 24, 81, 168, 207
Bangladeshi students 6, 110, Table
  5.2, 124, 126, 135, 140
behaviour, and Afro-Caribbean
  students *see* attitude,
  ethnocentrism, interaction,
  labelling and myth
Bengali Table 7.2, 191, 196
bidialectism 173–4, 177–83, 216
bilingualism 132, 173–4, 179–80,
  183–97, Table 7.1, Table 7.2, 205
black as group label 4, 5, 6, 7
Black Power 2, 9
black studies 148, 150
Bradford 114, Table 7.1, Table 7.2,
  188, 190, 210
Brazil 4
Bullock report (1975) 175, 194–5

Burnage High School, Manchester 153–4
busing *see* dispersal

Canada 153
census ethnic question 5, 7
Centre for Policy Studies (CPS) 115–16 *see also* new right
Certificate of Secondary Education (CSE) *see* examination achievement
Chicano movement (USA) 2
Chinese Table 7.2
City Road Comprehensive
    local community 6, 7, 14
    pupil population 14
    reputation 14
    staff 14
Cityside district 27, 49
class 14, 26, 50, 53, 59, 64, 71, 73, 107, 111–2, 123–5, Table 5.3, 127, 129–31, Table 5.5, 133, 135–6, 138, 140, 144, 153, 154, 178, 203, 207, 214
colour-blind, policy and practice of 29, 164, 199, 202, 209
    see also ethnocentrism, institutional racism and myth
Commission for Racial Equality (CRE) 5, 9, 22, 75, 77–8, 147, 158, 168, 193, 215
commitment to academic goals 31, 60, 61, 67, 90, 95–6, 97–9
Committee of Inquiry into the Education of Children from Ethnic Minority Groups *see* Rampton report (1981) and Swann report (1985)
community languages *see* mother tongue debate
Coventry Table 7.1, Table 7.2, 188
Creole 23, 50, 64, 177–83, 185, Table 7.2, 197, 205, 216
cross-curricular dimensions, skills and themes *see* national curriculum
cultural competence and confusion 23, 24, 37
curriculum, 142–72, 198, 203–5 *see also* hidden curriculum and national curriculum

demeanour,
    official expectations 25–6, 83–4, 88, 200
    styles of Afro-Caribbean 27–9, 49–50, 62, 64, 182, 200
    see also youth culture
Department of Education and Science (DES) 110, 122, 126, 144, 145, 149, 150, 165–9, 178, 184, 185, 189, 195–7, 204–6
detention 33, 34–5, Table 2.1, 38–41, Table 2.2, 42–3, 44, 55, 80, 84–5, 200
dialect *see* bidialectism and creole
diet 26
differentiation 25–6, 73, 81, 82, 85–7, 89, 95, 167, 168, 202, 207, 216
    see also polarization
disadvantage 45, 64, 66, 70, 100, 141, 202
discipline and 'trouble' 14, 19–44, Table 2.1, Table 2.2, 53–9, 72, 80, 82, 84–5, 92, 100, 161, 168, 198–200 *see also* Elton report and myth
discrimination
    indirect 9–10, 147 *see also* racism
dispersal policy 145–6, 147, 165, 204
dress 25, 26, 29, 50, 62, 69, 83–4, 96, 147, 182, 200

economic factors *see* class
Education Act (1944) 106
Education Reform Act (1988) 105, 166, 196, 206, 216 *see also* Local Management of Schools (LMS) and national curriculum
eleven plus examinations 107, 207
Elton report (1989) 191–2, 199
employment 69, 88, 95, 113–15, 120–1, 135, 143 *see also* unemployment
English
    as a second language (E2L) 144, 148, 168, 174–7, 197 *see also* standard English and language
Ethiopia 50
ethnic group, defined 4–5
ethnicity 7, 23, 27–9, 43–4, 48, 49–50, 53, 59, 62–4, 66, 68,

73–5, 78–9, 86, 100–1, 107, 140,
153, 177, 183, 184, 200–2, 212,
213
defined 7
ethnic minority
defined 5
teachers 14, 136, 148, 192, 209
ethnocentrism 25, 26, 29, 37, 42–4,
47–8, 70, 100, 155, 159, 162,
164, 183, 196, 200, 213
defined 10 *see also* racism
ethnography 13, 21, 22, 211 *see also*
qualitative research
European Community (EC) 188–9,
192, 196
examinations
achievement 30, 48, 59, 63, 66–8,
70, 72, 97, 107, Table 5.1, Table
5.2, 110–11, 113–15, 120, 122,
123–41, Table 5.3, Table 5.4, *5.1*,
Table 5.5, Table 5.6, 147, 176,
181, 190, 199, 203, 212
entry 92, 95, 96 *see also*
underachievement
expulsion from school 14, 19, 33, 50,
51, 56–9, 201
expectations, teachers' of pupils
25–6, 30, 48, 53, 56, 60, 63, 75,
80, 83, 87–8, 92–3, 100, 202 *see
also* labelling and myth

friendship choices 49, 52, 63, 73,
74–5, 78–9, 100, 200–2, 213
further and higher education 88, 106,
113, 114, 121

gender 2, 11, 14, 20–1, 26, Table 2.1,
40, Table 2.2, 53, 59, 64, 66–70,
73, 74, 79, 97, 101, 107, 123,
124, 127, 129–30, Table 5.5,
135, 138, 140, 151, 167, 168,
169, 195, 201–2, 203, 210, 212,
213
General Certificate of Education
(GCE) *see* examination
achievement
General Certificate of Secondary
Education (GCSE) *see*
examination achievement
Greek language Table 7.2

Greek students' achievements Table
5.2
grounded research 13, 210 *see also*
qualitative research
guidance 30, 90, 91, 92
Gujerati Table 7.2, 196

harassment and victimization
racial 36, 53, 54, 70, 75–8, 100,
137–8, 143–5, 201–2
sexual 70
Haringey 186–8, Table 7.1, Table 7.2
heredity *see* 'intelligence'
Her Majesty's Inspectorate (HMI)
160, 166
'Hightown grammar school' 81
hidden curriculum 157, 160–1
Hillgate group *see* new right
Hindi 185, Table 7.2, 196
Hindu students 74, 78, 132, 151, 185
see also Asian students
Honeyford affair *see* Honeyford in
name index
humour 70, 94 *see also* racist jokes

ideal client 25–6 *see also* teachers
immigration 143–4, 173
immigration controls 144
Indian students 6, 74, 110, Table 5.2,
124, 126, 185 *see also* Asian
students
industrial action, by teachers 214
initial teacher training (ITT) 165
Inner London Education Authority
(ILEA) 19, 110, Table 5.2, 115,
126, 136–7
integration 146–7, 148, 149, 151,
161, 165, 171, 204
'intelligence', IQ and racism 117–19,
120, 170, 207
interaction,
pupil–pupil 46, 49, 50–3, 62–3, 67,
73–9, 89, 93–5
teacher–pupil 10, 19–44, 48–9, 50,
53–5, 58–65, 68, 70, 74, 79–81,
86, 88–90, 93–6, 100, 116,
181–3, 199–202, 216
Interactionism 12, 33
interference 180–1, 183, 190
involvement, pupil adaptations and

97–9, 101 *see also* polarization theory

Irish,
  students 7, 124
  UK ethnic minority 5
Italian,
  language Table 7.2
  students 7
  UK ethnic minority 5

Jamaica 6
Jews, UK ethnic minority 5
jobs *see* employment

Kirklees 146

labelling 21–2, 24, 29, 30, 33–5, 38, 53, 56, 58, 92–3, 99, 113, 167, 207
labour market *see* employment
'Landley school' 21–2, 211
language 173–97, 205–6
  and ethnic identity 4, 50, 62, 64, 69, 145, 178–9, 181–3, 189–90, 200, 205, 206–7, 216
  centres 9, 174–6
  use 26, 27, 29, 62, 69, 73, 91, 132, 144–5, 147, 155, 157, 167, 200, 206–7 *see also* bidialectism, bilingualism, Creole, English as a second language and mother tongue
Linguistic Minorities Project (LMP) 173, 179–80, 184–90, Table 7.1, Table 7.2, 192–3, 205, 216
Local Management of Schools (LMS) 150
'Lumley' secondary modern school 64, 81

Manchester 153–4
media 2, 27, 49, 63, 72, 79, 133, 135, 136, 144, 153–4, 165
'messing about' and avoiding work 94–5
middle schools 20–1, 29–30, 77
mixed ability teaching 14–15, 60, 89
mixed race
  as group label 6
  students 6, 14, Table 2.1, 37, 40,

Table 2.2, 42, 53, 54, 62, 124, Table 5.6, 212
modern language curriculum 192–7, 205–6
mother tongue
  debate 174, 183–97, 205–6
  maintenance 188–92, 194
motivation 120–1
multicultural education 147, 148–53, 156–7, 158, 161, 164, 170, 171, 192, 195, 204, 209
  definitional problems 148–9, 159
  criticisms of 151–3, 154–5
Muslim students 74–5, 75, 78, 91, 132, 185, 213 *see also* Asian students
myth of an Afro-Caribbean challenge 25, 35–8, 42–4, 45, 56, 57, 59, 71, 80, 183, 200–2

National Anti-racist Movement in Education (NAME) 215
national curriculum 105, 142, 163, 166–71, 177, 195–7, 205–9, 215
National Curriculum Council (NCC) 169–70
National Foundation for Educational Research (NFER) 163
National Union of Teachers (NUT) 193
new right 115–19, 135, 136, 152, 155, 199, 203
Netherlands 153
newspapers *see* media
Nottingham 144, 212, 214–15
Notting Hill 144

opportunity, equality of educational 37, 105–23, 140, 146, 153, 162, 169, 190, 202–3, 208
  defined as achievement and outcome 106–7, 203
  defined as formal access 106
  defined as provision and circumstance 106
  liberal critique 112–15, 140
  new right critique 115–19
  radical critique 119–23, 140 *see also* disadvantage and underachievement

option choices 15, 52, 82, 86, 87, 89–90, 91–2, 97, 132, 138–9, 194–5, 214

Pakistani students 6, 74–5, Table 5.2, 124, 126, 135, 185 *see also* Asian students
parents 34, 210
  Afro-Caribbean 27, 36, 38, 42, 44, 45, 60–1, 80, 121, 136, 147, 178, 200, 208–9
  Asian 79–80, 100, 121, 185, 191, 208–9
  white 79, 145–6, 208–9
patois *see* Creole
permeation 150
Peterborough 186, Table 7.1, Table 7.2
polarization
  in City Road comprehensive 82–97, 100–1, 202
  theory of differentiation and 81–2, 97–9, 100–1
police 33
Policy Studies Institute (PSI) 131–8, 195, 214
Polish Table 7.2
political education 160
Post-Graduate Certificate in Education (PGCE) *see* initial teacher training
power 5, 8, 10, 14, 53, 112, 115, 153, 155
prejudice 8, 9, 42, 114, 148 *see also* racism
primary schools 20–1, 29–30, 215
progress, academic 131, 133–5, 141, 199, 207
pro-school pupils 31, 67, 81–2, 84, 86, 87, 89, 97, 99 *see also* commitment
Punjab 185
Punjabi 185, Table 7.2, 191, 194, 196
Pushtu Table 7.2

qualitative research, methods and uses 11, 12–13, 66, 74, 86, 138–9, 140, 192, 199, 208, 210–11, 212
quantitative research, methods and uses 11, 12, 73, 110, 120, 122–4, 126, 131, 132, 137–8, 140, 179–80, 185–6, 203, 208, 214

race
  biological 3–4
  defined 3–4
  social 4, *see also* racism
racelessness 68
Race Relations Act (1976) 147
racism 1, 5, 10, 31–2, 42, 44, 54, 55, 69–70, 72, 75, 90, 99–100, 113, 114, 117, 118–121, 143, 145–6, 147, 153–8, 161–2, 164, 198, 200, 202, 204
  as prejudice plus power 8
  institutional 9, 10, 116, 147, 152, 154, 157–8, 159–60, 162, 168, 176, 207
  popular 8–9, 164–5, 200
  scientific 3, 8
  see also ethnocentrism and harassment
racist jokes 22
racist stereotypes, *see* stereotypes
Ramadan 75
Rampton report (1981) 107, 110, 126, 181
Rastafarianism 65
religion 26, 75, 97, 147, 184
report cards 33–4, 35, 55, 211–12
resistance 28–9, 48–60, 64–5, 67–8, 70–1, 121, 139, 147, 201
riots
  (1958) 143–4, 214–15
  (1981) 214–15
Russian language 196

sanctions *see* detention, discipline, expulsion and report cards
Scandinavian students 7
Scarman report (1982) 214–15
school effects and effectiveness 11, 131–2, 135–7, 140, 203, 207, 208
Schools Council 114, 161, 175
Schools Language Survey (SLS) *see* Linguistic Minorities Project
Section 11 of Local Government Act 165
selection *see* banding, differentiation, mixed ability, option choices,

setting and streaming
sentence completion tasks 31, 50, 212
setting by ability 14–15, 30, 60, 61, 82, 88–9, 92
Sheffield 114
Sikh students 10, 74, 78, 132, 185, 212 *see also* Asian students
slavery 113, 178
social class *see* class
South Africa 5, 106
South Asian, *see* Asian
sport 25, 49, 113–14, 118
standard assessment tasks (SATs) 168–9, 207 *see also* Task Group on Assessment and Testing
standard English 171, 173, 177–8, 180, 184, 190
stereotypes
    racist 5, 10, 35–6, 37, 71–3, 79–80, 85, 99, 100–1, 113, 120–2, 137, 141, 146, 149, 163, 170, 171, 201–2, 204 *see also* labelling
streaming 21, 23, 81, 168, 181, 183, 207
strike *see* industrial action
subculture
    defined 46–7, *3.1*
    pupil 48–9, 63, 64, 66–7, 69–71, 74, 81–2, 84, 201
subject status 90–1, 92–3, 139, 194
surveys, *see* quantitative research
suspension from school 14, 19, 43, 51, 55, 56–7,
Swann report (1985) 5, 9, 77, 99, 107, 110, 124–6, 145, 149, 158–63, 164, 165–6, 170, 176–7, 181, 183, 188–92, 194–6, 204, 214, 215
    policy of *education for all* 158–63, 204

Task Group on Assessment and Testing (TGAT) 167–8, 207, 215–16
teachers 14, 42, 43, 57, 72, 76, 77–81, 113, 122, 132, 137, 143, 147, 149, 150, 155, 157–8, 161, 163, 167, 170, 176, 199, 204 *see also* ethnic minority teachers, ethnocentrism, expectations,

interaction, labelling, stereotypes
television *see* media
testing *see* 'intelligence', standard assessment tasks and Task Group on Assessment and Testing
'Torville' school 68
toughness and physical prowess 49–51, 53–4, 59, 63, 94, 96
Travellers, UK ethnic minority 5
truancy 37, 39, 63, 69, 86, 90–1, 93, 96, 97, 99
Turkish language Table 7.2
Turkish students' achievements Table 5.2, 140

Ukranians, UK ethnic minority 5
underachievement 22, 60, 62, 87, 99, 107–112, 119–25, 129, 133, 141, 199, 203
    defined 107–110
unemployment 114–15, 121, 214
United States of America (USA) 4, 68, 131
'Upton school' 21–2, 211
Urdu 91, 185, Table 7.2, 191, 192, 194, 196

'Valley View High School' 23–4
voluntary school movement 136

Waltham Forest Table 7.1, Table 7.2
West Indian, *see* Afro-Caribbean
'West Midlands School' 22–3
white
    as group label 7
    students 14, 21, 31–2, Table 2.1, 40, Table 2.2, 51, 52, 53, 59, 60, 62, 64, 71, 72, 75, 77, 78, 80, 85, 86, 94, 97, 100, Table 5.1, 110, Table 5.2, 120, 121, 124, Table 5.3, 126, Table 5.4, *5.1*, 129, Table 5.5, 133, Table 5.6, 135, 146, 179, 194, 202

Youth Cohort Study (YCS) 112, 126–30, Table 5.4, Table 5.5, 132
youth culture 27, 49 *see also* demeanour, dress, language and media

Name Index

Aggleton, P. 213
Aldrich, R. 215
Anjali, M. 21, 121
Anyon, J. 71
Arora, R.K. 183, 190, 195, 196, 205
Ash, R. 192
Ashrif, S. 151
Atkinson, P. 12, 13, 213

Bagley, C. 120, 153
Baker, K. 171, 196–7
Ball, S.J. 56, 67, 74, 81, 92, 97, 138, 211
Ballard, R. 85
Ballard, C. 85
Banton, M. 3, 4, 5, 9
Barnett, B.R. 138
Becker, H.S. 12, 25–6, 33, 46–7, *3.1*, 84
Bell, L. 105
Bennett, A. 12
Ben-Tovim, G. 215
Bhachu, P. 85
Bird, C. 82, 83
Blackledge, D. 33
Bloomfield, J. 138, 195
Boyle, Sir Edward 145
Brandt, G.L. 9, 154–7, 161, 215
Brittan, E.M. 72, 73, 85, 163
Brook, M.R.M. 184
Brown, C. 121, 124
Brown, P. 81
Bullivant, B.M. 152–3
Bullock, A. *see* Bullock report in subject index
Bulmer, M. 3, 5
Burgess, R.G. 12, 142, 213
Burgess, T. 179, 180
Burt, Sir C. 207

Byford, D. Table 5.2, Table 5.4

Carby, H.V. 154
Carmichael, S. 9
Carrington, B. 113–14, 210
Carter, S. 121
Carter, T. 158–9
Cashmore, E.E. 2, 144, 177, 214, 215
Cheshire, J. 181
Chevannes, M. 123, 136
Chitty, C. 166
Chivers, T.S. 151
Clough, E. 114–15, 121
Coard, B. 147
Cohen, A.K. 47
Cohen, L. 73, 149, 174–5
Cohen, P.S. 98
Cohn, T. 1
Collicott, S. 151
Coopers & Lybrand 150
Cox, C. 119, 155
Cox, G. 151
Craft, A. 123–6, Table 5.3, 129, 215
Craft, M. 123–6, Table 5.3, 129, 165
Cross, M. 5, 7

Demaine, J. 2, 3–4
Demuth, C. 157, 190, 194
Derrick, J. 174
Dhondy, F. 59–60, 145, 152
Dickinson, P. 5, 144
Dorn, A. 107, 166
Drew, D. Table 5.1, 112, 114–15, 121, 126–9, Table 5.4, *5.1*, Table 5.5, 132, 133, 203, 208, 214
Driver, G. 22–5, 37, 44
Drury, B. 212
Dunn, D. 21, 121
Dyson, D. 151

242

Edwards, V. 177–80, 181, 216
Eggleston, J. 21, 121, 167
Elmore, R.F. 105
Elton, Lord *see* Elton report in subject index
Etzioni, A. 98
Evans, P.C.C. 178
Evetts, J. 107
Eysenck, H.J. 117–18

Farah, C.E. 213
Faruqi, S. 121
Flanders, N.A. 20, 211
Flew, A. 115–17, 118–20, 214
Fordham, S. 68, 71
Foster-Carter, O. 146
Fowler, G. 140
Fuller, M. 66–8, 70, 214
Furlong, V.J. 82

Gabriel, J. 182
Gaine, C. 6, 164
Geer, B. 46–7, *3.1*
Genovese, E.D. 71, 178
Gherardi, S. 12
Gibson, A. 180–1
Giddens, A. 4, 11
Gill, D. 157, 170
Gillborn, D. 6, 33, 88, 105, 138, 191–2, 209, 211, 212
Giroux, H.A. 161
Glaser, B.G. 13
Goacher, B. 114–15, 212
Goffman, E. 92, 94
Gordon, P. 210
Gray, J. 11, Table 5.1, 112, 126–9, Table 5.4, *5.1*, Table 5.5, 131, 132, 203, 208, 214
Griffin, C. 66
Green, Andy 158
Green, Anthony 25–6
Green, P.A. 20–1, 22, 29–30, 199
Gurnah, A. 162

Halsey, A.H. 106–7, 207
Hamilton, C. 9
Hammersley, M. 12, 13, 67, 81–3, 98, 211, 213
Hansard 145, 166
Hargreaves, D.H. 33, 64, 66, 81–2, 97

Hatcher, R. 158
Haviland, J. 166, 168, 195
Hearnshaw, L.S. 207
Heath, A.F. 106–7, 207
Hegarty, S. 48, 124
Hester, S. 33
Hestor, H. 175
Hewitt, R. 179
Hodgkinson, K. 151
Honeyford, R. 79, 135–6, 138, 146, 199, 210
Hooper, Baroness 167
Hubbuck, J. 121
Hughes, E.C. 46–7, *3.1*
Hunt, B. 33

Jeffcoate, R. 5, 9, 112–13, 115, 149, 158, 161, 173
Jelinek, M.M. 73
Jenkins, R. 146
Jensen, A.R. 117
Johnson, L.K. 216
Joseph, G. 151
Joseph, Sir Keith 166

Kamin, L. 117–18, 207
Kawwa, T. 73
Kerry, T.L. 211
Kimberley, K. 170–1, 207
King, M.L. 2
Kirp, D.L. 165–6
Klein, G. 142, 150, 154, 168, 198, 205, 206, 215
Kysel, F. Table 5.1, 110, Table 5.2, 126, 203

Labov, W. 177
Lacey, C. 1, 56, 66–7, 71, 74, 81–2, 97
Lambart, A.M. 66, 213
Lashley, H. 151
Lawrence, D. 118
Lawton, D. 142, 166
Le Page, R.B. 178
Levidow, L. 157, 170
Linguistic Minorities Project *see* subject index
Little, A. 176
Lloyd, J. 154
Lowe, C. 167, 216

Name Index

Lynch, J. 143, 146–7

Mabey, C. Table 5.1
Mac an Ghaill, M. 5, 10, 65, 66–8,
    70–1, 72, 85–6, 142, 182, 183, 199,
    213, 214
Macdonald, I. 153–4
MacGregor, J. 171
Malone, M. 10
Manion, L. 73, 149, 174–5
Marks, J. 152
Mason, D. 2, 3
Matthews, A. 164–5
Maughan, B. 131, Table 5.1
McPherson, A.F. 11, 131
McRobbie, A. 66
Mellor, F. 33
Melo, A. 140
Meyenn, R.J. 66
Middleton, B. J. 23–4
Modgil, S. 151
Moreno, J.L. 74
Mortimore, J. 212
Mortimore, P. Table 5.2, Table 5.4,
    131, 212
Mukherjee, Tuku 5
Mukherjee, Tara 196–7
Mullard, C. 143, 146–7, 152–3, 154,
    215
Multicultural Teaching 150

Newsam, P. 115
Nixon, J. 33, 192, 209, 215
Nuttall, D.L. 11, 111–12, 136–7

Ohri, S. 121
Oldman, D. 115
Ouston, J. 131

Palmer, F. 115, 155, 214
Parekh, B. 99, 151
Phillips-Bell, M. 148
Powell, B. 195
Pratt, J. 138, 195

Quicke, J. 115, 151

Raffe, D. 11, 131
Ramdin, R. 144
Rampton, A. 159 *see also* Rampton
report in subject index
Ranger, C. 209
Reeves, F. 123, 136
Reid, M.I. 138
Rex, J. 2, 162–3
Reynolds, D. 131
Ridge, J.M. 106–7, 207
Rizvi, F. 153
Rosen, H. 179, 180
Rosenberg, H.A. 138
Rowley, K.G. 73
Ruddock, J. 33, 192, 209
Rutter, M. 11, Table 5.1, 131

Saifullah Khan, V. 85
Salisbury Review 79
Salkey, A. 216
Sarup, M. 215
Saunders, M. 157
Scarman, Lord *see* Scarman report in
    subject index
Schutz, A. 26
Scruton, R. 152, 215
Seale, C. 138, 195
Shakespeare, W. 88
Sharp, R. 25–6
Sharpe, S. 66
Shepherd, D. 216
Sivanandan, A. 147
Smith, D. J. 11, 19, 73, 121, 122,
    131–8, Table 5.6, 184, 195, 214
Solomos, J. 9
Spencer, D. 154
Stenhouse, L. 148
Stone, M. 148, 157
Strauss, A.L. 13, 198
Stubbs, M. 216
Sutcliffe, D. 178
Swann, Lord 158 *see also* Swann
    report in subject index
Swetz, F.J. 151
Syer, M. 33

Taylor, M. J. 22, 48, 124, 177, 178,
    179
Thatcher, M. 115
Tierney, J. 173
Times Educational Supplement 19,
    146, 158, 171, 196, 215
Tomlinson, S. 10, 11, 19, 73, 85, 91,

121, 122, 131–8, Table 5.6, 148,
175, 178–9, 184, 193, 195, 214
Troyna, B. 11, 119–24, 125, 126, 159,
165, 199, 210, 215
Turner, B. 12
Turner, G. 82, 83, 98
Twitchin, J. 157, 165, 190, 194

van den Berghe, P.L. 3, 4, 8

Wallman, S. 7
Watts, S. 151
Weber, M. 82

Weis, L. 66
Wellman, D.T. 8
Willey, R. 176
Williams, J. 144, 148–9, 164
Willis, P. 50, 51, 53, 56, 59, 66
Wilson, A. 6–7
Woods, P. 12, 66, 86, 91, 97, 138
Wragg, E.C. 211
Wright, C. 21–5, 44, 64–5, 68–9, 70,
85, 182–3, 199, 211
Wright, J. 175

Young, M.F.D. 142